The
Sponsor

Classics in Communication and Mass Culture Series

Arthur Asa Berger, Series Editor

Agit-Pop, Arthur Asa Berger

The Astonished Muse, Reuel Denney

Beyond Words, Kurt W. Back

Blind Men and Elephants, Arthur Asa Berger

Communication and Social Order, Hugh Dalziel Duncan

Desexualization in American Life, Charles Winick

Everyday Life in the Modern World, Henri Lefebvre

Farce, Jessica Milner Davis

The Flow of Information, Melvin DeFleur and Otto N. Larson

The Hollywood TV Producer, Muriel G. Cantor

Humor and Laughter, Antony Chapman and Hugh Foot

Jewish Humor, Avner Ziv

Life Studies of Comedy Writers, William F. Fry and Melanie Allen

Mass Media in Modern Society, Norman Jacobs

The Play Theory of Mass Communication, William Stephenson

Political Culture and Public Opinion, Arthur Asa Berger

Political Persuaders, Dan Nimmo

Polls and the Awareness of Public Opinion, Leo Bogart

The Public Arts, Gilbert Seldes

The Sponsor, Erik Barnouw

The Strategy of Desire, Ernest Dichter

Television as an Instrument of Terror, Arthur Asa Berger

Television in Society, Arthur Asa Berger

T.V.: The Most Popular Art, Horace Newcomb

The Uses of Literacy, Richard Hoggart

You Don't Say, Benjamin DeMott

Notes on Modern Potentates

The
Sponsor

Erik Barnouw

With a new preface by Deirdre Boyle

Transaction Publishers
New Brunswick (U.S.A.) and London (U.K.)

Library of Congress Catalog Number: 2003048421
ISBN: 0-7658-0547-2
Printed in the United States of America

Library of Congress Cataloging-in-Publication Data

Barnouw, Erik, 1908-
    The sponsor : notes on modern potentates / Erik Barnouw ; with a new preface by Deirdre Boyle.
        p. cm.—(Classics in communication and mass culture series)
    Includes bibliographical references and index.
    ISBN 0-7658-0547-2 (pbk.: alk paper)
        1. Television advertising—United States. 2. Television programs—United States. 3. Television broadcasting—Social aspects—United States.

HF6146.T42B35   2004
306.4' 85—dc21
                                                    2003048421

CONTENTS

List of Illustrations   ix

Preface to the Transaction Edition   xi

Acknowledgment   xvii

But First, This Message . . .   3

PART ONE   RISE   7

1   On the Eve of the Sponsor   9

2   The First 400   10

3   New System   14

4   Monopoly Games   20

5   National   21

6   The Dispossessed   27

7   Uprising   28

8   Two Worlds   32

9   Senator Truman   37

10   Transition   41

11   Qualms   48

12   Changing the Guard   55

13   Going Public   58

14   Demographics   68

15   Do You Agree or Disagree . . . ?   74

PART TWO   DOMAIN   77

   1   The Inner Fortress—the "commercial"   79

   2   The Outer Defenses—"entertainment"   101

   3   The Satrapies—"public service"   123

   4   Sphere of Influence—"culture"   149

PART THREE   PROSPECT   153

   1   Problem: Success   155

   2   The Medium and The Biosphere   156

   3   The New Liberation   159

   4   Genie from the Tube   161

   5   Jobs Wanted   169

   6   The Circuses   171

   7   Empires   174

   8   Fringe Medium   179

NOTES   183

INDEX   207

LIST OF ILLUSTRATIONS

TV-equipped tricycle—cartoon

No sales message—The Browning King Orchestra

Announcement of the formation of NBC

Inflating the credit bubble—a spend-now "singing commercial"

The Demographic Dial

Police car "as seen on TV"—cartoon

Exporting the wasteland—cartoon

The secret agent

"Don't you understand?"—cartoon

A Modern TV ad

Public service message for Radio Free Europe

Mobil underwriting—cartoon

"How about changing seats?"—cartoon

The Advertising Council claims "sponsorship" of a Yucca Flat atomic test

And circuses—the Goodyear blimp with a "public service" message

Step by step I find myself moving willy-nilly toward the proclaimed future. At the same time, I do keep wondering what sort of society will emerge from that new-age television. What kinds of humans will it help to shape?

ERIK BARNOUW, **Media Marathon**

PREFACE TO THE TRANSACTION EDITION

The world of television has changed since Erik Barnouw wrote his lucid analysis of the wide-ranging influence of the sponsor in broadcasting. Today hundreds of channels vie for the viewer's attention in a vastly expanded "new media" world where the Internet competes with television for the hearts, minds, and credit cards of the American citizenry. Although the media have changed in the last twenty years, the sponsor really has not, nor has his role diminished, although any sense of an individual operating in that role has faded into the impersonal mythos of massive corporate power. With the proliferation of new media formats and the rise of conglomerate control of the media industries, the sponsor's role has grown even more pervasive, complex, and influential. To understand why and how television advertising exerts such profound economic and ideological influence on American culture, this slim volume offers readers a wonderful point of departure.

Best known as the dean of U.S. broadcasting history, Erik Barnouw was also a participant in that history, working in radio and television before becoming a teacher, critic, filmmaker, and media historian. He landed his first job after college working for one of the big ten advertising agencies as a director-producer for network radio shows; there he learned firsthand how well the sponsor called the tune. His first program was a musical show aimed at women: *The Camel Quarter Hour*. It was sponsored by the R.J. Reynolds Tobacco Company for the Columbia Broadcasting System (CBS), which had just been bought by William Paley, a cigar manufacturer himself. As Barnouw explains in his fascinating memoir, *Media Marathon*, it took him a long time to sort out his feelings about the show and understand what it was all about. He writes:

> In the 1920s few women smoked. Cigarette makers became beguiled by the thought that if women could be persuaded to smoke, that would double the market.... At Erwin, Wasey & Company I never heard such strategies mentioned; perhaps medical reports already discouraged discussion. And I am sure no one on our tour was thinking of such matters. For all, the job was the focus. It was good to get a show off on time, get a good review, win a good rating, see your name on a marquee, get a police escort, move an audience, be received by the mayor, write a good report. These were enough. To any larger implications we were as oblivious as our audience. The obliviousness was a gold mine, and we troupers received our share of its yield. Along with our salaries each one of us received, each week, a free carton of Camels. We were content.

Although this young Princeton grad was happy to land a good job during the Depression, the older and wiser scholar and social historian had many further thoughts, and in *The Sponsor*, he shares his thoughts about the immoderate influence of sponsors on American society in a remarkably straightforward and informative book accessible to all.

The book, which can be read in one or two sittings, is divided into three parts: "Rise," "Domain," and "Prospect." It begins with analysis of the sponsor's central role in early radio when overt interference from the sponsor's booth was the norm and sponsors not only subsidized the air time for popular radio shows but also wrote, cast, and produced them. Barnouw next concentrates on advertising's influence on network TV programming, where the sponsor's impact was more subtle than in radio's heyday yet just as powerful. Finally, he considers how non-commercial sponsors—such as political, religious, educational, and public interest groups—exert their influence over social institutions and public mores. As Edward Bernays, the father of the PR industry, aptly noted: "The conscious and intelligent manipulation of the organized habits and opinions of the masses is an important element in a democratic society. Those who manipulate this unseen mechanism of society constitute an invisible government which is the true ruling power of our country." In *The Sponsor*, as in all his work, Barnouw helps thoughtful readers pause and reflect on the visible and invisible forces controlling our media and our selves.

Praise for *The Sponsor* on publication came from many quarters, including distinguished broadcasters apparently affected by McLuhan's hot and cold theories of media. "I haven't read a more stimulating and enlightening book about television. My mind still burns under its influence," Bill Moyers observed, while Daniel Schorr found it "a chilling record of how Americans have been manipulated via their air waves for the profit of a few." In 1978, when *The Sponsor* first appeared, a slew of books about television was being published, written by academics, public intellectuals, and disaffected media professionals. In an omnibus review of four such books, James Wolcott, in *The New York Review of Books*, singled out *The Sponsor* for his only praise. Noting that Barnouw had revisited topics covered in both his magisterial three-volume *A History of Broadcasting in the United States* and one-volume distillation, *Tube of Plenty* (1975), Wolcott stressed the power of the new material that "spiked" his narrative here.

One such example cited by Wolcott is worth recalling. It was on the power of ITT, which had been trying to repair its damaged public image after public exposure of its role in subverting the Allende government in Chile. To this end, ITT decided to sponsor a children's series called *The Big Blue Marble*, which showed children around the world involved in a pen-pal campaign. Once the series had aired, ITT then ran primetime commercials about the program, proclaiming with self-serving directness: "The Best Ideas Are Ideas That Help People." Barnouw wrote:

> *The Big Blue Marble* films cost $4 million to produce but were *given away* to television stations, with the result that they appeared mainly in fringe periods. Not so the corporate commercials *about* the *Big Blue Marble* series and other intercultural good deeds. These commercials appeared in prime time at a cost of $4.2 million in 1974, and of $3.7 million in 1975...the company's name did not apparently come up in a single television network evening newscast during the six months of 1975, when the good-deeds commercials were constantly on the air.

ITT's strategy worked. "According to [the Daniel Yankelovich, Inc. research company], the ITT 'cares about the general public' rating more than doubled during a twelve-month period, going from 20 percent to 43 percent." Exploiting the children's market was a fine way of rescuing reputation from public scorn. Wolcott reveled in Barnouw's pithy case study and ultimate disclosure that the American broadcasting empire is built upon just such cunning and calculation.

But what Wolcott and other reviewers further prized was Barnouw's prophetic awareness that storm clouds were gathering. "The sponsor, the merchant, has been living at the summit of our communication system. He has had things largely his way, and we are in trouble. He himself is aware of it. Impending change is in the air," Barnouw wrote in 1978. By the early eighties, when Ken Auletta's fine portrait of the end of an era of monolithic network broadcasting—*Three Blind Mice*—begins, the mighty three networks of CBS, NBC, and ABC were rapidly ceding audiences to local and cable competitors. No longer capable of commanding the attention of 92 percent of American households during prime time, the networks' audience share in 1984 had shrunk to 75 percent and by 1991 hovered at 60 percent and was sinking fast. Corporate raiders soon put an end to the dynasties that had run the monoliths. And by the year 2000, as Ben Bagdikian in *The Media Monopoly* points out, the twenty-three corporations that owned most major media outlets in America in 1984 had shrunk to six. With video games, home computers, and the Internet about to challenge American patterns of entertainment and information behaviors, Barnouw's astute warning in 1978 that change was on the way proved prescient if largely unattended.

Barnouw was the first historian to document the shifting course of sponsored broadcasting in America and arguably was that history's best critic. He captured a picture that was about to transform dramatically, and it would be up to other scholars to chart the changing landscape of broadcasting and advertising. Radio and television historians Michele Hilmes, William Boddy, and Susan Smulyan have written extensively on their special areas of broadcasting history, and sociologists and communications theorists like Stuart Ewen, Lawrence R. Samuel, and Roland Marchand have examined the history of advertising and its impact on American consciousness. Interest in political advertising on television has developed since 1984, when writers such as Edwin Diamond, Stephen Bates, and Kathleen Hall Jamieson began publishing updated analyses on presidential campaign advertising. Scholarship has abounded in Barnouw's pioneering wake, thanks in part to his modest ability to prepare the ground and then stand aside so that further work could be done. His generosity in supporting his juniors was much appreciated by many who found encouragement from him. This writer is one of many who can look back on Erik's inspiration and kindness with affection and gratitude.

In 2001, Erik Barnouw died at the age of ninety-three. His life and work had focused on the history of the twentieth century and most of its communications breakthroughs. His exceptional career included co-founding the Writers Guild of America, heading up the Library of Congress's Motion Picture, Broadcasting and Recorded Sound Division, organizing the Center for Mass Communication at Columbia University where he also was a professor, editing the *International Encyclopedia of Communications*, and producing the astonishing film *Hiroshima-Nagasaki, August 1945*. His classic texts on documentary film,

Indian cinema, early cinema, and broadcasting history set the standard for media scholarship and fine, clear writing for years to come, winning him numerous fellowships and prizes. Director, lyricist, painter, documentary filmmaker, raconteur, anti-nuclear activist, teacher, programmer, historian, memoirist—Erik Barnouw was a man of many talents and identities, which he cultivated in a life lived with passion, integrity, moral probity, energy, and profound commitment. Actively engaged in the life of the mind until the very end, his last book, *Media Lost and Found*, was published just months before his death. In this collection of essays, lectures, and other writings, Barnouw chronicled "the old media giving way to the new, and then being replaced by them, as the ghosts of the old media rise in new forms."

His thoughts at the end of his life were about the shape of things to come and how our new media would shape life to come. This interest was already apparent in the last line of *The Sponsor*: "While we make our media, our media make us." Erik Barnouw's lifelong effort to understand and explain the way our media make us who we are defined his life but did not limit it. His curiosity to know how the future would be shaped by new media is his legacy for new generations of media scholars and practitioners: we must continue applying the same energy, intelligence, wit, and judgment in an ongoing effort to reveal the latest strategies of media moguls and sponsors to manipulate the hearts, minds, and checkbooks of American society. Perhaps new readers of this luminous study will be inspired to take up the work that he began. At the start of a new millennium and on the brink of a dubious war, that work has never been more vital or urgent.

Deirdre Boyle
March 2003
New York, NY

ACKNOWLEDGMENT

The author is grateful for the opportunity he had to study, as a 1976 Fellow of the Woodrow Wilson International Center for Scholars, Smithsonian Institution, Washington, D.C., the role and influence of the sponsor in American television. He was free to pursue his inquiry wherever it led him. The resulting document is his responsibility.

He also owes a deep debt of gratitude to the many people in television—and surrounding territory—who helped and encouraged him in this exploration.

October 1977   E. B.
New York, N.Y.

The
Sponsor

> "Papa, what is the moon
> supposed to advertise?"
>
> CARL SANDBURG, **The People, Yes**

BUT FIRST, THIS MESSAGE . . .

The television sponsor has become semi-mythical. He is remote and unseen, but omnipresent. Dramas, football games, press conferences pause for a "word" from him. He "makes possible" concerts and public affairs broadcasts. His "underwriting grants" bring you folk festivals and classic films. Interviews with visiting statesmen are interrupted for him, to continue "in a moment."

His role and image have changed. There was a time when he clearly had human form. Performers saw him sitting in the "sponsor's booth," where he could order script revisions, which were promptly made. He was surrounded by attendant executives; sometimes he was accompanied by a lady. There were rumors that this or that program or star had been canceled—or saved—by the verdict of a sponsor's wife. The folklore of sponsor meddling fills volumes of radio and early television history.

But things have changed. One is not even sure now whether a sponsor is a person or some abstract corporate entity—"they"

3

rather than "he" ("IBM presents . . ."). If there is someone who sits at the corporate summit and makes decisions, he remains shadowy.

What sorts of decisions does he make? According to some network executives, he no longer makes decisions that deal with programming. Spokesmen for sponsoring organizations tend toward similar statements, but with a difference. They say they don't want to control programming, but insist on the right to decide with what programs their names or commercials will be associated. They leave it to broadcasting companies to provide suitable settings for this participation. The broadcasters do so.

Perhaps they are all saying that sponsorship has become so essential, so crucial to the whole scheme of things, that interference of the old sort is no longer necessary. A vast industry has grown up around the needs and wishes of sponsors. Its program formulas, business practices, ratings, demographic surveys have all evolved in ways to satisfy sponsor requirements. He has reached the ultimate status: most decision-making swirls at levels below him, requiring only his occasional benediction at this or that selected point. He is a potentate of our time.

Regardless of where decisions are now made, sponsorship is basic to American television. Even noncommercial television looks to it for survival. Yet the subject is seldom discussed. This may be because broadcasters are reluctant—understandably—to emphasize their dependent state. It may also be because a generation of Americans has grown up in a television environment so conditioned by sponsors that it has become difficult to imagine any other state of affairs. But considering the place that television has achieved in the life of our day, the subject demands analysis and appraisal.

The word "sponsor" evokes the business sponsor, but there are of course others, who in our society play a lesser role. They include officials in government and diverse non-profit units—educational, religious, philanthropic, political. All will be considered in this study. Their relative roles, here as elsewhere in the world, seem to reflect their relative power status. And the tube is an arena for their continuing interaction.

The first Part of our study will sketch the rise of the sponsor, in radio and then television, to his present state of eminence; this section is titled RISE. The second will examine his pervasive impact on television programming, with the emphasis on network programming, the main arena; this section is titled DOMAIN. The third and final Part will assess what the dominance has meant for our society, mores, and institutions—and may mean for our future; it is titled PROSPECT.

Our study is thus concerned with an instrument of power, exercised in forms seldom associated in the average person's mind with power, and perhaps all the more telling for that reason. For it provides delights to which men and women turn for relaxation, reassurance, and understanding of the world they inhabit—via images in color more real than life, defining what is good and great and desirable.

RISE

Do we move ourselves, or are moved by an unseen hand
at a game
That pushes us off from the board . . . ?

TENNYSON, **Maud**

ON THE EVE OF THE SPONSOR

When radio station KDKA, Pittsburgh, went on the air in No-
vember 1920 as a venture of the Westinghouse Electric and
Manufacturing Company, it set off extraordinary explosions.
Overnight the broadcasting age began throughout the United
States. Starting in radio, it promised to expand soon into tele-
vision; Westinghouse and others were experimenting with it.

During the months following the KDKA debut, the new
"radio" counters of department stores and electrical shops were
mobbed by people clamoring for sets and parts. And hundreds
of entrepreneurs rushed to secure broadcasting licenses and
build stations, which further stimulated the set-buying boom.
By July 1922 some four hundred stations were licensed, and
more were on the way. Newspapers were running columns and
whole sections on broadcasting, and many were planning stations.[1]

Although the broadcasting era had been launched, the time-
buying "sponsor" was not yet a part of it. None of the first four

hundred stations had sold time—for advertising or any other purpose. Most had not even contemplated such an idea. Thus "the American system of broadcasting"—built on the sale of time— was not a part of our first broadcasting boom.

But circumstances were setting the stage for the entrance of the sponsor. The circumstances can be understood by focusing briefly on those first four hundred stations. Who launched them? For what purpose? What were they broadcasting?

THE FIRST 400

The Westinghouse company, which had sparked the explosion, had been making radio equipment for years, mainly for the army and navy, which had been among the earliest users of wireless and radio. Before World War I they had shared the air with various others: ship-to-shore radio; professional experimenters like Reginald A. Fessenden, Lee de Forest, Edwin H. Armstrong, and others, some working in corporate laboratories, some on university campuses; and also with countless amateurs or "hams" who filled the air with code and chatter, and often enraged the military. The "hams" were accused of interfering with naval communication and even of such pranks as sending fake orders to admirals. To control the "hams" a licensing law was passed in 1912. Then, as the United States entered World War I, the amateurs were all ordered off the air and required to seal their equipment. Radio became an arcane military activity, on which the public was forbidden to trespass. Civilians could read about it in wartime fiction, which depicted radio as a tool of espionage and of heroic rescues on land and sea.[2]

Meanwhile an electronic industry was burgeoning via army and navy contracts, which made Westinghouse, General Electric, and Western Electric (subsidiary of the American Telephone and Telegraph Company) into young electronic giants. The army and navy wanted quantities of transmitters and receivers—for ships, airplanes, automobiles. They wanted mobile "trench transmitters" (using barbed wire for antennas), "pack transmitters," and compact receivers. They wanted submarine detectors, radio direction finders, and equipment for the recording and study of code transmissions. All of these used electronic vacuum tubes; assembly lines that had produced electric light bulbs before the war were now turning out vacuum tubes by the hundreds of thousands. Under wartime pressure, masked by military security, the technology of electronics leaped forward.

With peace, the assembly lines abruptly halted, as contracts ended. Radio seemed suddenly dead. Some of the "hams" began to unpack their sealed equipment, but the radio boom seemed over.

Then Westinghouse began to wonder: those compact, easy-to-operate receivers, which the company had made in such quantity for the Signal Corps, might the general public be persuaded to buy such sets, if a daily program service were made available? The KDKA experiment answered the question in spectacular style. So assembly lines started up again—at Westinghouse, General Electric, Western Electric. As a further listener incentive, all rushed to build additional stations.

So did the infant Radio Corporation of America, which had been formed in 1919—a year before KDKA—as a joint venture of GE, Westinghouse, AT&T, and United Fruit—the four corporations that controlled almost all electronic patents.* Curiously, the creation of RCA had not been prompted by any broadcasting visions. The purpose was to organize a U.S.-controlled international message service that, by using the air, could undercut British-controlled cables and make the United States supreme in international communication. Nationalistic impulses were behind the move, and the RCA board included a representative of the Navy Department, which had wanted a radio monopoly—if not under its own control, then at least in congenial hands. RCA quickly achieved a dominant world role in the message business, but the broadcasting explosion turned its attention elsewhere. It became the distribution arm for GE and Westinghouse radios (all sold under the RCA trademark),

---

* United Fruit had begun using wireless before the turn of the century to coordinate its scattered plantations and direct banana boats to profitable markets. It later acquired a radio manufacturing subsidiary and had valuable patents relating to crystal detectors.

and it launched RCA radio stations. RCA, GE, and Westing-house spotted their stations around the United States for wide coverage, to help build a nationwide audience. All saw their profit in the sale of sets, which seemed likely to go on forever, in radio and then television. There seemed no question that it could support their broadcasting services.

In their programming, the stations followed the KDKA lead. KDKA had opened with a news event—coverage of the 1920 presidential election returns, which had brought Warren G. Harding to the presidency. During the following days and weeks KDKA offered radio concerts; broadcasts from local churches; speeches by Secretary of Commerce Herbert Hoover and other Cabinet members; a prizefight broadcast; a pickup from a theater; talks on numerous subjects. Each day's schedule was brief—starting with an hour or so per day, then gradually expanding. But the diversity brought an overnight change to the meaning of "radio." For the military it had meant transmission of information and orders. Now it suddenly symbolized a coming age of enlightenment. It was seen as leading to the fulfillment of democracy. Government, it was said, would become "a living thing to its citizens." Broadcasting was called "the people's university." It would link rich and poor, young and old. It would end the isolation of rural life. It would unite the nation.[3]

Radio also seemed a key to prestige and influence. With diverse purposes, transmitters began to go up on the roofs of newspaper offices, colleges and universities, churches, theaters, hotels, department stores, banks, and other businesses. All, in one way or another, wanted a role in the new age. Each broadcasting station identified itself from time to time, as required by law. But each did so circumspectly at first, with a sense of entering a rather special realm.

Colleges and universities were particularly prominent in the surge, and this seemed logical. Many had conducted early technical experiments; now they foresaw radio facilitating lifelong learning. During 1922 some seventy colleges and universities went on the air. Some began to broadcast adult-education courses, for which credit could be earned by passing an exam and paying a fee. Churches likewise saw in radio an "outreach" opportunity, a chance to fulfill the scriptural injunction that the Word should be "proclaimed from the housetops."

For all these early broadcasters, there was one major worry: chaos was approaching. All stations were at first licensed to broadcast on the same wavelength; in each community, they were supposed to divide the available time. But as stations multiplied, the sharing became difficult, and in some cases acrimonious. Some defied each other and broadcast simultaneously. Interference between stations in different cities increased rapidly. Many of the early broadcasters urged Secretary of Commerce Herbert Hoover, who under the 1912 law was responsible for station licensing, to establish order in the ether.* But the law was vague as to his powers. Its intent seemed to be that anyone applying for a license had a right to one. The law did not make clear what restrictions the Secretary could impose. Hoover considered it "a very weak rudder to steer so powerful a phenomenon." He pressed Congress for new legislation, and meanwhile called leaders of the mushrooming industry to several Washington Radio Conferences to discuss the pandemonium, and what to do about it. All leading manufacturers attended, and urged Hoover to act resolutely. Hoover noted with interest what he considered a remarkable state of affairs—an American industry was begging for government controls.[4]

The public, oddly enough, was not greatly aroused over the ether turmoil. Tuning a radio was considered a challenge, and many people sat up far into the night, trying to separate one station from another. But with scores of entrepreneurs still applying for licenses, the bedlam was sure to intensify.

Amid the worry the American Telephone & Telegraph Company made a historic announcement. Issued in the month of the first Washington Radio Conference, it was apparently offered as a solution to the developing crisis. But if AT&T expected praise, it was due for disappointment. The first reaction was indignation.

---

* Originally the Secretary of Commerce and Labor was designated the licensing authority. After a separate Department of Labor was created in 1913, the Secretary of Commerce became the licensing agent.

NEW SYSTEM

In February 1922 AT&T announced that it would soon open a new kind of station, and eventually a nationwide chain of stations, to engage in "toll broadcasting." AT&T called its projected stations "radiotelephone" stations and likened them to phone booths. Just as one entered a phone booth, paid a fee, and talked to a friend, so anyone who might want to address the general public would be able to visit an AT&T station—a phone booth of the air—pay a fee, and address the world. AT&T envisaged thirty-eight such stations across the nation, to be linked by its long lines. A New York City station would be launched as soon as possible.

AT&T's announcement, dated February 11, 1922, said that the company would provide "no program of its own, but provide the channels through which anyone with whom it makes a contract can send out their own programs." It was the first proposal for putting air time on a for-sale basis.[5]

Western Electric, AT&T's subsidiary, made and sold transmitters; the other electronic giants, as part of their patent-pool agreement, had ceded this field to it. At the time that AT&T made its "toll broadcasting" announcement, the company apparently had a large backlog of orders for transmitters. According to an AT&T official, Edgar Felix, more than a hundred of these transmitters were destined for use in the New York area. Sensing that they could bring disaster to the air, AT&T began telling customers that it would be months or even years before delivery could be made, but that AT&T's "toll" stations would serve their purposes. Thus it tried to divert buyers from one-time transmitter purchases to continuing time purchases.

AT&T applied the policy to non-commercial as well as commercial applicants. When New York City in March 1922 appropriated funds for a municipal broadcasting station—to serve police and fire departments as well as education—AT&T urged the city to buy time instead—from the New York "toll" station about to be launched. Grover Whalen, chairman of the city's Board of Purchase, was indignant. "What! The great City of

New York subsidiary to a commercial company? Decidedly no!" The city later managed to import a used Western Electric transmitter from Brazil.

The first Washington Radio Conference proved similarly antagonistic, condemning the idea of "ether advertising." AT&T published, in the new *Radio Broadcast* magazine, a reply that was mollifying in tone but defended the proposed "experiment":

> The conference under Secretary Hoover's chairmanship agreed that it was against the public interest to broadcast pure advertising matter. The American Telephone and Telegraph officials agreed with this point of view. Their experiment is to see whether there are people who desire to buy the right to talk to the public and at the same time tell the public something it would like to hear. If this experiment succeeds, a commercial basis for broadcasting will have been established.

Most published reactions, like those at the Washington conference, were unfriendly. The trade periodical *Radio Dealer* condemned the AT&T plan for its "mercenary advertising purposes" and predicted a "man-sized vocal rebellion." *Printers' Ink*, perhaps reflecting the fears of periodicals supported by advertising, said the plan would prove "positively offensive to great numbers of people."

Secretary of Commerce Herbert Hoover, already considered a presidential possibility, was quoted as saying that it was "inconceivable that we should allow so great a possibility for service . . . to be drowned in advertising chatter." In a later statement he expressed the opinion that if a presidential message ever became "the meat in a sandwich of two patent medicine advertisements," it would destroy broadcasting.

But AT&T went ahead. After technical reverses—ascribed to skyscraper interference—it finally opened its first toll station on August 16, 1922, with the call letters WEAF.* It was almost two weeks before any sponsor ventured into the phone booth of the air.

On August 28 the Queensboro Corporation paid $50 for a late-afternoon 10-minute period on WEAF, and used it to extol

---

* It later became WRCA and WNBC.

suburban living and promote the sale of apartments in a housing complex in Jackson Heights, Long Island. Three weeks later, according to WEAF executive Edgar Felix, the Queensboro Corporation "reported sales amounting to $127,000, directly traceable to that one speech." It decided to buy four additional afternoon periods at $50 each and an evening period for $100.[6]

In spite of this success, WEAF made slow progress. In September only two other companies rented the phone booth: Tidewater Oil and the American Express Company. WEAF revenues for the first two months amounted to only $550. But gradually the tempo picked up. The approach of Christmas brought the Macy, Gimbel, and Hearn department stores into the phone booth.

An advertising executive, William H. Rankin of the Rankin agency, became curious about the medium but felt he should test it before recommending it to clients. So he bought a $100 evening period to discuss advertising. His talk brought a flurry of letters and phone calls, including one from a prospective sponsor, maker of the beauty product Mineralava. The event proved crucial in the evolution of sponsored broadcasting. In a program produced for Mineralava by the Rankin agency, the actress Marion Davies talked about "How I Make Up for the Movies" and offered autographed photos to those writing in. Letters came by the hundreds. Mineralava received brief, restrained mention. The response enabled the Rankin agency to enlist Goodrich for a sponsored *series*, and others followed. By the end of six months, WEAF had won sixteen sponsors of programs or series.[7]

Though some sponsors had negotiated directly with WEAF, AT&T insisted on paying their advertising agencies a 15 per cent commission, matching the commissions paid by print media on space purchases. This encouraged participation by advertising agencies, who began to show a decided taste for making the plunge.

There was a period of bafflement as to how to use this new access to public attention. Some advertisers, emulating the Marion Davies success, offered talks. An association of greeting card manufacturers sponsored a talk on the history of Christmas cards. Gillette provided a discourse on fashions in beards since mediaeval times, culminating in the triumph of the safety razor. The resemblance to a carnival pitch was close enough to cause uneasiness at WEAF, which longed for respectability. A talk on teeth and their care, offered by a toothpaste company, was delayed while executives argued whether anything so personal as teeth should even be mentioned on the air. They finally gave in, but kept devising new rules. Prices must not be mentioned. Samples must not be offered. Store locations were a taboo subject.

Then came a new breakthrough—a weekly 1-hour series launched April 25, 1923, featuring the Browning King Orchestra. The clothing firm Browning King was content to attach its name to an orchestra. No sales message was used; the programs did not even mention that Browning King sold clothes. During 1923-24 this Spartan example became the model for other series, all dedicated simply to "trade-name publicity": the Goodrich Silvertown Orchestra, the Cliquot Club Eskimos, the Gold Dust Twins, the Ipana Troubadours, the A&P Gypsies, the Kodak Chorus. Sales talks now tended to vanish from the air.

In a book about sponsored broadcasting, Edgar Felix later wrote that the audience "resents the slightest attempt at direct advertising" but is willing to refer to an entertainment feature "by a trade name." He added that a sponsor "does not earn the right to inflict selling propaganda in the midst of a broadcasting entertainment any more than an agreeable weekend guest may suddenly launch into an insurance solicitation at Sunday dinner."[8]

"Indirect selling"—via "trade-name publicity"—became the central doctrine of WEAF policy, and helped it to win increasing acceptance.

To some observers, even trade-name publicity was a scandal. Writing in *Century* magazine—June 1924—Bruce Bliven described radio as a medium of magnificent promise given to "outrageous rubbish." But audiences grew, and sponsors came in increasing numbers.

A factor in the growing success was crucial governmental help—from Secretary of Commerce Herbert Hoover himself.

NO SALES MESSAGE: Browning King, clothing firm, was content to attach its name to Anna Byrne's orchestra. On programs of *The Browning King Orchestra,* clothing was not mentioned. *NBC*

Hoover, urged on by the second Washington Radio Conference, held in March 1923, had taken drastic steps to reduce ether chaos. Dispersing stations among several wavelengths, he also adopted a plan that created, in effect, a hierarchy of stations. Some would be "clear channel" stations, free of interference over most of the country, and therefore able to use the maximum permitted power. Less privileged would be "regional" stations, which would share a wavelength with other regional stations, and were therefore limited to medium power. At the bottom of the hierarchy would be "local" stations, serving small areas, and therefore very restricted in power, and in some cases confined to daytime hours to minimize interference. Most were part-time stations.

AT&T took the position that the stations owned by others, including college-owned stations, were all "special-interest" stations, whereas a "toll" station was for *everybody* and should therefore have preferential treatment. Hoover apparently accepted this argument: WEAF won a clear channel. Most educational stations received "local" channels—a matter that caused increasing bitterness during following years.

But AT&T schedules began to represent the aristocracy of radio programming. In 1923 AT&T launched its second toll station, WCAP, Washington, linked by wire to WEAF, New York. AT&T began a series of spectacular "chain broadcast" experiments, while developing a special kind of cable for station interconnection. It generally refused the use of its cables for chain broadcasts by others. AT&T was rapidly winning unquestioned supremacy in programming.

All this put other stations under agonizing pressures. Their potential was limited, while their costs rose. During the early euphoria most stations had been besieged by volunteer performers, from the amateur to the famous, wanting their moment in history. And stations had used copyrighted material including music, news bulletins, fiction, and poetry, without permission or thought of royalties. It was all considered a benefaction. But in 1922 the American Society of Composers, Authors, and Publishers began to ask payment for use of ASCAP-controlled music; an annual license fee was demanded of each station. WEAF settled at once—for a $500 fee for the first year, due to rise sharply in later years. Literary copyright owners began to make similar demands. The salaries paid to WEAF's sponsored performers meanwhile spurred artist demands everywhere. WEAF's *Eveready Hour*, launched in December 1923 and soon featured in "chain" broadcasts, was said to have paid Will Rogers $1000 for a single performance. Such rumors sent all costs spiraling upward.

Alarmed at the escalation, RCA, GE, Westinghouse, and others began to think about selling time. But a curious battle developed: AT&T said they had no right to.

MONOPOLY GAMES

In giving its plan telephonic terminology, AT&T had been pursuing a tricky legal strategy. When joining GE, Westinghouse, and United Fruit in the organizing of RCA, the partners had formed a patent pool which protected each in its traditional line of work, while dividing new empires insofar as they could foresee them. Each had the use of all the patents—within its assigned sphere. AT&T had been assured of the sole right to operate a commercial telephone service. In adopting such terminology as "toll" and "radiotelephony," AT&T was warning its partners that it considered sponsored broadcasting a new phase of the telephone business, and therefore sole AT&T territory.[9]

The dispute brought furious behind-closed-doors argument, continuing for months. Since their whole relationship raised questions vis-à-vis antitrust law, none of the partners wished to air the dispute in public. Meanwhile GE, Westinghouse, and RCA adopted a modified sponsorship system. A *Schrafft's Tearoom Orchestra* was heard in New York on WJZ,* featuring musicians paid by Schrafft's restaurants, but this "sponsor" ("underwriter," a later generation would say) did not pay for time. Similarly, Wanamaker's store supported the *Wanamaker Organ Concerts*, but got free time. In the same way *Harper's Bazaar* provided fashion talks, and *Field and Stream* a sports

---

* Originally a Westinghouse station, soon transferred to RCA.

program. This trend was followed by stations throughout the country, and increasingly filled the air with trade names, and the press with protests. But in Manhattan boardrooms GE, Westinghouse, RCA, and AT&T officials faced each other with argument and counterargument, threat and counterthreat.

If a compromise was at last found—one that dramatically reorganized the industry—it was partly because of government action. In 1924 the Federal Trade Commission issued a formal charge that AT&T, RCA, GE, Westinghouse, United Fruit, and subsidiaries had conspired to create a monopoly in broadcasting and the manufacture of radio devices. The FTC planned hearings to examine the group's agreements and competitive practices. The announcement gave the accused a strong incentive to settle their quarrel, and loosen their close ties.

After long, stiff bargaining, AT&T agreed to sell WEAF for $1 million and withdraw entirely from broadcasting—but under terms that ensured it a continuing, lucrative revenue. A central broadcasting organization, the National Broadcasting Company, would be formed by RCA, GE, and Westinghouse. Their stations, and others that might affiliate with them, would be linked by AT&T lines, which would mean a telephone bill for the network of about $1 million for the first year, and rising sharply as the operations expanded. AT&T's WCAP, Washington, would be dissolved, with its time taken over by RCA's WRC, Washington. The new organization was incorporated early in 1926. With its founding, "toll" broadcasting was formally transferred to the national scene, though the telephone terminology was dropped.

The conferees argued briefly whether they should claim the *sole* right to broadcast on a sponsorship basis—continuing the AT&T claim. The idea was, however, forgotten.

Thus the system—soon to be known as "the American system of broadcasting"—entered its nationwide network phase. But its promoters dared not say so—not yet.

NATIONAL

In the dramatic full-page announcements—September 1926—of the creation of the National Broadcasting Company, such words as "advertising," "toll," and "sponsor" did not appear. To the reader, the rationale for the creation of NBC seemed to be the same as for the launching of KDKA, but looking to a nation-wide reach.

RCA estimated that 5 million homes already had radios while 21 million remained to be equipped. If programming of importance and highest quality were made available, *all* would want to buy. Therefore RCA, as the world's largest distributor of radios, had a stake in providing such programming. For this reason this "instrument of great public service" was being created. It would broadcast, throughout the United States, every event of national importance. Fine programs would be made available to stations coast to coast—not only those of RCA and its associates. An Advisory Council of distinguished citizens would watch over the service.

On November 15, 1926, from the Grand Ballroom of the Waldorf Astoria, in the presence of leaders of industry and finance, a galaxy of theater and concert stars—Mary Garden, Will Rogers, Titta Ruffo, Walter Damrosch, Weber and Fields, Vincent Lopez, and others—helped launch the network in a mammoth debut. By January 1, 1927, NBC had two networks in operation. It was a beginning of extraordinary promise.

The network's position was fortified a month later by passage of the Radio Act of 1927. This law has often been cited as establishing the commercial broadcasting system, but it scarcely did so. One sentence in the 7000-word document specified that a person or company paying for or furnishing a program had to be identified. But otherwise the law, like the NBC announcement, sidestepped the matter of "ether advertising"; it neither authorized nor forbade it. It said nothing about the sale of time. It made clear that no licensee could *own* the channel assigned to him. The channel was to be used for "the public interest, convenience, or necessity."[10]

But the law clearly empowered the commission to organize the spectrum—for television as well as radio—in the way Hoover had begun. Legal action of this sort had become a dire need when a Federal court ruled that Hoover had exceeded his authority—a ruling that had brought hellish confusion as stations

Announcing the

National Broadcasting Company, Inc.

National radio broadcasting with better programs permanently assured by this important action of the *Radio Corporation of America* in the interest of the listening public

THE RADIO CORPORATION OF AMERICA is the largest distributor of radio receiving sets in the world. It handles the entire output in this field of the Westinghouse and General Electric factories.

It does not say this boastfully. It does not say it with apology. It says it for the purpose of making clear the fact that it is more largely interested, more selfishly interested, if you please, in the best possible broadcasting in the United States than anyone else.

Radio for 26,000,000 Homes

The market for receiving sets in the future will be determined largely by the quantity and quality of the programs broadcast.

We say quantity because they must be diversified enough so that some of them will appeal to all possible listeners.

We say quality because each program must be the best of its kind. If that ideal were to be reached, no home in the United States could afford to be without a radio receiving set.

Today the best available statistics indicate that 5,000,000 homes are equipped, and 21,000,000 homes remain to be supplied.

Radio receiving sets of the best reproductive quality should be made available for all, and we hope to make them cheap enough so that all may buy.

The day has gone by when the radio receiving set is a plaything. It must now be an instrument of service.

WEAF Purchased for $1,000,000

The Radio Corporation of America, therefore, is interested, just as the public is, in having the most adequate programs broadcast. It is interested, as the public is, in having them comprehensive and free from discrimination.

Any use of radio transmission which causes the public to feel that the quality of the programs is not the highest, that the use of radio is not the broadest and best use in the public interest, that it is used for political advantage or selfish power, will be detrimental to the public interest in radio, and therefore to the Radio Corporation of America.

To insure, therefore, the development of this great service, the Radio Corporation of America has purchased for one million dollars station WEAF from the American Telephone and Telegraph Company, that company having decided to retire from the broadcasting business.

The Radio Corporation of America will assume active control of that station on November 15.

National Broadcasting Company Organized

The Radio Corporation of America has decided to incorporate that station, which has achieved such a deservedly high reputation for the quality and character of its programs, under the name of the National Broadcasting Company, Inc.

The Purpose of the New Company

The purpose of that company will be to provide the best program available for broadcasting in the United States.

The National Broadcasting Company will not only broadcast these programs through station WEAF, but it will make them available to other broadcasting stations throughout the country so far as it may be practicable to do so, and they may desire to take them.

It is hoped that arrangements may be made so that every event of national importance may be broadcast widely throughout the United States.

No Monopoly of the Air

The Radio Corporation of America is not in any sense seeking a monopoly of the air. That would be a liability rather than an asset. It is seeking, however, to provide machinery which will insure a national distribution of national programs, and a wider distribution of programs of the highest quality.

If others will engage in this business the Radio Corporation of America will welcome their action, whether it be cooperative or competitive.

If other radio manufacturing companies, competitors of the Radio Corporation of America, wish to use the facilities of the National Broadcasting Company for the purpose of making known to the public their receiving sets, they may do so on the same terms as accorded to other clients.

The necessity of providing adequate broadcasting is apparent. The problem of finding the best means of doing it is yet experimental. The Radio Corporation of America is making this experiment in the interest of the art and the furtherance of the industry.

A Public Advisory Council

In order that the National Broadcasting Company may be advised as to the best type of program, that discrimination may be avoided, that the public may be assured that the broadcasting is being done in the fairest and best way, always allowing for human frailties and human performance, it has created an Advisory Council, composed of twelve members, to be chosen as representative of various shades of public opinion, which will from time to time give it the benefit of their judgment and suggestion. The members of this Council will be announced as soon as their acceptance shall have been obtained.

M. H. Aylesworth to be President

The President of the new National Broadcasting Company will be M. H. Aylesworth, for many years Managing Director of the National Electric Light Association. He will perform the executive and administrative duties of the corporation.

Mr. Aylesworth, while not hitherto identified with the radio industry or broadcasting, has had public experience as Chairman of the Colorado Public Utilities Commission, and, through his work with the association which represents the electrical industry, has a broad understanding of the technical problems which measure the pace of broadcasting.

One of his major responsibilities will be to see that the operations of the National Broadcasting Company reflect enlightened public opinion, which expresses itself so promptly the morning after any error of taste or judgment or departure from fair play.

We have no hesitation in recommending the National Broadcasting Company to the people of the United States.

It will need the help of all listeners. It will make mistakes. If the public will make known its views to the officials of the company from time to time, we are confident that the new broadcasting company will be an instrument of great public service.

RADIO CORPORATION OF AMERICA

OWEN D. YOUNG, *Chairman of the Board*

JAMES G. HARBORD, *President*

freely increased their power and roamed the dial in search of favorable positions.* The National Broadcasting Company had
begged for peace in the spectrum; once again broadcasting leaders pleaded for government regulation.

The new law seemed to signal an era of stability and prosperity. Major corporations flocked to the new network. Concerts, classical and semiclassical, dominated its initial programming—with *The Ampico Hour, The Maxwell House Hour, The
Palmolive Hour, The General Motors Family Party, The Cities
Service Orchestra.* Continuing from AT&T days were *The Cliquot Club Eskimos, The Ipana Troubadours,* and others. *The
Eveready Hour* scored triumphs with its drama experiments,
especially a program on Joan of Arc starring Rosaline Greene,
which had to be repeated several times.

An air of dignity dominated the proceedings. In the evening
announcers wore tuxedos. They often began, "Ladies and
gentlemen of the radio audience. . . ." Some had quasi-English
accents.

NBC policies, following AT&T's example, began with ex-
treme caution. The company's first president, Merlin H. Aylesworth—recruited from the electric utility field—told a congressional committee in 1928 that NBC sponsors did not go in for
any "direct advertising." Asked to explain further, he said:
"These clients neither describe their product nor name its price
but simply depend on the good-will that results from their contribution of good programs." NBC had apparently adopted the
AT&T policy centered on "trade-name publicity."[11]

Almost as austere in its dedication—at least in regard to nighttime hours—was the first code of the National Association of
Broadcasters. The NAB had been formed in 1923 to combat
ASCAP demands but had expanded into other areas. Its first
code, proclaimed in 1928, stated: "Commercial announcements,
as the term is generally understood, should not be broadcast between seven and eleven p.m." The NAB apparently felt at this
time that business belonged to daytime hours, whereas evening
was a family domain.

---

* The case was *U.S.* v. *Zenith* (1926). Zenith had challenged the legality
of a Hoover order and had won the decision.

But this view soon began to erode. The 1929 stock market crash, and the business collapse that followed, undoubtedly contributed to the shift; resolute salesmanship now seemed needed. The competition of a new and struggling network, the Columbia Broadcasting System, also contributed. Making a perilous start, several times verging on collapse, CBS scrambled for business and soon welcomed whatever George Washington Hill, flamboyant president of American Tobacco, wanted said about Cremo cigars: that they cost five cents and were not made with spit. Between blaring numbers of the Cremo Military Band its announcer shouted: "There is no spit in Cremo!" CBS president William Paley, reviewing the evolution of the art of selling by radio, noted suavely: "Our specific contribution to this end is the permitting of price mention." NBC president Aylesworth apparently felt the pressure and told his Advisory Council:

> We believe that the interests of the listener, the client and the broadcaster are best served under our American system of broadcasting by frankly recognizing the part that each plays in the development. With this thought in mind, and after long consideration, the company has decided to alter its policy with reference to the mention of price in commercial announcements.[12]

But the mention of prices was only one rolling pebble in what was already becoming an avalanche. With AT&T no longer threatening to sue stations for unauthorized "toll radiotelephony," the time-for-sale system spread rapidly. Among ardent early broadcasters were drug companies. They had the example of fantastic successes scored by "Dr." John Romulus Brinkley, whose Kansas station earned untold millions selling drug products—also, goat-gland transplants performed at his private hospital—to solve diverse personal crises. Thousands wrote him of their troubles; Brinkley, alternating with hymns, inspirational guest talks, and country music, diagnosed especially interesting cases over the air, prescribing "Dr. Brinkley's No. 6" or "Dr. Brinkley's No. 17," and, via form letters, prescribed for others by mail. The American Medical Association condemned him as a quack but the Federal Radio Commission kept renewing his license, and even gave him a clear channel. His station seemed to be for *everybody*. In 1930 the license was finally voided but he set up a transmitter across the Mexican border and continued his profitable career. Drug promotion was meanwhile exploding on radio throughout the land. On CBS an anonymous Voice of Experience, giving advice to souls in distress, and sponsored by a group of drug products, was soon receiving 10,000 to 20,000 letters a week. He too discussed the most sensational problems on the air, while the rest were answered via some hundred standardized advice letters, designed to take care of most human problems. CBS also featured the astrologer Evangeline Adams, whose advice—on the air or by mail—was obtained by sending birth-date information and a boxtop of Forhan's toothpaste. Kolynos launched a comparable numerology series from Chicago. The Depression, with its millions of unemployed, provided fertile soil for such series.[13]

Merchandising schemes involving boxtops or other "proof of purchase" were also prominent in campaigns for packaged foods, especially campaigns addressed to children. Some 418,000 sent the folder from an Ovaltine can to get a picture of the heroine of the *Little Orphan Annie* series. And in the magazine *Chain Store Management*—June 1932—the Kellogg company told its dealers how merchandising via the *Singing Lady* program was helping them:

> Just think of this: 14,000 people a day, from every state in the Union, are sending tops of Kellogg packages to the Singing Lady for her song book. Nearly 100,000 tops a week come into Battle Creek. And many hundreds of thousands of children, fascinated by her songs and stories and helped by her counsel on food, are eating more Kellogg cereals today than ever before. This entire program is pointed to *increase consumption*—by suggesting Kellogg cereals, not only for breakfast but for lunch, after school and the evening meal. It's another evidence of the Kellogg policy to build business—and it's building.

The sales leverage exerted by the child audience was noted in another trade-paper advertisement, headlined, "And a little child shall lead them—to your product." But listeners of all ages seemed susceptible to sales messages spoken by a loved or trusted voice. Radio time salesmen and sales brochures stressed this in soliciting business.[14]

Radio was, in fact, winning a loyalty that seemed almost irrational. Social workers noted that destitute families, forced to give up an icebox or furniture or bedding, clung to the radio as to a last link to humanity. In consequence radio, though briefly jolted by the Depression, was soon prospering from it. Motion picture business was suffering, the theater was collapsing, vaudeville was dying, but many of their major talents flocked to radio—along with audiences and sponsors. Some companies were beginning to make a comeback through radio sponsorship. In the process, the tone of radio changed rapidly. To Senator Burton K. Wheeler, the air was turning into a "pawnshop."[15]

Protests were heard with increasing frequency. Among protesters were many who had played an early role in broadcasting, and now considered themselves dispossessed. These included labor, farm, and religious elements. But the largest group of disaffected were educators.

THE DISPOSSESSED

In 1927, as the Federal Radio Commission began its work, 732 stations were broadcasting. About ninety were operated by educational institutions.

The commission set out to reduce the total number of stations and to rearrange dial positions. In the course of an enormous shuffle, almost all stations operated by educational institutions received part-time assignments, in most cases confined to daytime hours—which many considered useless for adult education. In 1927 eight of the educational stations left the air, followed in 1928 by twenty-three others, and in 1929 by thirteen more. But some were determined to hang on.

They were under pressure to leave. Those sharing a channel with a time-selling broadcaster were constantly urged to sell their portion; such sales were routinely approved by the commission. These persuasions were often accompanied by other pressures. The time-selling station would constantly petition the commission for an extension of its operating hours, so as to improve its service "in the public interest." This would cause the commission to schedule a hearing on the proposed redistribution of hours, with the result that the college-owned station had to send a lawyer to Washington to fight for survival. This sometimes produced a new juggling of channels. The costs of constant Washington legal representation were murderous to most educational broadcasters.

When WCAC, Storrs, Connecticut, operated by Connecticut State College, finally gave up in 1932, its dial position had been shifted by the commission eight times in five years. Originally licensed in 1923 and operating full time, its hours and power had been whittled down while it was compelled to share time successively with WTIC, Hartford; WDRC, Hartford; WICC, Bridgeport; and WGBS, New York. When it finally gave up, Connecticut College spokesman Jerome Davis wrote:

> For ten years this station has sought to secure the right to operate a more powerful station and one free from commercial interference. For ten years this station has continued to broadcast into whistle-ridden channels, vainly hoping that some provision would be made for state broadcasting needs.

The college finally concluded that "a significant state educational project" was not possible under these circumstances, and made plans to withdraw.[16]

A *Harvard Business Review* study concluded that "the point seems clear that the Federal Radio Commission has interpreted the concept of public interest so as to favor in actual practice one particular group . . . the commercial broadcasters."[17]

The process left a trail of bitterness, which in 1934 produced the most serious challenge to be faced by sponsor-supported broadcasting.

UPRISING

As the Franklin D. Roosevelt administration entered office in 1933, its activism gave dissidents hope for a new radio deal. When the Administration proposed a new law to replace the Federal Radio Act of 1927, their moment seemed at hand. Roosevelt's aims were actually quite limited: he wanted a new commission, a Federal Communications Commission, which would supervise not only radio and television but also the telephone industry, which had been under the Interstate Commerce Commission. The deep involvement of AT&T in broadcasting made the move seem logical.

But the dissidents offered an amendment that was far more drastic. Sponsored by the influential Senator Robert F. Wagner of New York and Senator Henry D. Hatfield of West Virginia, it promptly won the endorsement of the National Education Association. College presidents, school superintendents, teachers, clergy, and farm leaders lined up behind it.[18]

The Wagner-Hatfield proposal shocked the industry. It provided that *all* existing station licenses be declared "null and void" ninety days after passage of the Act. During that time a new distribution of channels would be made, with one-fourth of all channels allotted to "educational, religious, agricultural, cooperative, and similar non-profit-making associations. . . ." These would have to be "equally as desirable as those assigned to profit-making persons, firms, or corporations."

Passionate argument supported the bill. Dean Thomas E. Brenner of the University of Illinois declared that the Depression had brought on a "sickness" of the national culture, and that recapture of the broadcasting channels was essential to any cure. In a Senate committee hearing, Father John B. Harney of the Paulist Fathers described the treatment given to educational interests as "beggarly and outrageous," and castigated the commission for its habit of basing allocations on financial resources. "Oh yes—income, income—we will do everything we can for you." Such standards, he said, had created an "overlordship" of "commercialists."

Perhaps the most pungent campaigner for the reform bill was James Rorty, a former copywriter for the Batten, Barton, Durstine & Osborn advertising agency, who had, in effect, defected from advertising. As the debate moved to a crisis he published *Our Master's Voice*, a book whose title was derived from an RCA trademark. He attacked advertising in general, but his imagery centered on radio as a sort of screeching gargoyle "set at the top of America's skyscraping adventure in acquisition *ad infinitum*."

> The gargoyle's mouth is a loudspeaker, powered by the vested interest of a two-billion dollar industry, and back of that the vested interests of business as a whole, of industry, of finance. It is never silent, it drowns out all other voices, and it suffers no rebuke, for is it not the voice of America? That is its claim and to some extent it is a just claim. . . .

Countless Americans, said Rorty, had grown up listening to that voice as to an oracle:

> It has taught them how to live, what to be afraid of, what to be proud of, how to be beautiful, how to be loved, how to be envied, how to be successful.

To Rorty the atmosphere seemed saturated with a never-ending "jabberwocky" from hundreds of thousands of loudspeakers.

> Is it any wonder that the American population tends increasingly to speak, think, feel in terms of this jabberwocky? That the stimuli of art, science, religion are progressively expelled to the periphery of American life to become marginal values, cultivated by marginal people on marginal time?[19]

Powered by such rhetoric, the Wagner-Hatfield bill was seen headed for victory. A headline in the business-oriented *Broadcasting* magazine warned: "POWERFUL LOBBY THREATENS RADIO STRUCTURE."[20]

But the bill had a vulnerable feature. Most of the non-profit groups supporting it were in financial straits, and not in a position to support stations from their operating funds. They had therefore included in the bill a proviso that a non-profit licensee could "sell such part of the allotted time as will make the station self-supporting."

It was indeed ironic that the campaigners should look for salvation to the very system they were denouncing. Proponents defended the idea: many non-profit publications, including scholarly journals, received part of their revenue from advertising. But opponents saw it as a target. Senator Clarence C. Dill of Washington, one of the authors of the Radio Act of 1927 and defender of the status quo, expressed moral outrage over the proposal. Wasn't there too much advertising already? Wasn't everybody agreed on that? Now the educators proposed still more of it. "That," said Dill, "is not what the people of this country are asking for!" Thus he neatly turned the concern with "overcommercialization" into an argument for the status quo.[21]

Such attacks were accompanied by more positive moves. Broadcasters pointed out that they had unsold periods that could be devoted—without charge—to educational projects. Why didn't educators make proposals? To underline this point, the *University of Chicago Round Table*, a local Chicago series, was given a berth on one of the NBC networks, the NBC-red; this move came during the Wagner-Hatfield battle. At the same time the other NBC network, the NBC-blue, announced a weekly *America's Town Meeting of the Air*, to emanate from the non-profit Town Hall in New York with national leaders debating major issues. CBS had already, during the first rumblings from educators, begun an *American School of the Air*, a daily series which schools were invited to use in the classroom. There was much talk of "cooperative broadcasting." The Wagner-Hatfield proponents saw all this as a reaction to temporary pressures, and stuck to their guns. But some educators were impressed, and felt that broadcasting was entering a new, promising phase.

In the end Congress voted to instruct the FCC to study the whole question of educational needs, and to report back. The maneuver defused the uprising. In the Senate the Wagner-Hatfield bill lost, 42-23.

But the educators had scored gains. Throughout the following decade the promises made by broadcasters in Senate hearings served as hostages. "Cooperative broadcasting" became part of the administrative language of the industry. Stations were asked, in license-renewal proceedings, about their "public service" broadcasts and what non-profit groups had participated in them. The trend created a secondary type of sponsor, a non-profit type, who might pay program costs but got free time.[22]

But the commercial system had also scored gains. The defeat of the educational uprising had, by implication, established the commercial system as the official system—even though the new law, like the old, sidestepped the issue, and said nothing about commercial sponsorship.

The "cooperative broadcasting" formula brought a period of peace and rising prosperity. And it tended to divide network radio into two separate worlds.

TWO WORLDS

During the 1930's less than half the time available to networks was usually sold out.* Unsold network time was filled with "sustaining" programs. Before Wagner-Hatfield this generally meant music by a staff orchestra—the most economical "filler." Afterwards it seemed essential to devote some of these periods to license-protection programs of a public service nature. Some proved to have other, unexpected values for the networks. They broadened the listening audience, disarmed critics, and gave broadcasting a meaning far beyond entertainment. And some proved to be financially profitable.

One of the two worlds was programmed and controlled by advertising agencies, serving their clients. This was turning into a big-money world, and it provided the networks with their total revenue. The other half reflected the nation's non-profit structure: education, religion, social services. It lived on skimpy rations, necessarily seasoned with dedication.

The two worlds used the same studios and were served by the same studio engineers. But they tended to draw on different writers and directors. There was little interaction between the two worlds. Yet they served as valuable supplements to each other.

Sponsored broadcasting, an observer noted, was often in danger of sliding into prostitution. Educational broadcasting, on the

---

* At CBS and NBC the day was divided into "network time" and "station time." Network time consisted of about twelve hours, in four segments (one of them was "prime time"), which the network could sell to national sponsors. MBS (Mutual Broadcasting System), launched in 1934, was more loosely organized; it never reached competitive status.

other hand, was in danger of dying an old maid. Their cohabitation was unusual but, for the moment, seemed practical and useful.

In the sponsor-controlled hours, the sponsor was king. He decided on programming. If he decided to change programs, network assent was considered *pro forma*. The sponsor was assumed to hold a "franchise" on his time period or periods. Many programs were advertising agency creations, designed to fulfill specific sponsor objectives. The director was likely to be an advertising agency staff employee. During dress rehearsal, an official of the sponsoring company was often on hand in the sponsor's booth, prepared to order last-minute changes. In "Radio City"—completed in 1933—every studio had a sponsor's booth.

The "concerts" of early network days were no longer dominant. Most sponsors now preferred comedy, variety, or drama. Quiz programs were on the rise. The Hooperatings, inaugurated in 1935, showed that comedians—Eddie Cantor, Bob Hope, Jack Benny, Edgar Bergen and Charlie McCarthy—were the surest guarantee of a large audience. But sponsors chose other programming for various corporate reasons.

Thus Boake Carter, an often vituperative news commentator, was sponsored for five years by Philco, 1933-38, and then by General Foods and others. His political views were generally anti-Roosevelt, anti-labor, and isolationist. His views, and the vigor with which he expressed them, apparently helped him to win sponsors and later to lose them. A CIO boycott of Philco products persuaded Philco to drop him. Both his hiring and firing were warmly protested by listeners. But a sponsor's right to make decisions of this sort was not widely challenged at the time.[23]

Similarly political was the *Ford Sunday Evening Hour*, a concert series featuring "intermission talks" by Ford executive William J. Cameron. He lauded the ideas of Henry Ford and philosophized about American institutions, often nostalgically. This gave him opportunities to disparage unemployment insurance, surplus profits taxes, and other measures and proposals of the Roosevelt administration. The series was often attacked, but continued for years.

Political in a more subtle way was *Cavalcade of America*, a history series sponsored by E. I. du Pont de Nemours & Co. It began as an effort at image-repair. The company felt traumatized in the mid-1930's by a Senate investigation of munitions profits in World War I. This showed that du Pont had derived more than a billion dollars from war contracts for a wartime profit of $237,908,339.64—which had sent du Pont stock from $125 to $593. The findings produced indignation—among those who became aware of them. From du Pont they brought a prompt countermeasure: *Cavalcade of America*, designed and produced by the Batten, Barton, Durstine & Osborn advertising agency. It began in October 1935, shortly before the Senate committee report reached print, and continued for two decades. It sought to blur the "merchants of death" image by superimposing another—of a company concerned with "better things for better living." It engaged such talented young writers as Arthur Miller and Norman Rosten, and university professors to check their scripts. It handled history fairly punctiliously insofar as individual programs were concerned. Corporate strategy lay in the careful selection and vetoing of topics. War stories were banned; no shot was to be fired on the du Pont version of American history. The emphasis was on individual achievements in scientific research, and the quest for a better life. Improvements in the lot of women were dramatized periodically. The series was always idealistic in tone; no iconoclasm was permitted. Each program tended to be a tribute to a hero or heroine. Absolute taboos included government projects such as the TVA, which the sponsor considered socialistic; labor history; and, for a long time, the Negro.* Except for science and the role of women, history tended to end in the nineteenth century.

The exclusions were the heart of the sponsorship strategy. They had political ramifications, and were periodically protested by labor and black groups. But most people were quite unaware of the exclusions. They reacted to what they heard—generally,

---

* The ban on Negro topics lasted until 1948, when the company agreed to a program on Booker T. Washington—who had felt the Negro should "keep his place" until better educated.

with approval. Memories from school history courses were coming to life on the air, in stellar productions. The series won many educational awards.[24]

If political projects of this sort, well financed by corporate sponsorship, were widely tolerated, it was because many other voices and views were reaching the air. They did so through the forums and round tables organized early in the decade. They did so also through the substantial news operations that the networks—notably CBS—began to organize in 1935.* These were giving expression to such diverse voices as Edward R. Murrow, William Shirer, Eric Sevareid, Howard K. Smith, Elmer Davis, Raymond Swing, Fred Bate, Max Jordan. Their words, whether in "news bulletins" or "commentaries" or "news analyses," conveyed a variety of opinions. Opinion emerged also in drama, as in the powerful *The Fall of the City*, a verse parable on Nazism by Archibald MacLeish, which foreshadowed Hitler's march into Vienna. It was broadcast in 1937 on the CBS series *The Columbia Workshop*, which was scheduled at 7 p.m. Sundays—a period CBS could not sell because it was opposite Jack Benny on NBC. The audience reached by *The Fall of the City* was small by radio standards but huge by any other, and its impact was electric. It helped launch the radio career of its young narrator, Orson Welles. More significantly, it attracted to radio other major poets—Stephen Vincent Benét, Edna St. Vincent Millay, and others—who suddenly saw the medium ushering in a new era of poetic drama. They, too, began to contribute to the ferment of ideas.

This ferment was complex and chaotic, but real. If Boake Carter's observations were often virulently anti-British, they were effectively countered by Edward R. Murrow and others. If General Mills, sponsoring H. V. Kaltenborn on CBS in 1939, demanded that he not criticize Franco, and fired him when he would not agree, Norman Corwin's unsponsored verse play

---

* News programs heard previously on the networks, by Lowell Thomas, H. V. Kaltenborn, Boake Carter, and a few others, were individual ventures not backed by news departments. The newsmen relied on various sources, including newspapers. After a press-radio "war" in 1933-35, the networks took up news-gathering.

They Fly Through the Air, also on CBS in 1939, was able to heap anger and scorn on the Franco campaign. If the commentator Fulton Lewis, Jr., on MBS, regarded Hitler with considerable equanimity (he sent Hitler advice on how to keep the United States out of the war), contrasting views were heard on the same network from Raymond Gram Swing. If *Cavalcade of America* tended to picture America in white, elitist terms, the CBS sustaining series *The Pursuit of Happiness* made a point of its ethnic diversity, introducing such talents as the black ex-convict "Leadbelly" (Huddie Ledbetter), the "borscht circuit" comedian Danny Kaye, the hobo laureate Woody Guthrie, and scheduling a radio premiere of "Ballad for Americans" in a powerful rendition by Paul Robeson.[25]

Network leaders had mixed feelings about the ferment and clash of opinions. At Washington hearings they emphasized with pride that sustaining schedules were serving a balancing function, performing services that sponsored programs could not be expected to handle. On the other hand, the clash of views brought angry letters, and protests from groups and sponsors and people in government. The networks sometimes tried to mute the debate. CBS made a distinction between news *analysis*, which it encouraged, and news *commentary*, which it decried. But the distinction seemed to affect form more than substance. Kaltenborn described a policy discussion to which he had been summoned by CBS vice president Edward Klauber, in which Klauber requested him to stop saying "I think. . . ." Instead he was to use such phrases as, "The opinion is held in well-informed quarters. . . ." Klauber pointed out that Kaltenborn could "put over the same idea" in that way with less offense.[26]

Despite nervous tremors, the American system of broadcasting during 1935-40 was serving a forum function. It was a time of world turmoil and contentiousness, and the system reflected it. At its apex were commercial operations of enormous popularity, successful in merchandising, and supporting the entire system. In their shelter were varied non-commercial ventures, reaching smaller but substantial audiences, and serving diverse interests.

Some thirty scattered non-commercial stations, mostly supported by state universities, still continued to operate, but their reach was minimal. If the average listener were asked, during 1935-40, about "educational broadcasting," his mind would probably turn not to those stations but to the "public service" programs on the networks, living as guests in the house of the sponsor.

Thus the sponsor-supported system had, by 1940, won a secure place and growing prosperity. It seemed headed for a glittering future.

Then came developments which seemed likely, for the moment, to topple the entire system—but which, in the end, extended its domain into new fields.

SENATOR TRUMAN

Even before the United States became a World War II combatant, consumer products began to disappear from the market; from 1938 on, rearmament became a central concern. After Pearl Harbor, many leading sponsors had nothing to sell to the public. The making and selling of cars, refrigerators, washing machines, radios, television sets, and other equipment yielded to war production. Oil and gas were so strictly rationed that sales promotion was unnecessary, and seemed wrong. Yet major companies involved in these products continued to advertise—to maintain their position for the postwar years, they said.

Behind this were economic factors of which the public was unaware, but which disturbed the Senate committee investigating the defense program—the "Truman committee" under Senator Harry S. Truman of Missouri.

Truman noted that the total costs of advertising, including costs of radio programs, television experiments, time purchases, agency commissions, and publicity, were being deducted by the sponsors as necessary business expenses. Why *necessary*, asked Truman—when the U.S. government was the sole customer?

Donald M. Nelson, chairman of the War Production Board, said advertising was not necessary to do business with the government. Yet advertising funds were pouring into radio in increasing volume.

Another tax factor was at work. To prevent profit bonanzas

of the sort that had descended on du Pont during World War I, the Federal government had adopted an "excess profits" tax that could go as high as 90 per cent. The move had wide public support.

But it meant that if a sponsor spent $1 million on a radio series, he was spending money that would otherwise go almost entirely to the government in taxes. The net cost of the series might be only 10 per cent of the apparent cost. The remainder was really subsidized by the taxpayer.

Truman objected to this. By all means let them advertise, he said, but let them pay for it "out of their own pockets," and not charge it to the taxpayer.

Commissioner of Internal Revenue Guy Helvering announced—October 1942—that corporation tax returns were being examined to disallow excessive deductions.

A furious battle developed, continuing for months. Lobbyists, representing both sponsors and broadcasting companies, converged on Congress and the executive agencies. The prosperity—even the existence—of the broadcasting industry seemed at stake.[27]

But the struggle began to intersect with another struggle, with curious results.

Government agencies were coping with a tangled forest of problems. Americans *had* to be persuaded to save cans, buy war bonds, learn nursing, black out windows, change eating habits, avoid rumors, become air raid wardens, write letters to soldiers, curb travel. How achieve all this?

Sponsors of all leading network programs began to receive a deluge of requests from government agencies and volunteer services. Would Bob Hope please plug the nursing campaign? Would Bing Crosby do a war bond announcement? If Mary Margaret McBride would only explain about saving cans, the campaign would be won. An "avoid rumor" message by Walter Winchell could save thousands of lives. Such requests began before Pearl Harbor, and became a deluge thereafter. Some producers said that if they honored all requests there would be no time for the programs. Print media received similar appeals, but radio was especially inundated. Advertisers saw the barrage as a burden, a duty—and an opportunity.

They asked the Office of War Information, set up early in 1942 under commentator Elmer Davis, to sift through the campaigns to establish priorities. They themselves would form a unit, the War Advertising Council, to allocate the messages to specific media, in accordance with the priorities. On radio the messages might take any form the producer might determine: dramatized, musical, or straight, delivered by announcers or program stars.

Within weeks the system was in operation, and a stream of messages poured forth from the air! Advertising leaders began to speak of their industry as the "information industry." They issued release after release detailing its war services. A 1943 brochure proclaimed that it had already contributed "$100,000,000 worth of talent and time" to the war effort. The brochure was titled *This Is an Army Hitler Forgot!*, and carried photos of dozens of stars. Secretary of Commerce Jesse H. Jones was persuaded to issue a statement on "the many values of advertising to a free nation fighting to maintain its freedom." On behalf of the Commerce Department he praised the war work of the "great information industry . . . essential ingredient of a free society."

The industry was successfully outflanking the tax people and the Truman committee. By mid-1942 victory was in sight. The Administration agreed that advertising costs would be deductible if "reasonable." No great effort was made to define "reasonable." Advertising costs, it seemed, were deductible.[28]

This helped to raise radio prosperity—notably network prosperity—to dizzying heights. Newspapers were experiencing a paper shortage and could not accommodate increased advertising; they were, in fact, reducing it. But radio was available, and was now enriched—financially and culturally—by a wave of institutional sponsorship. General Motors, with no cars to sell, sponsored the recently created NBC Symphony Orchestra under Arturo Toscanini. United States Rubber, with almost no tires to sell to the public, was financing the New York Philharmonic on CBS. Allis Chalmers, in a similar plight, was bringing the Boston Symphony to the American people. The Atlantic Refining Company had resolved to leave the air but, instead, decided to sponsor football on eighty-three stations. The Ford Motor Company, which was making tanks, inaugurated a daily news program on NBC-blue, titled *Watch the World Go By*—a deft reminder of its earlier slogan, "Watch the Fords Go By."

For listeners it was an extraordinarily fruitful period, with little salesmanship; national attention was riveted on radio. For networks it was the most prosperous time they had yet known. For non-profit groups it was fine: they continued to receive time allotments, although these tended to be moved toward the fringes of the schedule as time-sales mounted. For sponsors it was a gratifying period of *noblesse oblige*, at minimal and partly subsidized cost. They were seen as patrons of the arts, Renaissance-style.

But they had achieved something else that was perhaps, in the long run, more significant. When the war ended, advertisers, agencies, and media determined to continue the War Advertising Council as the Advertising Council. As the Office of War Information passed out of existence, the Advertising Council itself assumed the task of determining priorities. The processing and distribution of "public service announcements," or "PSA's," became part of the established machinery of the advertising industry. It held high prestige. The annual meetings of the Advertising Council regularly heard addresses by the President of the United States, praising the industry's services to the nation.

The power to decide what messages are of social importance and must have wide distribution (and which are not) is a considerable power. That it had become part of the domain of sponsors and advertising agencies, who already controlled most network time by purchase, seemed odd to some observers, and even preposterous. But sponsors and agencies had not in the first instance sought a role in this matter. Because of their dominance of the most valuable time—including prime time—the role had been virtually thrust upon them. It was a case of power gravitating toward power. Soon it was taken for granted.

The contentiousness of the prewar years subsided during the war, though not entirely. Purol, sponsoring H. V. Kaltenborn during the war years, found he could still rouse listener indignation—as well as enthusiasm—at frequent intervals. But the company stuck with him, and refrained from pressure, even in the form of advice. Sponsor relations were going through a period of remarkable harmony. Raymond Swing, preparing his commentary on the Nazi invasion of Luxembourg, Belgium, and the Netherlands, was so tortured by the thought of a middle commercial for White Owl Cigars that he offered to step aside for another newsman; instead White Owl waived the middle commercial. Middle commercials were never again heard on the series.[29]

Wartime broadcasting reflected an unprecedented air of consensus. This was exemplified by an appearance of Wendell Willkie on the NBC sustaining series *Words At War*, produced with the cooperation of the Council on Books in Wartime—a unit organized by the major publishers. Each week the Council made available to NBC, without charge, for dramatization, a new book dealing with the war. One of the first programs, featuring Willkie himself, dealt with his book *One World*, about his journey around the world following his defeat in the 1940 presidential election. The program, broadcast in 1943, reenacted his talk with Stalin; then Willkie reported his favorable impressions of the Soviet Union and his strong conviction that it had "survival value." Such words from a former Republican presidential nominee were strange and dramatic, but symptomatic of the moment. They seemed to find acceptance. Shortly afterwards the *Words At War* series, in spite of such previously unthinkable program matter, won Johnson's Wax as sponsor.

Government statements, as in the army's *Why We Fight* films, adopted a similar attitude toward the Soviets. There were some, like the House un-American activities committee under Representative Martin Dies of Texas, who protested all this, charged subversion in high places, and predicted a day of reckoning. But during the war such charges were generally shrugged off. Consensus ruled. But it could not long survive the peace.

TRANSITION

The American system of broadcasting had enormous prestige as the war ended. It was holding the nation spellbound. Its economic arrangements had fostered rapid expansion and brilliant technology. It had served war needs. And it had established a *modus vivendi* between commercial and public service interests.

Now television was on the way. A brief prewar start—aborted for war reasons—followed by wartime advances in electronics had set the stage for a television explosion, just as World War I had set the stage for radio. This time sponsors, too, were ready. Their advertising agencies had experimented with programs and commercials.

The sponsor-supported system evolved for radio offered a pattern for the age of television. Few doubted it would be followed. But the decade 1945-55 became one of constant upheaval and conflict, with numerous overlapping transitions.

The main transition was, of course, from radio to television, as television erupted in a gold rush atmosphere. It won the national spotlight with astonishing speed and soon spread abroad as many American companies became multinational—partly in consequence of the Marshall Plan and other aid programs.

But there was, at the same time, a transition from war production to the production of consumer goods. This wiped out the rationale for most institutional advertising and brought sharp merchandising competition—at home and, later, abroad. This consumer goods explosion, held back briefly by the Korean War, increased the number, length, and stridency of commercials, and brought back much of the "pawnshop" atmosphere of the early 1930's. It was abetted by a wave of quiz and game shows, in radio and then in television, in which contestants were showered with consumer goods—prizes that had a dramatic impact of their own after the austerity of the war years. Radio's *$64 Question* became television's *$64,000 Question*, in which the "consolation prize" for losers was a Cadillac. Such prizes were donated by manufacturers in return for product descriptions on the air. Thus sponsor commercials were surrounded by mini-commercials for subsidiary sponsors. There were also *sub rosa* sponsors. Drama writers and directors were advised that if they could make potato chips a part of any happy party scene, a $100 check would be forthcoming from a publicity agent—who had, in fact, a long list of products that could earn similar pay-offs—

Money, money, who wants money?
You know the answer when you do.
At General Public Loan
We're your kind of people
And we like to do business
With people like you.

Cash—at your convenience!
Cash—at your command!
When you need money
For any good reason
We're the kind of people who understand.

Money, money, who wants money?
You know the answer when you do.
At General Public Loan
We're your kind of people
And we like to do business
With people like you.

INFLATING THE CREDIT BUBBLE: a spend-now "singing commercial," *c.* 1960.

parallels to the "payola," or commercial bribery, that was becoming endemic to disc-jockey programs in radio. Along with feverish product promotion went credit promotion—"buy now, pay later." Banks and loan companies virtually begged people to borrow money. Thus the ascetic war years were replaced by a frontier boom town atmosphere, with a scramble for stakes large and small.[30]

The period saw, at the same time, a transition from consensus to paranoia, as the cold war took charge of the American scene. Within months after the coming of peace three ex-FBI men, organized as American Business Consultants, Inc., were peddling along Madison Avenue a newsletter titled *Counterattack*, listing "pinks," "reds," "subversives," "fellow travelers," "dupes"—terms used interchangeably—who should be shunned by agencies and sponsors. The operation was financed by Alfred Kohlberg, a leader of the "China Lobby" and later an ardent backer of Senator Joseph McCarthy. The newsletter seemed to have little immediate impact, but won enough subscribers to become a financial success, so that competing blacklist operations began to spring up. Their impact grew after the onset of the Korean War in 1950. That year American Business Consultants issued *Red Channels*, a book purporting to expose "communist influence" in network programming and naming 151 of the most honored men and women in the broadcasting industry as part of it. "Citations" enumerated their deeds: they had aided Negro civil rights drives, opposed Franco, favored recognition of the Mao Tsetung regime, spoken out against the hydrogen bomb, criticized the House committee on un-American activities, and favored a détente with the Soviet Union. Such views and activities were now depicted as treasonable, and elements of an international "conspiracy." Senator Joseph McCarthy, adding his fulminations to the hysteria, helped to fasten on television in its childhood years a terror of "controversial" people and "controversial" topics—a phobia that tended to stunt its development.[31]

It was also a period in which the *modus vivendi* between sponsored and public service broadcasting collapsed. To finance the costly transition to television, networks pared expenditures on sustaining radio programs; many hours were given over to disc-jockey programming. CBS scrapped its *School of the Air* and *Columbia Workshop*. The NBC Symphony Orchestra, no longer supported by General Motors, had a brief television trial and was then marked for dissolution. *America's Town Meeting of the Air* disappeared in similar fashion. Early network television ventures included items intensely admired by educators, such as *Amahl and the Night Visitors* by Gian-Carlo Menotti, produced by an NBC opera unit; *What in the World?*, a notable archaeology series; and *Adventure*, a CBS series involving the cooperation of various museums. But escalating time sales pushed such projects aside. Educators grew restive, and began once more to agitate for special channels. In 1950 they formed a Joint Committee (later renamed "Council") for Educational Television and won Ford Foundation support for its agenda. At the FCC Frieda Hennock, its first woman member, championed the Council's cause, and in 1952 the FCC was persuaded to earmark 242 television channels for non-commercial use. This time, mindful of Wagner-Hatfield experience, the educators did not ask the right to solicit advertising support. Thus they met less opposition from commercial interests—none from those who already held licenses, because channels enjoined from commercial use would reduce competition for the advertising dollar. Commercial stations were even inclined to donate surplus equipment—and win a tax deduction. And they felt happily relieved of the kinds of obligation incurred by the Wagner-Hatfield battle. They were "off the hook."[32]

The American system of earlier days had now fissioned into two systems. The commercial system was booming. The non-commercial system, on the other hand, began in agonizing poverty. Educators had scored a victory, but some felt they had won an electronic tin cup.

Along with these transitions was still another—from live to film, east to west. The 1945-55 decade saw television begin almost wholly with live production, with strong theater influence; by the end of the decade network schedules were 80 per cent on film. In the early years the major Hollywood studios had boycotted the medium, withholding both their films and their contract talent. By 1954 they sensed that history was passing them by. Warner Brothers, leading the way, signed a contract to produce for ABC-TV; starting with *Cheyenne*, it struck gold with numerous profitable western series, and the other studios followed, while also unloading their backlog of feature films. Hollywood quickly replaced New York as chief program source for the small screen—in drama, comedy, variety. The stress was now on "action-adventure" drama: the pursuit of evil men.[33]

All these transitions were overshadowed and propelled by the irresistible advance of television. It surpassed all predictions. In cities where television began, other media experienced agonies. In 1950-51 film theaters closed in waves: 70 closings in eastern Pennsylvania, 134 in southern California, 61 in Massachusetts, 64 in the Chicago area, 55 in Metropolitan New York. On radio, ratings plummeted; even Bob Hope, a leader for two decades, found his radio audience evaporating:

1949	23.8
1951	12.7
1953	5.4

Now no major sponsor dared stay out of television. Some who made the plunge issued astonishing success stories. Hazel Bishop lipsticks, doing a $50,000 annual business, took up television in 1950; solely through television advertising, sales zoomed to $4,500,000 in 1952, and continued up. There were many such tales, especially in the drug and cosmetic field. For the 1954-55 season, NBC and CBS were sold out months ahead. *Sponsor* magazine advised: "So far as nighttime availabilities on NBC or CBS are concerned, forget about it. There just aren't any." Even ABC, a late television starter, was doing brisk business.[34]

All these transitions were setting the stage for another, which was to take longer: a change in business relations, modifying the role of the sponsor—in ways whose ultimate effect was not immediately clear.

Network leaders had long chafed over the degree of control they had yielded, early in broadcasting history, to advertising agencies and sponsors. Aside from philosophical questions, it had resulted in schedules that were haphazard and often senseless. William Paley, at CBS, was determined that television should evolve differently. So was Sylvester L. ("Pat") Weaver, Jr., who in 1949 became NBC vice president in charge of television, and in 1953 took over the presidency. He argued for a "magazine concept"—a system under which sponsors would buy only inserts in programs produced by the networks, or by independent producers for the networks, under network control. He launched *Today* and *Tonight* on the "magazine" basis, and both became large money-earners for the network. But these were in fringe periods, and served a miscellany of sponsors. Many major sponsors, long-time inhabitants of prime time, resisted the Weaver idea. So did many people in his own sales department. For years they had sold broadcasting to sponsors on the basis of a "gratitude factor"—the osmosis of affection and trust from program to product. The magazine concept undermined accepted doctrine.

Semi-official industry pronouncements also decried the magazine approach. A vice president of the Association of National Advertisers warned that if advertisers "could not be identified with the particular program of their choice, they could not justify, for simple economic reasons, their present investment in television and would feel impelled to withdraw." The magazine concept, said a former president of the National Association of Broadcasters, "could not possibly be of benefit to anyone involved."[35]

The argument seemed arrested in mid-air. Many sponsors continued with their established vehicles and procedures. As costs rose, alternating sponsorships were becoming common: thus *Philco Television Playhouse* and *Goodyear Television Playhouse*, as scheduled 1951-55, were really the same Sunday evening drama series with sponsors alternating—each spending $25,000 to $35,000 per program, aside from time costs. The arrangement scarcely reduced the amount of sponsor control. ABC-TV pioneered with shared sponsorships, in which each sponsor dominated a segment of a program. The arrangement involved some diminution of control, but the arrangement seemed to satisfy many sponsors with moderate-sized budgets.

When Weaver left the NBC presidency in 1955, his magazine concept seemed to have made little headway. But other factors were beginning to come into play. As the boom expanded, and as television came to be recognized as an unprecedented force in American society, the role of the sponsor was increasingly called in question.

QUALMS

Feelings of dissatisfaction were intensified by an accumulation of disputes and crises.

Early television sponsors who experienced huge successes included the Block Drug Company, maker of the chlorophyll toothpaste Amm-i-dent and many other products. In 1950 it began to sponsor *Danger* over CBS; within a year, Amm-i-dent became number two among the hundred toothpastes on the market. Block used the series also to plug mouthwashes, liniments, and shampoos, and all prospered. Block became one of the most euphoric of sponsors, pouring $20 million into television in the next five years, and often sending advertising agency executives thousands of miles to persuade additional stations to carry the series—using "under-the-counter" payments if necessary. It cost Block $8000 to get onto an Iowa station, but sales jumped $25,000 in that one city, so "it was worth it," according to a Block executive.*

Amid the heady successes, Mr. Leonard Block received a letter from Laurence Johnson, a supermarket executive in Syracuse, N.Y., and an officer in the National Association of Supermarkets. Johnson—a fanatic red-hunter—noted that the cast credits on the *Danger* series had sometimes included performers who, he said, were listed in *Counterattack* as politically suspect. Johnson therefore made what he called an "offer."

In his supermarkets he would arrange side-by-side displays of Block's Amm-i-dent and its chief rival, Lever Brothers' Chloro-

---

* During this period many cities had only one station, which could accept programs from any of the three networks. This put station executives in a bargaining position. They sometimes found themselves strenuously wooed —and bribed—to influence their choice. The Block payments are detailed in *Sponsor*, May 30, 1955.

dent. In front of each display would be a sign. The Chlorodent sign would say that Lever Brothers used only "pro-American actors" and shunned "Stalin's little creatures." The Amm-i-dent sign would explain why Block used "communist fronters"; Mr. Block himself was invited to write it. The letter went on: "Would not the results of such a test be of the utmost value to the thousands of supermarkets throughout America . . . ?"

As a final blackmailing fillip, Johnson added: "This letter will be held awaiting your answer for a few days. Then copies will be sent to the following. . . ." Here he listed business and patriotic organizations that included the United States Chamber of Commerce, the Sons of the American Revolution, the Catholic War Veterans, the Super Market Institute of Chicago—and many others.

Mr. Block reacted with panic: his expanding empire seemed threatened with catastrophe. He quickly reassured Mr. Johnson. He ordered casts to be checked thenceforth against blacklists and newsletters recommended by Johnson. The Block Drug Company was not alone in all this. Sponsor after sponsor was falling into line, nudged by Johnson's letters and offers of "polls," and bombardments from other sources as well. Johnson's missives, sometimes reenforced by personal visits, seem to have been especially effective.[36]

The Laurence Johnson successes make clear one reason why blacklists quickly conquered television and radio. Products sold through supermarkets accounted for more than 60 per cent of broadcast revenues. Manufacturers of such products were especially vulnerable to pressures that threatened their place on supermarket shelves. The networks, which proved equally susceptible to Johnson's "offers" and polls, were vulnerable to pressures that threatened their most lucrative customers. That television programming decisions should hang on such pressures clearly held appalling implications.

The pressures of the day went deeply into editorial policies. In 1955 U.S. Steel was sponsoring a series produced by the Theater Guild under supervision of the Batten, Barton, Durstine & Osborn advertising agency—one of the most conservative agencies. As in the *Cavalcade of America* series, BBD&O kept the series free of race-relations stories.* Not only were these considered inimical to business; interest in the subject was now regarded—by many, including the FBI—as a likely symptom of communist leanings. This explains the extraordinary brouhaha over *Noon on Doomsday*, by Rod Serling.

Serling had been stunned by the Emmett Till case, which took place in 1955. The episode involved a fourteen-year-old black youth in Mississippi who had whistled at a white woman, which had prompted two white men to seize him, shoot him, and dump his body into the Tallahatchie River. In the face of overwhelming evidence, a local jury had acquitted them, but the community had later treated them coolly. Serling was interested in the phenomenon of a town closing ranks against outside pressures. He felt the community was saying, "They're bastards, but they're *our* bastards." When Serling discussed this with the Theater Guild as a story topic, he readily agreed—in the interest of a sale—to remove the racial factor by making the black youth "something else." The victim became an old pawnbroker; the killer, a neurotic malcontent lashing out at the old man as a scapegoat for his own shortcomings. The play, skillfully written by Serling, was accepted by the Theater Guild, the advertising agency, and the sponsor, and went into rehearsal.

But Serling casually told a reporter that the story had been originally suggested by the Emmett Till case, and the reporter mentioned this in a newspaper column. Then all hell broke loose. Serling found himself in endless meetings with executives of the Theater Guild, the Batten, Barton, Durstine & Osborn advertising agency, and U.S. Steel; all became involved in script revisions. Everything frightened them. It was said that Southern White Citizens Councils were threatening a boycott against U.S. Steel. Serling was assured this was no idle threat; they

---

* It should be noted that "controversial" issues are highly changeable. In the 1950's advertisers readily asserted that they could not afford to have their products known as "Negro products." This influenced programming and commercials. By the 1970's Negro purchasing power was considered formidable, and black participation in commercials and programs had become mandatory. Behind these shifts was one unchanging element: the assumption that merchandising factors must determine editorial policy.

had carried out boycotts, he was told, against Ford and Philip Morris. The Southern location therefore had to be changed. An unspecified location was not good enough; it had to be New England. To prove it was New England, the play had to open on a white church spire. Anything that might suggest the South had to be changed. Plot details were changed throughout rehearsal; the play emerged as an absurdity. The hysteria was bizarre, but perhaps also ominous. It cast doubt on the sanity of prevailing editorial processes.[37]

Not all sponsors were so given to instant terror. The case of Alcoa and *See It Now* exemplified remarkable steadfastness. In 1951 Alcoa decided to sponsor an Edward R. Murrow series for reasons similar to those which had impelled du Pont toward a history series. Alcoa had been the subject of a Federal antitrust suit, having been found to control 90 per cent of the aluminum market. Losing the case, Alcoa considered its image tarnished. It approached Edward R. Murrow, a figure revered for his World War II radio reports and honored for integrity. He was invited to launch an Alcoa-sponsored television series, which became *See It Now,* produced by Murrow in collaboration with Fred W. Friendly. Irving W. Wilson, President of Alcoa, told them: "You do the programs, we'll make the aluminum. Don't tell us how to make the aluminum, and we won't tell you how to make the programs." The promise was kept. During the first two years this caused few problems. But the increasing influence of McCarthyism troubled Murrow, and he became determined to focus on it. Late in 1953 he began a series of programs dealing with McCarthyism, including one on Senator McCarthy himself, in which McCarthy was offered time to reply—an offer he accepted. After the first of the McCarthy programs, Wilson told Murrow: "I wouldn't ask you not to do such programs, but I would hope you wouldn't do them every week." "Neither would we," said Murrow. During the following months they did several. The programs polarized public opinion and brought on Alcoa a flood of vituperative mail, pressure from dealers, denunciations from columnists. The mail ran five to four against Murrow, but Alcoa held firm. A year later—in 1955, when the hubbub had subsided—Alcoa withdrew its sponsorship, explaining that an increasingly competitive market called for a shift from institutional advertising to sales promotion. CBS continued *See It Now* on an intermittent basis, occasionally sponsored or partly sponsored, until 1958, when it was dropped from the schedule. Its budget—$90,000 for a 1-hour program—could not be recouped through partial sponsorship.

Alcoa's fidelity in the face of pressures remains legendary. But the sequence of events raises questions. Must the existence of such a series, which leading critics considered a historic contribution to the democratic process, and which had apparently helped mitigate prevailing hysteria—must such a series depend on the appearance of a courageous sponsor? Or on a sponsor with image problems? Is television journalism to be a by-product of public relations crises? In the end the much-discussed Alcoa ordeal—its "years of sitting on the hot-seat," as *Sponsor* magazine called it—made most sponsors wary of documentaries, particularly when produced by a free-thinking entity like the Murrow unit.[38]

They were less averse to documentaries they could control. Documentaries of this sort were beginning to appear in local telecasts throughout the country, distributed mainly by Modern Talking Picture Service and other distributors of "public relations films." The key to their operation was that the films were "free"—to schools, churches, clubs, theaters, television stations. For each use the distributor received a fee from the sponsor—usually $15 for a theater or television booking, lesser amounts for other uses. A sponsor, having spent $50,000 on the production of a half-hour film, might spend $250,000 subsidizing its distribution over a few years.

These films, on a large range of subjects, specialized in an almost subliminal type of advertising. A magnificent film on skiing might end with scenes of evening conviviality; on the table you would notice a bottle of Old Crow Bourbon, and its sponsorship would be fleetingly credited at the end. In a film on hunting techniques you might notice, in passing, equipment made by Remington Arms. Some films were highly informative, such as one on the history of the automobile—with some of the more triumphant moments reserved for Ford cars, the sponsor.

Not surprisingly, AT&T, inventor of sponsored broadcasting, had also pioneered business-sponsored film distribution. Modern Talking Picture Service had begun in the 1920's as an AT&T unit. Spun off in the 1930's under antitrust pressure, it continued to grow. By the 1950's it could report that 53,000 schools and colleges, 36,000 churches, and 28,000 clubs and groups were using its films. Theaters devastated by television were beginning to save rental costs by filling available gaps with free sponsored shorts. Television stations were likewise turning to sponsored items to fill fringe periods. Network affiliates used them to help fill "station time." By 1956 Modern claimed that 99 per cent of American television stations were using its films.[39]

But in the late 1950's it was not sponsor influence over fringe periods but sponsor control of network prime time that was causing concern. The control pointed up an essentially fictitious aspect of the whole structure of broadcasting. The Attorney General mentioned it in a 1959 report to the President. He pointed out that individual stations were "legally responsible" for what they broadcast, but that they had long surrendered control over much programming to the networks, who had in turn sold it to advertisers and their agents.[40]

The FCC was well aware of all this, but preferred to dwell on less thorny problems. In 1959 it finally authorized a staff study of "television network program procurement," in which advertising agency executives and others were queried about program decision-making.

Their testimony showed fascinating ambivalences. Some, aware of legal quicksands, tended to minimize their own role. Others, apparently fearful that they would seem not to be earning their substantial agency commissions, tended to magnify it and to insist on its importance, as a matter of responsibility. "When we are representing a client and his investment," said Nicholas Edward Keesely, vice president of the Lennen & Newell agency, "we have to bend backwards to be sure that you don't get into these areas. . . ." He meant danger areas, such as those he had confronted in a *Playhouse 90* drama sponsored by one of his agency's clients, the natural gas industry. The play dealt with the Nuremberg trials.

The script came through and this is why we get paid, going through the script. In going through the script, we noticed gas referred to in a half dozen places that had to do with the death chambers. This was just an oversight on somebody's part. We deal with a lot of artistic people in the creative end, and sometimes they do not have the commercial judgment or see things as we are paid to see, and we raised the point with CBS and they said they would remove the word "gas," and we thought they would, and they did in some cases, and at the last minute we found that there were still some left in. As a result—and this was just, I think, stupidity—the show went on the air where the word "gas" was deleted by the engineer. . . .

Q. The objection with respect to the word "gas," did it come from you originally, or was it on the part of your clients?

A. It came from us. This is our job.

Q. That's part of your job?

A. Darn right.[41]

Those executives who minimized their own role generally insisted that interference was very seldom necessary. Vice president C. Terence Clyne of the McCann-Erickson agency—which was spending about $100 million a year on television and radio on behalf of various clients—said:

Actually there have been very few cases where it has been necessary to exercise a veto, because the producers involved and the writers involved are normally pretty well aware of what might not be acceptable.

Q. In other words, they know already before they start writing and producing what the limitations are, the subject matter limitations, that you will accept and your client will accept—is that correct?

A. That is correct.[42]

This view, expressed again and again, was meant to reassure. Yet the vista of a generation of producers and writers so attuned to sponsor wishes that they automatically avoided "areas" considered, at the moment, controversial, was scarcely inspiring. The tamed artist was perhaps as ominous a phenomenon as the vetoing sponsor.

By and large, the testimony of the agency program chiefs did not suggest a renaissance in the making. A vice president of the Ted Bates agency, Richard A. Pinkham, offered this glimpse of sponsor supervision:

> I can give you what I hope will not be an indiscreet example.
> . . . Last year two tobacco companies had similar programming.
> Each issued a tobacco policy for his show. These were on two
> separate shows. One company manufactured a filter cigarette,
> and his policy indicated that the heavy must smoke non-filter
> cigarettes.
> Q. The heavies are villains?
> A. Villains. Whereas the manufacturer of the non-filter cigarette
> insisted that the heavy smoke a filtered cigarette. It sounds
> ridiculous, but it's not at all. . . . It's amusing, but not ridicu-
> lous. The association of the product that might be recognized as
> the client's product with a villain, a murderer, or whatever, is
> certainly something to be avoided.[43]

The agency witnesses were followed by "non-industry" witnesses—teachers, clergymen, journalists, and others. Almost all
blamed shortcomings of television on the dominance of the advertiser—often in scornful language. They spoke of "moral
bankruptcy," of the invasion of the home by an "everlasting
peddler," creating a culture "not worth living for and not worth
dying for." Their testimony came at a time when each network
carried only fifteen minutes of evening news and was without a
regular documentary series; the massive "escapism" was roundly
condemned. Some witnesses demanded "total divorce" of programs from advertiser influence. It seemed a replay of the Wagner-Hatfield assault.

In the end dramatic events—a major scandal—forced the networks to take action.

CHANGING THE GUARD

Late in 1959 Charles Van Doren, who had repeatedly denied
"irregularities" in winning $129,000 during his appearances on
the *Twenty-One* series—in which he had seemed to perform mi-

racles of concentration and recall while perspiring in an isolation booth—finally admitted that all answers had been given him in advance. His recantation of perjured testimony brought a stream of other recantations—some hundred contestants, producers, and others had apparently lied to a grand jury. The scandal rocked the industry, and reached into sponsorship levels. Charles Revson, whose sponsorship of *The $64,000 Question* had enabled Revlon cosmetics to engulf the products of Hazel Bishop, Inc., had repeatedly given orders as to which contestants should win —and thus continue on the series—and which should be disposed of. He left details to the producers, but was furious if his instructions were not carried out.[44]

Amid congressional hearings, FCC probes, grand jury proceedings, and lawsuits, all three networks launched reorganizations. They revised surveillance procedures: NBC's "continuity acceptance" unit became the "standards and practices" unit, with enlarged duties. CBS president Frank Stanton decreed that everything on CBS must now be "what it purports to be." He even ordered that canned laughter and applause be identified as such, but this was soon rescinded.

A program upheaval followed. Big-prize quizzes were canceled. Some were replaced by episodic film series from Hollywood, but there was also a return of the documentary. Each network, to restore something of its "public service" image, ordered a documentary rebirth. Only a year after the demise of *See It Now*, CBS instructed Fred Friendly to start a new and similar series, *CBS Reports*. NBC instituted a documentary series under the title *NBC White Paper*. ABC launched a *Close-Up* series. Some network executives looked on these as a costly, though momentarily necessary, form of window-dressing, but others saw hope of occasional sponsors more intent on prestige than ratings. There were encouraging signs in that direction. ABC secured Bell & Howell as sponsor for some of its *Close-Up* programs. Bell & Howell also became a partial sponsor, along with Goodrich, of *CBS Reports*. At NBC, president Robert Kintner was finding Gulf Oil ready to sponsor frequent news specials and occasional documentaries.

But a change of greater potential significance involved scheduling. All three networks moved toward full control of their schedules. "We will be masters in our own house," said Stanton. The networks would do the scheduling and let sponsors know what was available. CBS said it would consider programs from any source; it would look for "the best programming . . . whatever the source." But independent producers were now on notice that programs must be licensed to the network, not the sponsor. The network, having determined its schedule, would deal with sponsors and their advertising agencies.

The pronouncements were welcomed by many. The networks obviously had a broader constituency than any sponsor, and were considered far more likely to rise above merchandising considerations.

However, having made his sweeping declarations, Stanton began to trim them. Apparently "the best programming . . . whatever the source" would not apply to documentaries. In the documentary field, CBS announced that it would schedule only its own productions. This was asserted to be necessary in the interest of "standards," but seemed to independent documentarists a determination to corner for its own productions the limited sponsor funds available for documentaries. The other networks announced similar policies.[45]

Stanton also seemed at pains to mollify sponsors. In 1960 he explained:

> Since we are advertiser-supported we must take into account the general objectives and desires of advertisers as a whole. An advertiser has very specific practical objectives in mind. He is spending a very large sum of money—often many millions of dollars—to increase his sales, to strengthen his distribution and to win public favor. And so in dealing with this problem, it seems perfectly obvious that advertisers cannot and should not be forced into programs incompatible with their objectives.

It seemed a promise to provide programs "compatible" with advertiser objectives. But he went further. He observed that advertisers and their agents often wanted to "participate" in the creative process, and he felt they should be allowed to. What did all this mean?[46]

The year 1960 did bring changes. In May *Broadcasting* magazine, discussing the coming season, reported: "Four out of five
shows in prime time will be licensed to the networks which
carry them, and sold in turn to advertisers." This reversed previous practice.[47]

There was a simultaneous shift, continuing throughout the
following decade, toward the purchase of spots instead of complete programs. Program costs, which rose to at least double
those of the 1950's, were a factor in this. By 1970 the sponsor
of a 1-hour drama in prime time was likely to have to pay
$200,000 for the program and a similar amount for the time—
depending on the number of stations involved—for a total investment of around $400,000. Under the new system the net-
work sought a comparable revenue from such a program by
selling six 1-minute insertions for around $70,000 each. For
greater flexibility, the networks soon adopted the policy of let-
ting each one-minute gap be used for two 30-second commercials. This meant that the sale of six minutes could result in as
many as twelve 30-second commercials.* The system encouraged a dramaturgy full of intermediate climaxes, to create sus-
pense for commercial breaks. How else the spot-selling system
might affect programming was not at once clear.

But meanwhile another arena was winning sponsor attention—
educational television or, to use its later name, "public" television.

GOING PUBLIC

The educational television system decreed by the FCC in its
1952 channel reservations had almost died of malnutrition in
infancy. The Ford Foundation helped early stations into existence via construction grants; but that support had to be

---

* As of 1970, the NAB Television Code allowed 10 minutes of "non-
program material" in a prime time hour; this included commercials but also
"billboards," promotional announcements for other programs, and credits
in excess of 30 seconds. The allowance for other hours was 16 minutes
per hour.

matched by local or regional funds, and these proved elusive in many cities, the large as well as the small. In New York, Washington, and Los Angeles, all channels in the standard VHF waveband were already in use, so that only UHF channels were available. Sets already bought could not receive these without expensive converters. Building an audience would be slow, up-hill work.

The New York State Regents nonetheless recommended state-supported stations in New York City and other locations, but Governor Thomas E. Dewey sidetracked and buried the proposal. The Washington fund-raising efforts likewise failed throughout the 1950's. In Los Angeles a UHF station was started in 1953 but collapsed within months. For a decade the non-commercial system had no affiliates in the three major news and talent centers. And it was invisible to most Americans.

In San Francisco the availability of VHF channel 9 offered a more hopeful outlook. A station was launched in 1954, but with such scant funds that it sometimes limited itself to one hour a day of telecasting. Within a year its board of trustees, failing to find enough backing, voted to dissolve the station. The staff, however, pleaded for a chance to save the day, and staged an on-the-air auction of donated items that proved a financial and social success, sufficient to help the station turn the corner. On-the-air auctions became a standard device for educational television, for raising funds and pushing membership drives. They meant survival for some stations, in a few cases raising 25 per cent of their subsistence budgets.

That the system survived was mainly due to Ford Foundation contributions.* In addition to construction funds for individual

---

* The Ford Foundation simultaneously launched an experiment in commercial television. It financed the 90-minute series *Omnibus*, hosted by Alistair Cooke and available for commercial sponsorship, to test the proposition that an uncompromisingly intelligent and challenging series could win sponsors. In five seasons of Sunday afternoon programs it won many awards, a loyal following, and sponsors. The Foundation had spent approximately $8.5 million, recouping $5.5 million from sponsor payments. But the project had not visibly influenced other producers or sponsors, and the Foundation decided to end its experiment. The producer Robert Saudek continued the series for a time as a private venture.

stations, it financed establishment of a program service—which acquired the name National Educational Television, or NET—and kept it going until the late 1960's with annual grants, usually in the range of $3 to $6 million. NET provided stations with the nucleus of a schedule, and gave the system the semblance of a network. However, the system had no cable interconnection; such linkage was far beyond its means. Instead the programs came to each station on film—a package of some five hours a week at first, gradually expanded to double that amount. The shipment was routed from station to station to save print costs. About 1960 the system began to shift to videotape.

Funds were so scarce at first that program budgets averaged $4500 per half hour. For a time NET relied on off-the-tube films of local productions, which for financial reasons were likely to be lectures or round tables. Film series commissioned by NET were gradually added, necessarily on a small scale. The style and poverty of the system were interrelated. Only the long-range hopes and determination of a cluster of station and NET leaders, reinforced by Ford Foundation injections, kept the system alive.

For years, some of the reserved channels remained unused. Entrepreneurs anxious to plunge into commercial television pressed the FCC to release the channels for commercial use. *Broadcasting* magazine editorialized: "One day the FCC must take another look at the Communications Act in relation to these socialistic reservations."[48]

Some stations survived through support from local or state education systems. This usually required production of televised courses for classroom or supplementary viewing. These gave subsistence support, but the academic programming did not readily arouse excitement among a general audience—the sort of excitement that could spark viewer contributions.

Some stations began to look to business corporations for program help. In 1957 KTCA-TV, launched to serve the St. Paul–Minneapolis area, persuaded the Minneapolis Farmers and Mechanics Bank to "underwrite" a series titled *Money Matters*. The bank ran advertisements to promote the series. Along with a brief credit, the bank's picture appeared at the start of each program. The commercial stations of the area were outraged by what they considered a "doublecross." All four stations had helped KTCA-TV come into being, via funds and technical help. Now they saw the "non-commercial" station beginning to tap the sponsorship resources of the area. "What I'd like to say is unprintable," said the president of commercial KSTP-TV. About the same time WGBH-TV, Boston, ran a series on *The Facts of Medicine* prepared with the cooperation of Harvard University and produced with a grant from the John Hancock Life Insurance Company, which received a credit. The *Wall Street Journal*, citing this and a number of other such projects, observed that "non-commercial" television was being put to "solid commercial use." Its headline declared: "Non-commercial TV Sells Stock, Pianos, and Trains Workers."[49]

The FCC, however, took a different view. Its regulations governing non-commercial licensees (in FM and TV) did not forbid programs donated by others. They did forbid "commercial announcements of any character" in connection with such programs, but a "credit" did not fall into this category. The Communications Act of 1934, like the Radio Act of 1927, *required* identification of anyone "furnishing" a program. A credit was therefore not only proper, but mandatory.

Thus "trade-name publicity," which had once been the mainstay of commercially sponsored broadcasting, was now becoming a feature of "non-commercial" broadcasting—one that had the FCC's blessing and was certain to grow in importance.

It entered NET operations in 1959 when Field Enterprises, Eli Lilly & Co., IBM, and other companies made grants for programs to be distributed to the system. In 1961 NET mailed to 2000 business corporations its first public appeal for such funds, in a booklet titled *The Fourth Network*. That same year Humble Oil, a division of Standard Oil of New Jersey, underwrote the distribution and promotion of *An Age of Kings*, a 15-week BBC-TV series in which eight of Shakespeare's plays of English history were presented as one continuous pageant. Its extraordinary quality struck fire with NET audiences, and the winning over of a huge oil company—later known as Exxon—seemed an auspicious event for educational television. Still, much of its schedule remained severe and uninviting. *Newsweek* critic Joseph Morgenstern said it was "a virtuous bore," and added:

Its best friends know this in their heart of hearts, and quietly repine. Its worst enemies know this in their purse of purses, and quietly rejoice. . . ."

During the 1960's the idea of Federal backing for the educational system gained currency, but slowly. To many people the idea connoted "socialism" and "government control." A cautious first step was taken in 1961 with authorization of Federal aid for station construction—not programming. But the funds helped the system expand. It finally acquired outlets in Washington (1961), New York (1962), and Los Angeles (1964). By 1966 it consisted of a hundred stations and was becoming a national presence—one that might attract more underwriters.[50]

It also, on occasion, struck an independent note, reflecting views not aired over commercial television. It was often this note that brought viewer response—and gifts. With the escalation of the Vietnam War, the cleavage between commercial and noncommercial television became more evident; eventually it became an issue.

The funds NET received annually from the Ford Foundation were "unrestricted" funds; decisions as to subject matter and treatment were up to NET. NET producers felt that one of their chief obligations was to provide an "alternative" to commercial television; they sometimes spoke of their own system as "alternative television." Viewer response encouraged them in that direction. As the Vietnam War rose in fury, an alternative seemed increasingly demanded.

The Vietnam escalation of 1965-67 found commercial network television hewing fairly steadily to the Administration line. Newscasts often seemed to be pipelines for government rationales and declarations. President Johnson—who had a broadcasting background—was close to network leaders and in constant touch with them. He was known to watch three television sets simultaneously, one for each network. Anything he considered damaging to the war effort would bring an instant White House phone call to a network president or newsman.

The network monopoly over documentaries now became significant. Some were sponsored by corporations that were also major Defense Department contractors. Some programs were preoccupied by the grandeur of military hardware in action, and with Administration reports on successful action. Though a groundswell of opposition to the war was building at home and throughout much of the world, network television seemed at pains to insulate viewers from its impact. Foreign protests, such as mass demonstrations in London, were usually categorized as "leftist." American anti-war marches were often ignored in newscasts, or pictured in a brief vignette centered on a bearded youth, as though to identify the event as a "hippie" activity. Much sponsored entertainment was jingoistic. The escalation years brought a flood of spy and secret-agent drama, followed by a surge of military drama—mostly on World War II—in which military life was dramatized as glorious or amusing or both. Children's series were saturated with similar themes, reinforced by commercials for toys like Mattel's Fighting Men and their guns and tanks—"everything real fighting men use"—and the G.I. Joe army toys, including "a ten-inch bazooka that really works" and gas masks "to add real dimension to your play battles."

Through newscasts, viewers had the illusion of a daily close-up look at war, but the vignettes conveyed almost nothing of how it had all begun or what it was all about. In campus teach-ins, Administration statements were increasingly denounced as deception, and network television as a "cover-up." A 1967 Louis Harris poll noted "a growing television boycott" among the college-educated. A dissident subculture was finding expression in mimeographed bulletins, posters, marches, underground films, cabarets, songs. Many of the songs—"Eve of Destruction," "The Universal Soldier," "Waist Deep in the Big Muddy"—were banned by networks and most stations. The subculture seldom penetrated the fortress of network prime time but began to find occasional expression in NET programming in such series as *Black Journal, NET Journal, The Creative Person*, and—explosively—in the film *Inside North Vietnam*, a British documentarist's report on his 1967 visit to "the enemy."

Broadcast by NET early in 1968, it apparently had wide impact.[51]

It is ironic that these anti-war, anti-Administration programs erupted precisely at a time when the Administration had finally resolved on a policy of Federal sponsorship of the system. The conjunction was not entirely accidental.

Early in 1967 a Carnegie Commission on Educational Television, formed by the Carnegie Corporation with Administration encouragement, had published a report recommending government support. It suggested that the term "public television" be used, to encompass "all that is of human interest and importance which is not at the moment appropriate or available for support by advertising. . . ." It urged establishment of a Corporation for Public Broadcasting which would receive and disburse Federal funds—for interconnection via cable and/or satellite, and for programming.

There was surprise when President Johnson, intent on maintaining a war consensus, embraced the Carnegie plan and encouraged its rapid progress through Congress. It became law in November 1967. Reasons for his interest were perhaps reflected in subsequent actions. As chairman of the new Corporation for Public Broadcasting he appointed Frank Pace, Jr., a former Secretary of the Army and a former chief executive officer of General Dynamics—a pillar of the military-industrial complex. Chairman Pace expressed enthusiasm for his new post and said he had already commissioned research on an important idea— how public television might be used for riot control. The President's support had stirred high hopes among educational-television leaders; now they wondered if the system was being bear-hugged into extinction.[52]

The Carnegie Commission had recommended a system financed by an automatic source of revenue—such as a tax on television sets, or fees levied on commercial uses of the spectrum— that is, any arrangement that would insulate the system from the pressures involved in annual appropriations by Congress. This recommendation was not followed. The system was launched with a minimal first-year appropriation of $4,500,000. But the wisdom of the ignored recommendation was soon demonstrated.

The scheduling of *Inside North Vietnam* was announced by NET shortly after the Public Broadcasting Act became law, and as the Corporation for Public Broadcasting was being formed. The result was a letter to NET signed by thirty-three Congressmen, not one of whom had seen the film, demanding instant cancellation of the proposed broadcast. It was hinted that a change in NET management would be necessary if the broadcast went forward. One Congressman stated that he would never again vote for a public television appropriation bill if NET went ahead with its plan. Phoned warnings to the stations conveyed the same message. NET did go ahead with the broadcast, to wide acclaim. Its management survived, but only briefly.[53]

The withdrawal of Lyndon Johnson defused the anti-war agitation for a time, but it revived when the secret invasions of Laos and Cambodia, ordered by President Nixon at the start of his Administration, became known. The following months brought a number of NET programs that apparently infuriated the White House. They include *Who Invited US?*, a documentary on U.S. interventions abroad; a *Behind the Lines* program on FBI use of *agents provocateurs* to infiltrate anti-war groups, and to create justification for FBI attacks on them; and especially *The Great American Dream Machine*, a jovial variety series that specialized in short satirical items, often anti-war and anti-establishment. It sometimes featured lampoon commercials. The series brought to public television a political-cabaret note that won intense response among dissenters.

The trend brought a 1972 collision. President Nixon vetoed a two-year public television appropriation, then a modest one-year appropriation. White House spokesmen made it clear what public television would have to do to get an appropriation signed. It would have to reorganize, with stress on "grass-roots localism." The bulk of Federal funds would have to go directly to the individual stations. The system must stop thinking of itself as "The Fourth Network." It should deemphasize public affairs—which could, it was suggested, be left to commercial broadcasters. And every Federal dollar would, under any reorganization, have to be matched by two and a half dollars from other sources. While public television leaders agonized over their crisis, trying to work out a reorganization, they faced starvation budgets. The field was swept by resignations. But rescuers were in the wings: the oil companies.

It happened to be a time of oil crisis. The years 1972-75 brought a confrontation between giant oil companies and the countries where the oil was; then an embargo, a huge jump in oil and gasoline prices, a resultant jump in other prices, all precipitating government investigations, which led to revelations of years of illegal oil company gifts to American leaders, and high-level bribery abroad. Also, enormous and apparently mounting oil profits.

It was the sort of combination—an image problem plus a glut of money—that had given birth to du Pont's *Cavalcade of America* and Alcoa's *See It Now*. This time public television was the beneficiary. It acquired, with help from Mobil, brilliant imports from Britain under the titles *Classic Theater* and *Masterpiece Theater;* from Exxon, *Theater in America, Dance in America*, and a series of one hundred classic films; from Gulf, *The Incredible Machine* and other National Geographic specials; from Arco, *In Performance at Wolf Trap* and *The Adams Chronicles*. All were well financed and lavishly produced. They represented various combinations of Federal and corporate funds, with the latter predominating. Federal policy had virtually pushed public television in this direction. To organize similar matching combinations, station representatives began steady pilgrimages to the offices of major corporations.[54]

Public television was acquiring a polished, highly professional look. It was beginning to have style. It was building an audience, whose size occasionally jolted commercial networks. *The Incredible Machine*, thanks to heavy advertising support contributed by Gulf, swamped opposing commercial programs in a number of cities, including New York. But within the field the euphoria was mixed with trepidation. Some stations, for fundraising purposes, were hiring former time salesmen from commercial television. These were visiting the same corporations they had visited for commercial television, with a pitch only slightly different. A KQED-TV, San Francisco, brochure addressed to potential underwriters assured them that KQED viewers were "well above the average income . . . they have plenty of disposable income, and they spend it." They were, said the brochure, "the people you want to think positively about your company. . . ." WNET-TV, New York, was using a flip-chart titled "Public Television—A Viable Alternative." Its fund raisers were finding advertising agencies increasingly receptive to proposals. "They are impressed by those who are already in public television," one fund raiser explained. "We always tell ad agencies that we are in the public relations business, not the advertising business, so we're not competing." But the channeling of projects through advertising agencies suggested that public television was indeed becoming an aspect of advertising—certainly in the minds of underwriters.[55]

Business corporations and their agencies were becoming a visible force in public television. They had not, in the first instance, sought this role. It had been virtually thrust upon them. As in the case of the public service announcements of the Advertising Council, it was a case of power begetting power.

The Federal Communications Commission enunciated principles to govern the business participation. Identification of an underwriter might be done at the beginning and end of a program. On long programs, identification at hourly intervals was permissible. It should use only the company name, not its logo. An underwriter should not, thought the FCC, be associated with a program closely related to his products. The Public Broadcasting Service, in charge of the cable interconnection, interpreted this to mean that the *Woman Alive!* series must not be underwritten by Ortho, inasmuch as its diverse products included a contraceptive pill. But PBS later became more permissive, and approved Avon as underwriter. PBS welcomed corporate advertising in other media to build an audience for programs underwritten by the corporation, but such promotion was to be kept separate from product advertising.[56]

Some program people were still apprehensive. The corporate grants were almost all for "cultural" projects, remote from current issues. Projects of this sort—often valuable—were also being aided by the National Endowment for the Arts and the National Endowment for the Humanities. But would all this "cultural" material, increasing in volume, gradually edge issue-oriented

programs out of the PBS schedule? Funds available for such programs were, in any case, in decline. With the Ford Foundation
phasing out its participation, "unrestricted" funds were mainly
those raised by some stations via auctions and memberships
drives. And these were seldom sufficient for large-scale film production. Under PBS the stations organized a program cooperative to channel some of their funds into ambitious national projects; but in the computerized balloting to select these projects,
the experimental or controversial generally fell by the wayside.

There was another worry. Would the private gifts, the subscriptions, the support given to fund-raising auctions—would
these dry up as the system acquired an increasingly glossy, busi-
ness-supported look, sprinkled with commercial credits?

There was still another worry. Would the splendid gifts of
the oil companies and others subside as their public relations
struggles entered a calmer period?

But amid such concerns, the whiff of success was welcome.
To commercial television interests, on the other hand, the rise
of underwriting had disquieting aspects. The poor relation was
becoming a competitor, perhaps a threat. If the resentment of
the commercial broadcasters was not more vocal, a reason may
have been that their own prosperity seemed inexhaustible. The
money kept coming.

DEMOGRAPHICS

By the 1970's network-sponsor economic relations focused almost entirely on the buying and selling of spots—mostly in 30-
second and 60-second units.

Some aspects of earlier days remained. A few daytime serials
were still sponsor-owned, sponsor-controlled. And a prime-time
special might likewise be sponsored by one sponsor, who might
even have initiated it and brought it to the network, in the old-
time way. But this applied mainly to such major companies as
IBM, Exxon, Mobil, Xerox. By and large, television business had
settled down to the buying and selling of gaps—30-second and
60-second gaps—in a network schedule. It involved virtually the

entire schedule. The "sustaining program" had disappeared from broadcasting terminology.

Although the system resembled spot-selling arrangements in other countries, the American system had developed characteristics of its own. A central point was that a sale designated a particular *program*—not merely a time period. The advertiser had taken the position that he must have program settings suitable to his messages and purposes, and the networks had accepted this as reasonable. From this flowed many consequences.

One was the disappearance of fixed prices. The rate card became virtually obsolete. A slot in a program that had, at the moment, a top Nielsen or Arbitron rating could be sold for a higher price than a slot in a program with a lower rating. Thus the business gravitated toward endless bargaining. Prices fluctuated as on a stock market.

A sharp rise in ratings brought a rise in asking price. When NBC decided in 1970 to schedule a series around the comedian Flip Wilson—then a relatively unknown quantity—network time salesmen began by selling 30-second slots for about $35,000 each. As the program won unexpected success and climbing ratings, the asking price went to $40,000, $45,000, $50,000, and beyond. On any single broadcast, one spot might have been sold at the lowest, earliest price; others at later prices. On some series, ratings and prices went down instead of up.

The buying and selling was generally done in clusters or packages. In view of the staggering number of spots involved, this seemed inevitable. For the sponsor it was also a way to hedge his bets. Unexpected failures could be balanced by unexpected successes. There was safety in this "scatter" buying.[57]

In the bargaining process, a sponsor might indicate through his advertising agency that he was ready to invest $1,400,000 in time purchases for Mouthwash X; the network was asked to provide a suggested list of available slots. Some would be rejected as unsuitable, others accepted. Eventually there would be agreement on a spectrum of spots, and on a package price. A specific dollar value would be assigned to each spot; this was essential because a program cancellation would require the network to make a refund, or provide a comparable spot. The spots in a package might have wildly diverse price tags, reflecting their ratings and other bargaining factors. They might include 30-second slots in a football bowl game at $90,000 each; in a popular mystery series at $55,000 each; in an evening news series at $18,000 each; in a documentary prime-time special at $14,000 each; and in an early-morning show at $4000 each.

A documentary special, even in prime time, was likely to go at a "bargain price" unless some sensational element was involved. A special could not have a track record, so its rating could only be guessed at. And most sponsors were in any case reluctant to consider a slot in what might prove controversial; some flatly refused to take the risk. The network kept including such items in proposed packages at low rates—which often *did* turn out to be bargain prices in terms of viewers reached.

In the 1960's a sponsor generally felt that he ought not to pay more than $4 per thousand homes reached. He generally relied on Nielsen ratings, based on "audimeters" installed in a sample of homes, as an indication of the number of homes reached by a program.

Nielsen gradually began to supply additional information, which brought a change in the game. Nielsen began to supplement the audimeter information with data obtained from diaries kept by another sample of homes, which received a modest fee for filling out and returning the Nielsen diaries. Ratings computed from the diary sample served as a check on the audimeter ratings; in addition, the diaries gave information as to which family members watched each program. Since the make-up of every Nielsen family was known to the company, its computers could now analyze a program's audience in terms of sex, age, economic and educational status, urban or rural location, and other factors. The age and sex information was especially valued by advertisers. By the early 1970's this *demographic* information began to dominate trade talk, and the buying and selling of 30-second and 60-second slots.

Slot-buying began to seem highly scientific. Nielsen could tell a sponsor the male/female composition of his audience and break it into age groups: 18-24, 25-34, 35-49, 50-64, 65-plus, etc. From another service, the Brand Rating Index, the sponsor could get similar demographic information on his retail customers, for any of his products. Sponsorship became a matching game.

CBS even suggested it. In 1971 it sent its sponsors and their advertising agencies a promotion piece titled *Where the Girls Are.* Its cover featured a revolving disk, which would reveal at a glance the age distribution of retail buyers of 91 different products—all products bought mainly by women. "And the pages inside," said the brochure, "show you how you can apply this handy information to Nielsen's new audience reports by age of lady viewer."[58]

Network executives now tended to survey their schedules in terms of demographic product demands. Negotiations resembled transactions to deliver blocs of people. An advertising agency would be telling a network, in effect: "For Shampoo Y, our client is ready to invest $1,800,000 in women 18-49. Other viewers are of no interest in this case; the client doesn't care to pay for irrelevant viewers. But for women 18-49 he is willing to pay Z dollars per thousand. What spots can you offer?"

Gone were the days when a sponsor based his decisions on personal reactions to programs. Now he did not even need to watch programs. He watched charts and computer terminals. A number of sponsors acquired computer terminals linked to Nielsen computers in Dunedin, Florida, for prompt reception of Nielsen computations. It was a far cry from the sponsor's booth. The sponsor seemed to have become detached from the realm of programming—but his every decision influenced it.

At networks, programs now tended to survive to the extent that they served the demographic requirements of sponsors. Many sponsors were mainly intent on reaching women, whose decisions in supermarkets and drugstores spelled success or failure. Some looked for women 18-49; others wanted women 25-64. On the other hand, the makers of expensive cars, computers, and business machines needed male viewers in their prime—an elusive group. For their attention *en masse,* a 30-second slot in a Super Bowl game could be worth $100,000 or more. Newscasts and occasional documentaries, while considered essential for license protection, reached a smaller, older audience, of lower market value, but useful for some institutional advertising

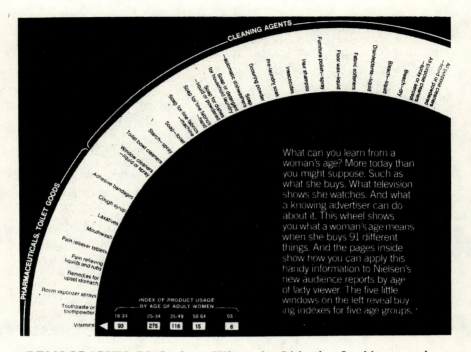

Labels around the wheel (clockwise from top):

CLEANING AGENTS
Soap—automatic dishwashers
Soap or detergent for household laundry
Soap for dishes—liquid or powdered
Soap for fine fabrics
Soap for fine fabrics—machine
Scouring powder
Pre-laundry soak
Insecticides
Hair shampoo
Furniture polish—spray
Floor wax—liquid
Fabric softeners
Disinfectants—liquid
Bleach—liquid
Bleach—dry
All purpose cleaners—spray or powdered
All purpose cleaners—liquid or aerosol
Starch—spray
Toilet bowl cleaners
Window cleaners—liquid or spray

PHARMACEUTICALS & TOILET GOODS
Adhesive bandages
Cough syrup
Laxatives
Mouthwash
Pain reliever tablets
Pain relieving liquids and rubs
Remedies for upset stomach
Room vaporizer sprays
Toothpaste or toothpowder
Vitamins

What can you learn from a
woman's age? More today than
you might suppose. Such as
what she buys. What television
shows she watches. And what
a knowing advertiser can do
about it. This wheel shows
you what a woman's age means
when she buys 91 different
things. And the pages inside
show how you can apply this
handy information to Nielsen's
new audience reports by age
of lady viewer. The five little
windows on the left reveal buying indexes for five age groups.

INDEX OF PRODUCT USAGE
BY AGE OF ADULT WOMEN

18-24	25-34	35-49	50-64	65
93	275	116	15	6

DEMOGRAPHIC DIAL—from *Where the Girls Are*. In this promotion piece CBS urges sponsors to match program demographics with product demographics, and offers the dial to help them. Note the age spread of vitamin buyers. Laxative buyers offer a contrasting pattern: (18–24) 38, (25–34) 51, (35–49) 85, (50–64) 126, (65+) 210. Result: laxative makers buy economical newscast slots, reaching an older audience. Makers of vitamins, perfumes, shampoos, deodorants bid for younger audiences. (*CBS Television Network*.)

and for products aimed at older buyers: denture cleaners and fixatives, stomach settlers, laxatives, pain relievers, decaffeinated coffee. But older viewers were not big spenders; a network needed relatively few programs for that market. *Gunsmoke*, while still high in ratings, was found to be reaching too old—and too rural—an audience, and was dropped by its network. It was no catastrophe in the history of drama, but it signaled the rising power of demographic data.[59]

The sponsor, said network executives, makes no program decisions. It was true that he bought only slots. But with every "yes" and "no" he turned thumbs up or thumbs down on a program. His decisions helped some programs to survive and others to die. They were pushing the documentary into limbo. They were helping create a dramaturgy reflecting the demographics of the supermarket.

In the early 1970's major sponsors won an extraordinary new concession. In view of large expenditures and steady patronage, a sponsor like Colgate could receive an "assurance"—the network did not like to use the word "guarantee"—that at the end of each three-month period the sponsor would not have spent more than Z dollars per thousand women in the proper demographic range. If the cost went higher, bonus spots would be provided.[60]

Everything at the network seemed to revolve around the yes's and no's. A low-rating program had become a menace. Wrong demographics were a menace. To maximize income, these had to be sloughed off. Pressure to this end came from sales executives, who received bonuses based on sales income; from affiliates, whose local sales were likewise affected by ratings and demographics; from stockholders, whose stock prices could reflect rating fluctuations; from top network executives, whose contracts had stock-option clauses. The system had become a closed-circuit escalation machine.

The sponsor, from whom the money flowed, had left the sponsor's booth, but had taken his influence along with him.

DO YOU AGREE OR DISAGREE . . . ?

From time to time interviewers of the Roper Organization have asked people:

> Q. Now, everything considered, do you agree or disagree that having commercials on TV is a fair price to pay for being able to watch it?

In 1974 most people agreed, seven to one, that it was a fair price. This "poll," paid for by the National Association of Broadcasters, was perhaps less a search for information than a propaganda ploy. To answer it, people had to accept the premise that "having commercials" was the price—the only price—they were paying.[61]

Of course the facts are otherwise. Aside from the cost of his receiving equipment, the viewer pays the entire cost of programming: he subsidizes it as taxpayer and as consumer. The channeling of most of the funds through the merchandising process gives the viewer the impression that it is free; it also makes the sponsor, as we have seen, a major influence.

That influence pervades programming: from the commercial to the entertainment that forms its setting; from the public service announcements of the Advertising Council to the offerings of public television. In the following section we will try to assess this influence in a more detailed way, genre by genre.

The sponsor may be viewed as a potentate with a strong influence over currents of thought in our society, exercised mainly through television, in various ways and in various degrees.

Over one instrument of his hegemony, the commercial, his power is of course absolute; it may be considered his inner fortress.

Programs surrounding his commercials are strongly influenced by him and may be considered his outer defenses.

Adjacent services, such as news, documentaries, and public service announcements, are less decisively influenced but may be looked on as semi-independent satrapies.

And finally there is the realm of cultural programming, a significant sphere of influence.

A study of these forms will comprise our next section.

Wherever television has been established—under whatever system—its influence has exceeded expectations, and has posed unanticipated problems and perils.

The luminous screen in the home carries fantastic authority. Viewers everywhere tend to accept it as a window on the world, and to watch it for hours each day. Viewers feel that they understand, from television alone, what is going on in the world. They unconsciously look to it for guidance as to what is important, good, and desirable, and what is not. It has tended to displace or overwhelm other influences such as newspapers, school, church, grandpa, grandma. It has become the definer and transmitter of a society's values.

In all these functions, it has gone beyond anyone's hopes or intentions. It has given the domination of its images and words an importance impossible to overstate.

TWO

DOMAIN

Drawing by Lorenz; © 1976 The New Yorker Magazine, Inc.

> The only part of television which has fulfilled
> its promise at all is the commercial.
>
> PAUL GOODMAN

THE INNER FORTRESS—the "commercial"

The word is in quotation marks because it is—has become—a euphemism. "Commercials" used to describe and promote products and still do, but they have meanwhile assumed a host of other functions. Often produced and exhibited at staggering cost, a network commercial is likely to promote not only a product but a way of life, a view of the world, a philosophy. Commercials are the main instrument of corporate image-glossing, military recruitment, political campaigning, and tourist solicitation and propaganda by foreign countries. Often, under the guise of merchandising, commercials are deeply involved in ideological conflict. They have a fateful, *de facto* role in education, and an impact on the world of religion. Along with all this, the "commercial" is a central element of television entertainment, outshining most other elements. Its success in this may be the key to its other successes.

Before a child can talk, it may try to echo a television jingle. Songs, slogans, and humor from television commercials have be-

79

come the folk media of our time. The dialogue of the teenager reflects an obsession with television commercials even more than with its entertainment features. Even in commuter train and barroom, the talk echoes television commercials.

A business textbook, *The Television Commercial: Creativity and Craftsmanship*, by Albert C. Book and Norman D. Carey, calls the commercial "an American art form . . . ahead of most TV programs in being in tune with the United States." Commercial jingles have been anthologized in *Great Songs of Madison Avenue*, a *New York Times* book publication. A Roper report tells us that 74 per cent of viewers often find commercials "fun to watch." Each year some fifty commercials—out of 40,000 or so produced—win Clio Awards (named after Clio, the muse of history), presented at an annual American TV Commercials Festival.[1]

Clearly the status of the commercial—in spite of continuing, occasionally vituperative attacks—has changed since AT&T first broached the idea. The extraordinary stellar casts involved in today's commercials reflect the change, and have undoubtedly furthered it. In the heyday of radio few top-rated performers were willing to do commercials. Today's television commercials are populated by an international who's who. Before he died, Paul Getty, reputedly the world's richest man, filmed a commercial endorsing a brokerage firm. Sir Laurence Olivier, star of stars, demonstrates a camera. A former Republican vice presidential nominee, William Miller, plugs a credit card. Yankee superstar Joe DiMaggio, one-time husband of Marilyn Monroe, explains how to make coffee. Ricardo Montalban serves as luxury car salesman. Henry Fonda pushes vinyl flooring. The list goes on and on.

Far from feeling demeaned by commercials, celebrities of all sorts now seem to covet and relish the selling role. Aside from lavish fees, some have won new fame through bravura performances—such as Robert Morley's pitches for British Airways, Jonathan Winters's plugs for Hefties, and O. J. Simpson's stylish performances for Hertz, the "superstar in rent-a-car." Commercials not only exploit, but seem to confer status. Frank Perdue, proprietor of Perdue's Chickens, became sufficiently celebrated through his sad-eyed delivery of his own commercials to become a talk-show guest. Some actresses have risen to film stardom via commercial stints. For yesterday's celebrities, commercials are now considered a comeback route. Out of the distant past comes George Burns, brilliantly selling cat food; then Joan Fontaine plugging beauty products; and baseball great Bob Feller proclaiming his rejuvenation by a hair-color formula while two beautiful young girls clutch at him.

It may seem a jovial game to viewers, but the huge stakes involved reflect the central role now played by commercials. The endorsing star may have a contract that runs to six or seven figures; like Bing Crosby, orange juice salesman, he may be a member of the company hierarchy. The production budget for a single 30-second commercial is likely to run from $20,000 to $200,000; some have gone higher. A 30-second canned-soup commercial featuring Ann Miller and other dancers in choreography by Busby Berkeley is said to have cost $250,000. If programs were produced on this scale, a 90-minute program would cost $45 million—more than a *Cleopatra*. By 1972 members of the Screen Actors Guild were earning more from commercials than from theatrical films and television films *combined*. Earnings that year came to $62,330,895 from commercials, $38,555,-730 from filmed television programs, $22,194,342 from theatrical motion pictures. The commercial had become, as an advertising executive put it, "the focal point of creative effort."[2]

The production cost of a commercial is, of course, only a start. The subsequent showing of a 30-second commercial in prime time may cost a sponsor from $10,000 to more than $100,000. And since most commercials are used many times—scores or even hundreds of times—one commercial may represent a multi-million-dollar venture.

Can it be worth it? What does it all mean? To the casual viewer the statistics seem incomprehensible, suggesting a world totally beyond his ken. And they are incomprehensible unless one glimpses the changes that have come over American business in recent decades—to some extent, augmented by television.

Business spokesmen often pay lip service to "market forces." Orthodox economic theory pictures a need or demand over which the entrepreneur has no control but which he seeks to satisfy by what he produces. But this picture, while it seems to survive in college textbooks and may apply in small businesses— especially local or regional businesses—is obsolete for the large corporations that dominate network television. Most of these live in a different world. Of the top 100 network sponsors of 1975, 81 were multinational corporations. Some have supply sources, manufacturing operations, and markets spanning several continents. Their global deployment holds potential for enormous power and profit—and disasters. With assembly lines dependent on distant suppliers, scattered labor forces, complex webs of regulations and levies, and ultimately on wide merchandising operations, they feel they cannot leave themselves at the mercy of "market forces." Such companies, to ward off governmental interference, may invoke classic economic doctrine, but meanwhile their total effort is toward control—of supply at one end, demand at the other.[3]

To manufacture a product without at the same time manufacturing a demand has become unthinkable. Today the manufacture of demand means, for most large companies, television— its commercials as well as other program elements. The growing scale of mass production has inevitably made advertising more crucial, but this understates the situation. As society becomes more product-glutted, the pressure on the consumer to consume—to live up to higher and higher norms of consumption— has become unrelenting.

The pressure, as various observers have noted, centers on selling the unnecessary. The merchandising of necessities— which, to some extent, will be bought anyway—can seldom sustain the budgets applied to the unnecessary, unless the necessary is cloaked with mythical supplementary values. The focus is on the creation of emotion-charged values to make the unneeded necessary.

All this is now so taken for granted that it is seldom discussed. The young writer entering advertising assumes that hope and fear are the springs he must touch—hope of success and fear of failure in sex, business, community status. As a dramatic medium that can draw on the resources of every art, and has as its stage the privacy of the home, television has unparalleled opportunities for this psychic pressure. It has intensified as the 30-second commercial has become the dominant vehicle, favored over the roomier 60-second form. There is scarcely time now for technical persuasions, documentation, "reason-why" advertising. Everyone knows what the job is: instant drama, posing threat and promise.

An important corollary is that the promise should be an undeliverable promise. Everyone knows that soap will clean hands, a razor remove hair, and a car transport you from one place to another. To promise such things means little or nothing. But there is no sure formula for being irresistible, for winning and holding those you love, or for rising to the top of the business or social circle. These are promises worth dangling.

That this calls for a certain amount of "well-considered mendacity," as John Kenneth Galbraith calls it, is clear to everyone. Here the role of humor becomes especially important: it gives the game a quality of charm rather than fraud. This helps all concerned. The creators of advertising can claim that no one takes it all very seriously; it is all more or less in fun. The viewer can adopt a similar attitude. The viewer's self-respect requires a rejection of most commercials on the conscious level, along with some ridicule. Beneath the ridicule the commercial does its work.

"Will the bags under my eyes be gone when I get back from Miami?" asks a man in an airline commercial. "They may not be gone, sir," he is told, "but they'll be a whole lot tanner." The humor is disarming. Dubious technical claims are avoided. But the commercial may well prod a yearning for rebirth in the Florida sun.

The creation and management of demand are only one of the tasks of the commercial. For the multinational corporation, a more pressing task is legitimation of its vast and often mysterious operations—which require, for success, an environment of confidence.

The global corporation derives its power from selective deployment. Its ability to shift supply resources, subassembly lines, and manufacturing sites, and to juggle merchandising and ac-

counting procedures to utilize—and press for—favorable circumstances is the key to its power and its growth. Multinationals
have achieved budgets dwarfing those of many countries where
they do business. But the stakes are so great that the temptation
to use any and all means to eliminate uncertainties is almost irresistible. In a moment of hubris, the president of the International
Telephone & Telegraph Company told his stockholders that
ITT had

> in its time met and surmounted every device employed by gov-
> ernments to encourage their own industries and hamper those of
> foreigners, including taxes, tariffs, quotas, currency restrictions,
> subsidies, barter arrangements, guarantees, moratoriums, devalu-
> ations—yes, and nationalizations.[4]

This boast was made in 1962 when multinationals were sharply
on the rise. Later years brought reversals and crises—for ITT,
Lockheed, United Brands, and many others, including major oil
companies—followed by revelations of methods used to overcome obstacles: bribery, subsidies to foreign political parties,
negotiations for CIA interventions, and other means. By the
1970's many multinationals had image problems and were faced
with investigations, demands for antitrust moves, and legislative
proposals for divestiture. As already noted, one response to this
was lavish underwriting of public television series. But the companies also counterattacked via television commercials. When
comedian Bob Hope, golf companion of U.S. Presidents, appeared on the tube again and again to ask—

> HOPE: Who owns America's oil companies? Fourteen million
> Americans, trusting in companies like Texaco! We're working
> to keep that trust! . . .

he was not in quest of sales, but of public confidence. Mobil,
combating divestiture through various media, ran commercials
that displayed some of its vast installations, then posed a question:

> ANNOUNCER: Some people want to break up the big oil com-
> panies. Is smallness really best? Think hard. . . . It's *your*
> country.

Are people influenced by such tidbits of plea and argument? As with commercials in general, most people are sure they are not influenced. The argumentation merely merges in the audio-visual wallpaper that is the backdrop of our lives. But the damaging news items that worried oil companies were, in most cases, broadcast only once, with utmost brevity, in non-peak hours. Texaco's "trust" pitches were broadcast repeatedly in peak hours, in high-rated programs. Whatever impressions were left by the news items, they were soon overlayed with layers on layers of brisk reassurance from Bob Hope, an American institution.[5]

ITT's use of television commercials in 1974-75 and its apparent success in serving the company's purposes are worth study. ITT was little known to the general public before Harold S. Geneen became its president in 1959, when an extraordinary expansion and diversification began, giving the company an aura of glamour. But in the early 1970's its reputation appeared to suffer devastating damage. In 1972 its $400,000 offer to underwrite the Republican convention was linked by investigators with Nixon administration settlement of an antitrust case in a manner favorable to ITT. A year later it was shown to have been deeply involved with the CIA in disruptive tactics against the Allende regime in Chile, and even to have offered the CIA $1 million to help finance the disruptions. That same year publication of *The Sovereign State of ITT*, by Anthony Sampson, further spotlighted the company's manipulations of governments, political parties, and media on an international scale.

In 1974, on the heels of these revelations, ITT announced plans for a series of children's programs titled *The Big Blue Marble* to "promote international understanding." It showed enchanting scenes of children in many lands, and involved a pen-pal campaign. At the same time the company launched a series of prime-time commercials, many of which publicized ITT as provider of *The Big Blue Marble* and showed scenes from it, while others featured American students abroad under international scholarships provided by ITT—reflecting, like the *Big Blue Marble* spots, a warm intercultural feeling. All the spots featured the slogan "The Best Ideas Are Ideas that Help People."

The *Big Blue Marble* films cost $4 million to produce but were *given away* to television stations, with the result that they appeared mainly in fringe periods. Not so the corporate commercials *about* the *Big Blue Marble* series and other intercultural good deeds. The commercials appeared in evening time at a cost of $4.2 million in 1974, and of $3.7 million in 1975. In 1975 the campaign was also extended to other countries—in America, Europe, Asia, Africa. The allocation of funds suggests that *The Big Blue Marble* and the scholarships existed primarily to give the company warm-hearted themes to trumpet in peak-time commercials. The impact of the strategy is worth noting.

ITT engaged the Daniel Yankelovich, Inc., research company to do periodic studies of public attitudes toward ITT. The studies included a question as to whether the company was thought to "care about the general public." During the spot campaign the company's "cares about the general public" rating went up substantially. Similar studies by the Gallup Organization, gauging the "social responsibility rating" of various large companies including ITT—*not* done for ITT—showed similar results. The unfavorable impression of the news items had apparently been blurred and blotted out by the "commercials."

ITT had been mentioned frequently in television newscasts of 1973, and also in 1974, when the "ITT case" was mentioned constantly in the Watergate hearings. But the company's name did not apparently come up in a single television network evening newscast during the first six months of 1975, when the good-deeds commercials were constantly on the air. These were shown some forty-four times on evening newscasts during that period. They sometimes appeared simultaneously on all three networks.

The 1974-75 barrage of commercials apparently achieved its aim. According to Yankelovich, the ITT "cares about the general public" rating more than doubled during a twelve-month period, going from 20 per cent to 43 per cent.[6]

The global corporations developed, during their rapid rise, a sense of mission. They saw themselves as creating an integrated world, organized on a rational basis. They pictured themselves as principal forces for peace and development. Their chief obstacle, as many saw it, was the obsolete nationalism fostered by nation states, which worked toward fragmentation. Armed with this world view, the multinational corporation has no guilt feelings about its power, wealth, or operating methods. These were needed to achieve its mission. An almost religious zeal infused the sense of mission. The global corporation, according to Courtney Brown, former Dean of the Columbia University Graduate School of Business, was the "prologue to a new World Symphony." Many corporate commercials have striven to spread this gospel, which is seen as an essential shield for global operation. The purpose is legitimation of power. This is behind the ceaseless repetition of "We're working to keep that trust!" and "Is smallness really best?"[7]

The involvement of commercials in political argumentation raises numerous issues. One is a tax issue. Propaganda is not tax deductible, whereas most advertising is. But the line between them, as we have seen, can be fuzzy. For tax purposes the cost of making and showing commercials is generally deducted as a business cost—which means that the citizen is in effect subsidizing much of the barrage of argumentation aimed at him. Harvey J. Schulman, attorney representing various public interest groups demanding "access" to the air, has called the Internal Revenue Service handling of this problem a "multi-million-dollar scandal."[8]

Another issue relates to the fairness doctrine. In 1967 the attorney John Banzhaf III argued before the FCC that broadcasters accepting cigarette advertising, which invariably linked cigarettes with romance and vigorous health, should be obliged to carry—free of charge, as a matter of the public interest—messages on the association of cigarettes with lung cancer and other diseases. When the FCC found validity in the idea, "counter-advertising" by various health agencies began to assault the cigarette—so persuasively that Congress decided to ban cigarette advertising from the air after 1970. In consequence both the cigarette commercials and the counter-commercials vanished from the air. But the idea of fairness-doctrine applicability to commercials did not vanish. Environmental groups wanted to answer automobile commercials promoting high-powered—and highly polluting—automobiles. They also wanted to answer fuel company commercials promoting their off-shore drilling, strip-mining, and nuclear-power operations.

The networks tried to ward off the problem by restraining advertiser and would-be respondent alike. They cited a policy—often proclaimed but irregularly followed—of refusing to sell time for "issue advertising" except in political campaigns. Mobil Oil vice president Herbert Schmertz called this policy "outrageous" and said the company was being deprived of "First Amendment rights." He wanted Mobil commercials to present in detail the company's views on the energy crisis. The networks argued that such issues were adequately covered in their news, documentary, and discussion programs, but Schmertz dismissed this coverage as inadequate. He considered news programs "entertainment." Mobil even offered, on several occasions, to pay for reply time for its critics, if Mobil were permitted to express itself fully in its "commercials." The networks declined the offer and stuck to their policy—a threat, as Schmertz saw it, to "free speech." But the environmentalists were no happier with the deadlock. They too considered the coverage in network-controlled news, documentaries, and discussion programs superficial and inadequate—and argued, moreover, that many commercials which the networks accepted as legitimate "product advertising" were already touching on controversial issues—off-shore drilling, strip-mining, nuclear power.

As for the FCC, it seemed in a state of terror over the Pandora's Box it had opened with its Banzhaf ruling. In 1971 it issued an official declaration that the cigarette problem was "unique" and that to extend it to product advertising in general would "undermine the present system, which is based on product commercials, many of which have some adverse ecological effects." This was a curious, damaging concession, which seemed to confirm what the environmentalists were saying. A similar self-damaging statement came from NBC, which estimated that the three networks would have had a $69.4 million loss for 1970 instead of a $50.1 million profit if they had been required to give time for "counter-advertising" of the sort initiated by the Banzhaf ruling. Again, the argument made network commercials seem highly questionable, although the purpose of the statement was to urge the FCC to stand firm.[9]

In subsequent declarations the FCC seemed determined to steer clear of issues posed by commercials. It apparently felt it could leave those to the industry's "self-regulation" system built around the NAB Television Code, and to the Federal Trade Commission—with its jurisdiction over false and misleading advertising. Both of these regulatory arrangements had, however, a long record of ineffectuality.

The FTC has had periods of zeal, but the procedures imposed on it have tended to keep it relatively impotent. The FTC reviews the scripts and story-boards for thousands of commercials each year. It may look into procedures used in tests and demonstrations, request substantiation of claims, and even ask for "corrective" advertising. Hearings may lead to a cease-and-desist order, which the company can then challenge in court. Such challenges may take years to resolve. By the time a cease-and-desist order is actually implemented, the campaign in question has usually been replaced by another.

Sometimes years of struggle lead to FTC victories in which principle is vindicated but practical consequences are minimal. Finding that the action of Carter's Little Liver Pills had nothing to do with the liver, the FTC ordered the company to stop intimating that it did, and to drop "liver" from its name. It took sixteen years of litigation to make the order stick. Users of the product may not have attached significance to the change, or even noticed it.[10]

Geritol involved a similar sequence of events, in which the FTC won—but won little. In 1965, after long investigation, the FTC ordered the makers of Geritol to stop claiming that the product would cure "tired blood" resulting from iron deficiency. In a unanimous nineteen-page decision, the commission said that "tiredness is not a generally reliable indication of iron deficiency" and that, in any case, Geritol would do little to cure most run-down feelings. When the company nonetheless re-introduced the theme, the FTC brought suit, which was finally settled in 1976 with payment of a $125,000 fine by the J. B. Williams Company—Nabisco subsidiary and maker of Geritol. But by that time Geritol had switched (with enormous success) to a very different campaign.[11]

Instead of people with "run-down" feelings, each commercial now showed a radiantly healthy young woman saying such words as "I'm in love, and I take Geritol!" or "I'm married, and I take Geritol!" She would explain that looking after yourself is important, so she got plenty of rest, enough exercise, "and Geritol—every day!" Some of these commercials featured couples clinging to each other, giving the impression that their love life was ecstatic, and interrupted only momentarily to film a commercial. One such 30-second production, introduced during the 1976 World Series between the Cincinnati Reds and the New York Yankees, featured Cincinnati's Pete Rose and his wife. These commercials seemed to be FTC-proof. They made no technical claims. They did not specify, or even suggest, to what extent the radiant bloom was the result of "plenty of rest," "enough exercise," "looking after yourself," being "in love," or Geritol. But while making no claims, their impact was probably accurately reflected by Pete Rose when he told exultant Cincinnati crowds, welcoming the Reds from their World Series victory, "The Yankees didn't take their Geritol!"

The success of the campaign suggests the increasing irrelevance of most FTC review, which tends to be word-oriented. In the new commercial dramaturgy, verbal promise is a secondary matter, vague and understated, while situation and imagery work on a more visceral level.

The FTC has sometimes tried to cope with deceptive visual persuasions, but found itself in a quagmire. In an early action of this sort, it objected in 1956 to a Rolaids pitchman dressed in a white coat—clearly intended to suggest medical approval of Rolaids. But a consistent policy of this sort could hardly be developed in a world populated by authority-cloaked figures of all sorts, real and mythical, live and animated—including "teachers," "policemen," "superstars," "business leaders." Although the "doctor" was banned, a "schoolteacher" in a classroom continued for years to ask "How do I spell relief?" and to answer it by writing on a blackboard "R-O-L-A-I-D-S."

Some FTC regulatory actions have been directed toward

studio methods used in "demonstrations." It questioned whether it was proper, in filming a commercial for Campbell Soup, to put clear-glass marbles in the soup to make the vegetables cluster near the surface. And whether it was proper, in picturing a pudding garnished with "whipped cream," to use shaving cream instead because it has greater resistance to studio lights. And whether, to demonstrate that Colgate Rapid Shave cream was so moisturizing that it would enable you to shave sandpaper, it was proper to use plexiglass sprinkled with sand, rather than sandpaper. FTC experimenters had actually tried to shave sandpaper, and found it harder than the commercial had indicated.

Most such FTC efforts do not seem to have generated wide support. Even the U.S. Supreme Court seemed more amused than disturbed over the great sandpaper embroglio ("COURT MUSES GAILY ON SHAVES," reported *The New York Times*).[12] The widespread admiration for "chicane," discussed long ago by Thorstein Veblen, may help to explain this.

Yet in one area of controversy, a groundswell of indignation and support has been evident. This concerns advertising addressed to children. Leading the attack has been a Boston-based organization formed in 1968—Action for Children's Television, led by Peggy Charren.

In appearances before the FCC, FTC, and congressional committees, ACT began to attack commercials in children's programs on various grounds: use of beloved hero-figures for product huckstering; nutritional miseducation in candy and food commercials; deceptions in toy commercials; and the immorality of promoting over-the-counter drugs to child audiences. It even declared advertising in children's programs to be inherently exploitative and a disservice to society.[13]

Beginning in 1971, the organization filed with the FTC a series of petitions focusing on "edibles." It pointed out that 98 per cent of the nation's children suffer from tooth decay, that sugary foods play a leading part in this, and that meanwhile commercials for sugared products (along with those for mechanical toys) overwhelmingly dominate the commercials addressed to children. These sugary commercials were seen as tantamount to a crusade for bad teeth; also for malnutrition, resulting from the diversion of appetite and purchasing power to worthless and harmful products; also, for food habits that in later life lead to obesity, digestive troubles, and problems of the heart and arteries.

ACT noted that in a specific seven-hour period on a single Saturday—October 28, 1972—the CBS-TV outlet in Boston showed sixty-seven commercials for sweetly flavored products, mostly candies and snacks.* There were also commercials for cereals—generally considered an essential part of a healthy diet. But it was pointed out that most cereals promoted on children's programs were sugared cereals, some being 50 per cent sugar—as much as some candy bars.

In the commercials surveyed, such products were regularly associated with love, joy, fame, power.

ACT cited a 1971 study of twenty-eight hours of children's programming that included not a single commercial for fruits, vegetables, meats, or milk. Their absence was also a message, in the opinion of the nutritionist Joan Gussow. She pictured television as selling a diet "that makes it impossible for a child *not* to go wrong."

Although most viewing by children involves programs that are not "children's programs," many advertisers have found "children's programs"—clustered on weekends and late afternoons—especially effective as sales vehicles because most children watch them *without* parents, free of any parental counter-advertising. Moreover, mothers are subsequently found to yield to children in product selection to an overwhelming extent—to children five to seven years old, 88 per cent of the time for cereals, 52 per cent for snack foods, 40 per cent for candy, 38 per cent for soft drinks. For older children, the percentages were

---

* Among the products promoted relentlessly on children's programs ACT mentioned Milky Way, Baby Ruth, Kit-Kat, Hershey Bar, Junior Mints, Butterfingers, Mr. Goodbar, M&M's, Kellogg's Pop-Tarts Pastry, Kellogg's Danish-Go-Rounds, Chips Ahoy, Oreos, Devil Dogs, Ring-Dings, Yankee Doodles, Yodels, Big Wheels, Hostess Cupcakes, Hostess Twinkies, Nabisco Sugar Wafers, Charm Big Tops, Holloway Milk Duds, Holloway Black Cows, Nestlé Crunch, Nestlé $100,000 Bar, Nestlé Triple Feature Bar, Tootsie Pops, Tootsie Rolls, Life Savers, Turkish Taffy, Clark Bars, Zagnut Bars.

even higher, according to a Harvard Business School study. As sales agent, the child is supreme.*

ACT told the FTC: "The United States is a nation of nutritional illiterates. Probably the single most influential contributor to this problem is television advertising."

Along with its campaign on "edibles," ACT demanded a halt to the promotion of over-the-counter drugs in children's programming. In 1971-72 three major drug companies were promoting vitamins directly to children, selling them as sweet and colorful. Some were shaped like popular cartoon characters. Hudson Pharmaceutical Company was plugging Spiderman Vitamins, using Marvel Comics superhero Spiderman as product salesman. The product was criticized by ACT as adding to the sugary assault and also as promoting pill-popping in quest of power. It was said by physicians to pose an overdose danger.

ACT meanwhile continued—in statements to the FTC, FCC, and congressional committees—to urge a ban on all advertising in children's programs.

These crusades gave the industry tremors of anxiety. To head off government action, the NAB in 1974 adopted amendments to its Television Code. These ordered an end to selling by program hosts, and shortened the time for commercials on children's programs from 16 minutes to 10 minutes per hour—later, to 9½ minutes per hour. In commercials for sugared products, the Code Administration began to demand insertion of phrases like "as part of a balanced diet"—or a visual equivalent such as an orange or glass of milk somewhere in the picture. Various drug companies agreed to discontinue vitamin promotion on children's programs.

A subsequent campaign for Spiderman vitamins was stopped by an FTC consent order which stated that "children are unqualified by age and experience" to make decisions about vitamins.[14]

---

* An advertising executive for Oscar Mayer & Co. once explained it this way. He depicted women as weak on brand loyalty, then added: "But when you sell a kid on your product, if he can't get it, he will throw himself on the floor, stamp his feet and cry. You can't get a reaction like that out of an adult." *Advertising Age*, July 19, 1965.

The FCC remained largely on the sidelines but issued a Policy Statement. It called on stations to "limit advertising to children to the lowest level consistent with their programming responsibilities"—as though such advertising and programming were inseparable responsibilities. It also resolved to gather, through the renewal application forms, more information on children's programming, including the amount of advertising.

Throughout these struggles, industry moves seemed designed to save, rather than correct, the situation spotlighted by ACT. As in other disputes, the NAB tried to head off the issue with a Roper study. In 1971 Roper interviewers asked 1993 people:

> Q. How do you feel—that there should be *no* commercials on any children's programs or that it is all right to have them if they don't take unfair advantage of children?

The sociology magazine *Transaction* commented: "The saving grace of that last clause! A poll-taker's masterpiece—to insert as a given that which is in dispute." With the stated proviso, 74 per cent of the 1993 people felt—quite predictably—that it was "all right to have them."

The NAB, reporting the poll result, headlined its release: "ROPER FINDS THREE OUT OF FOUR AMERICANS APPROVE PRINCIPLE OF COMMERCIAL SPONSORSHIP FOR CHILDREN'S TELEVISION PROGRAMS."[15]

The achievements of the ACT campaigns gave heart to many, but also tended to defuse the problem. They left the situation largely unchanged. Hosts on most children's programs were no longer plugging products but were replaced by other selling heroes, real and mythical. Sugared vitamins were gone from these programs, but sugared foods and candies remained in profusion, sharing the spotlight at Christmas time with mechanical toys. Most stations reduced the minutes allotted to commercials, but sold them at a slightly higher rate. Advertisers adjusted to the situation by concentrating on shorter commercials, sometimes selling several items in one 30-second spot. The total number of commercials remained approximately the same, though taking less time. Network revenues from commercials on children's programming actually increased in 1975 under the new limits, setting an all-time high of $90,805,400. Thus children's programming remained a lucrative advertising bait. Its success had its own irresistible momentum.

The FTC decision that child audiences required separate policies, as being "unqualified" to evaluate advertising, was considered by some to be an important breakthrough. But the implication that adult audiences *were* qualified for such evaluation is hardly borne out by the record. Numerous case histories of drug advertising illustrate the point, as does the history of cigarette advertising. In 1920, at the dawn of broadcasting, few women smoked; it was not considered a "feminine" activity. Realizing that the cigarette market could be doubled if this idea were overcome, cigarette manufacturers began in the 1920's to direct advertising toward women. Many of the radio and television campaigns of later years pursued this strategy—apparently with staggering success, creating a worldwide market of feminine addicts. Reports linking cigarettes with cancer began to circulate at mid-century, but massive television advertising— generally linking cigarette smoking with health, romance, social poise—continued successfully for two more decades. Audience response scarcely involved an "evaluation" process.

Television advertising has been successful to an extent that may pose dangers for itself as well as society. Few major corporations now dare to be absent from the tube, and the pressure has made virtually every hour salable—at rising prices. Regardless of price, many major corporations make time purchases far in advance. The constant price rise has tended to favor the most powerful enterprises and eliminate the marginal. It has posed huge obstacles to new enterprise except by the powerful. The absorption of smaller companies into conglomerates—usually multinational—has been one of the consequences. The trend to concentration, while hailed by some, is increasingly deplored and attacked by others.

The preemption of the schedule for commercial ends has put lethal pressure on other values and interests. The rising and increasingly indignant demand on the networks for "access" is one result.

The effect on politics has been devastating. Except for the minimal coverage provided in news programming—including, on rare occasions, debates—candidates for office win access to the medium only by accepting the role of sponsor, buying time at commercial rates. For broadcast purposes the candidate for major office—President, Governor, Senator—no longer plans campaign speeches; he plans and produces "commercials." The cost squeeze has made 30-second and 60-second "commercials" the principal campaign vehicles. The time frame has almost eliminated issues in favor of the kind of dramaturgy that sells products; the same advertising agencies, directors, and script writers are recruited for this. The cost factor favors wealthy candidates and those who are adept in attracting campaign con-tributions—a basic element in political corruption.

Television's success in squeezing the political process into the framework of commerce is primarily an American achievement. No major European country permits sale of time for political purposes. The prevailing pattern in Europe is allocation of free time on the basis of a mathematical formula—such as votes in a previous election, or party representation in a legislative body. The candidate who merchandises his candidacy with "commer-cials" in paid-for time is an American contribution to the electoral process. This may well be one of the most dangerous effects of the success of broadcast advertising.[16]

The sales effectiveness of the medium has not only altered values and customs; it has evolved its own cosmography.

In the world of the commercial, the work of Creation has been largely a disaster, functionally and aesthetically. Almost everything done in the making of man and his environment was a mistake; fortunately, man himself has invented products to correct the errors.

Hair, for example, grows where it shouldn't ("unsightly hair") and fails to grow where it should, leading to social and business disaster. Fortunately, man has evolved a host of prod-ucts for both problems. When hair does grow in the right places, it tends to grow wrongly. Many women, for example, are mortified by "skinny eyelashes." Again—fortunately—a whole industry has been developed to make them look thicker and longer. Additional industries take care of other problems. For the unfortunate races on whom Nature has bestowed curly hair, man has developed straightening products; for those with the humiliating heritage of straight hair, curling products. Hair is almost always wrongly colored: dark hair must be bleached, white hair darkened; fortunately, products are available for both problems. There are also products to give oily hair "the dry look" and dry hair "brilliant highlights." Skin involves similar aesthetic failures, which man has succeeded in remedying. Women need no longer be disadvantaged by "pale eyelids"; products that correct the condition are available. Products are also available for "moisturizing" dry skin and drying oily skin. The insufferable pallor of normal lips can be remedied by various products, which can also add orange, lemon, raspberry, or other flavors. Man has been especially inventive about odors; he has identified and named special odors for almost every zone of the body from "bad breath" to "foot odor." All require special products and commercials for them, including vaginal sprays. It used to be thought that the smell of a clean body had an aphrodisiac effect, involving natural secretions, but these are now obliterated by man-made products, with secretions and odors borrowed from other animals or from plants or minerals. Some of these irritate human tissues, but man has developed a host of products to soothe and counteract the irritations. The foods provided by Nature have, like the human body, proved to be failures. They include coarse ingredients that man has learned to remove, thus providing bread that is delightful to squeeze. The removed ingredients can later be processed into products to be sold as diet supplements. If the refined foods cause constipation, obesity, anemia, or other disruptions, a host of products is available for corrective purposes. The innumerable products needed to correct the failures of Nature are made by huge companies employing hosts of people in production, promotion, and distribution. They work under much pressure to keep

things going. The human apparatus designed by Nature is noto-
riously prone to waver under pressures of this sort; fortunately,
man has invented liquids and pills by which people can stimu-
late themselves or calm themselves as needed. Televised messages for beers and wines were produced and exhibited in the
United States in 1975 at a cost of around $140 million; for stom-
ach settlers and other digestive aids, $50 million; for pain re-
lievers and sleeping pills, $100 million. One of eight commercials
was for a drug product. Three drug companies were among the
ten largest network advertisers. For decades self-medication merchants have been among the leading sponsors—in network and
local broadcasting.

Commercials have worked—with success—toward revision of
many traditional tenets of our society. As we have seen, rever-
ence for nature has been replaced by a determination to process
it. Thrift has been replaced by the duty to buy. The work ethic
has been replaced by the consumption ethic. "Conspicuous consumption," once considered an unworthy tendency of leisure
classes, has been sanctified and democratized, and is right for
everybody. Modesty has been exorcized with help from the
sexual sell. Restraint of ego has lost standing. If one does not
proclaim oneself "the greatest," one is suspected of not being
much good. The reluctant candidate, willing to serve, is passé;
a candidate must repeatedly extol his capacities for leadership.
Self-love is consecrated ritual. The woman caressing her body
in shower or bathtub has become a standard feature of commercials. A woman applying perfume says: "It's expensive, but
I think I'm worth it!"

The chorus of claims and promises involves endless repetition.
If you can't afford "frequency," advises an advertising leader,
don't bother advertising. Don't worry if a commercial irritates
some people. If they "like" it too much, there may be something wrong with it. Commercials challenge each other on innumerable points (e.g. the battle of *roll-on* vs. *spray* vs. *cream*
deodorants), but never on the basic principle: you must buy.
So far the collective message is successful. It apparently holds its
audience in thrall. But sponsors are well aware that this might

not be so if the message were undermined by surrounding programming.

A degree of sponsor control over the surrounding territory—
most of which is categorized as "entertainment"—is therefore
considered crucial to the success of the message. We turn now
to those outer defenses.

> Give a small boy a hammer, and he'll soon
> find a lot of things that need hammering.
>
> CHARLES EAMES

THE OUTER DEFENSES—"entertainment"

The word is in quotation marks because it has no precise meaning but is, rather, a strategy word. It is used to deprecate the social significance of what is presented. As used for decades by Hollywood and today by networks and sponsors, it implies that there is no message—messages being for Western Union—and no purpose of any sort other than to fill leisure time and make you feel good. It is the relaxation you deserve after your hard work. Nowadays it goes with a beer and encourages you to have more than one.

The aura surrounding the word is important because it tends to lull critical faculties. Diversion being the order of the day, we are not inclined to question or even identify unspoken premises of the game. This enables "entertainment" to play a leading role in shaping attitudes and ideas, including political ideas.

This goes against accepted doctrine, which associates "propaganda" with such forms as the documentary, the public affairs program, the discussion program. But these forms confront their

subject matter openly. They therefore raise our resistance, perhaps even our hackles, and make us determined not to be "brain-
washed." They readily lead us to the charge of "propaganda."
There is irony in this: we are most likely to invoke the word
"propaganda" when a program is failing as propaganda.

"Entertainment" programs—plays, cartoons, game shows, variety shows—work differently, and can be far more effective
propaganda precisely because they are received as something
else—"entertainment."

If popular "entertainment" has generally been the preferred
setting for sponsor messages, the reasons have included not only
its popularity but also its apparent innocuousness—along with
other reasons to be discussed presently.

In previous centuries "entertainment" was a once-in-a-while
thing. Someone might read aloud, or play a musical instrument;
for the fortunate, there might be an occasional visit to a theater.
Today's television has no relation to those occasional *divertisse-
ments*. It is not surcease from daily routine, it *is* daily routine. It
is an environmental presence. For the first time in human history, people are constantly confronted by living images of themselves, doing things that seem to be good or bad, beautiful or
ugly, desirable or undesirable, and that rivet attention.

A child becomes aware of television at a remarkably early
age. It is the brightest thing in the house. Like the hearth of
earlier times, it tends to be the focus of home life. It is itself
full of life. The child becomes aware of television "uncles" and
"aunts" and strange animals who talk to him from its luminous
region, and are somewhat like extensions of the family, though
of another order. Before long his attention is drawn especially
to scenes of activity that seem to represent a universe beyond
home walls.

Some of this involves creatures that are like people but different. They are omnipotent. They can have pianos fall on them,
be flattened on a sidewalk, then reassemble themselves and strut
away. They can be hurled through the air, fall from buildings or
airplanes, and bounce painlessly. The child's awareness of its
own impotence, and its constant preoccupation with surmount-
ing it, may give these superhuman creatures special interest. The

obsession with impotence/omnipotence will remain to some degree for years—perhaps forever.

According to Nielsen statistics, children from three to five years of age who are at home spend an average of fifty-four hours a week in front of television—almost 64 per cent of their waking hours.[1]

By the time children are ready for school their main interest has generally shifted from animation creatures to beings that are clearly real, involved in actions that also seem real. The viewing now centers on various "action-adventure" series, offering glimpses of a wide world; also, to some extent, on "situation comedy," more familiar in setting. The child identifies with several of the heroes and heroines, and feels on closer terms with them than with many people in the neighborhood. He also knows many of the commercials by heart. This programming will constitute most of the viewing throughout elementary school and into the high school years. By the end of high school a youngster has spent about 12,000 hours in a classroom but may have spent 24,000 hours watching television—mostly stories and commercials. Their conflicts and crises have helped shape his conception of the world and its inhabitants.

The action-adventure and situation-comedy series are both categorized as *episodic series*. Such a series has one or more continuing characters but not a continued story—it is not a *serial*. An episode in a typical episodic series is complete—always a variation of a specific series formula. The genre permits participation by innumerable writers. There is no chronology; episodes can be repeated in any order.

Halfway through high school some youngsters—around half, according to observations of sociologist Wilbur Schramm—acquire an awareness of news, documentary, and public affairs programming, to which they have previously been oblivious. The other half remain almost immune to these, sticking with the episodic drama into adult years.[2]

Periodically during recent decades Roper interviewers have asked people from what source they learn "what's going on in the world today—from the newspapers or radio or television or magazines or talking to people or where?" Since 1963 most have said "television," and the percentage has risen since then. Television also appears to be the most trusted. Many people seem to rely almost totally on television.[3]

Television leaders take understandable pride in these findings, and generally consider them an achievement of television news programming. But is this likely? Before meaningful involvement in any news programming, a child may have seen ten or twenty or thirty thousand episodes of drama, most of which seem to concern "what's going on in the world today." Many of the action-adventure series deal with crime, espionage, and war, often in quasi-documentary fashion. Some crime series are "based on" the files of this or that police department; its actual buildings and badges are shown. On some, "only the names are changed to protect the innocent." At the end of each program of *The FBI*, allegedly dramatizing true victories over crime, we are told the exact sentences meted out to the criminals, even though a writer may have invented the case. The seal of the FBI is shown, and its Director thanked for his cooperation. In spy series there are references to various countries, and we see their famous buildings. The air of authenticity is everywhere.

Operating on a borderline between fact and fiction, producers aim at "showmanship" rather than deception, but the results may be similar. Disentangling fact from fiction may be almost impossible for many viewers. The question, "What is real, and what isn't?" may not even occur to the younger child. The older may ask the question, and arrive at a point of regarding a program as a "show" involving "stars"—while still feeling, unconsciously, that it is essentially "true," telling it "like it is." This is not confined to children. The spy series *The Man From U.N.C.L.E.* brought many letters to the United Nations applying for jobs at U.N.C.L.E. And for the thousands who line up in Washington to tour the J. Edgar Hoover building of the FBI, the legendary portrait presented on *The FBI* seems to have prevailed over the massive revelations of the early 1970's concerning FBI illegalities.[4]

The point is that for those growing up today, episodic drama plays a journalistic role for a decade before recognized news media can have an impact. For many it continues to play such a role into adult life, and to prevail over recognized "journalism."

Its ability to do this is not mysterious. Whereas news programs offer isolated tidbits of information, almost always out of context and incomprehensible to the uninformed, the action in episodic drama can be quickly understood, and invites emotional identification. In action-adventure it is at once clear that a good man is in a contest with one or more evil persons—gangsters, smugglers, murderers, cattle rustlers, enemy agents—and that the fate of a family, city, country, or the world may depend on the outcome. The formula guarantees emotional participation.

Such programming undoubtedly forms patterns of ideas and attitudes about the world. These may later determine what information, from the barrage offered by newscasts, will stick and what not stick; what will be believed and what not believed. Mental patterns of "reality," once established, seem to be fortified by selective perception and retention. On television it is drama, not news programming, that takes the lead in setting patterns.

Its hold over audiences is enough to explain its popularity with sponsors, but other factors are also involved. Among various forms of drama, the episodic series has played an especially crucial role in the evolution of sponsorship—a role that can best be understood by a look back.

In the early 1950's, during television's first boom years, the dominant form of sponsored drama was not the episodic series, but another kind of drama series, the *anthology* series—represented by *Philco Television Playhouse, Goodyear Television Playhouse, Studio One, Kraft Television Theater, U.S. Steel Hour, Playhouse 90*, and a dozen other series of similar nature. These featured independent plays without linkage of characters or subject matter. The series represented a *carte blanche* invitation to writers to write about something that interested them. This soon drew an avalanche of submissions that brought to the fore many new writers including Paddy Chayefsky, Gore Vidal, Reginald Rose, and others—as well as new directors and actors. The series had their ups and downs, yet in a few short years produced an extraordinary body of work. A number of the plays, in published collections, continue to draw admiration. Some led to theater successes such as *Twelve Angry Men* and *Visit to a Small Planet;* others to notable feature films—*Marty, Bachelor's Party, A Catered Affair, Edge of the City, Patterns, Requiem for a Heavyweight.* On television these series held high Nielsen and other ratings: *Philco Television Playhouse* was among program leaders for five successive years. At times, four of the ten top ratings were won by anthology series.[5]

Yet beginning in 1955, the anthology series were abruptly jettisoned in favor of episodic series, and virtually passed out of existence. The reasons for this transition tell us a great deal about commercial sponsorship and its possible social impact.

In spite of large audiences and critical acclaim, the anthology programs made sponsors restive. Like most programs of the early 1950's, these series were produced "live" and therefore tended—like the theater, their major influence—to encourage compact plays with indoor settings, and to favor psychological over physical confrontations. As in Ibsen's dramas, the dilemmas sometimes had wide social implications, which might make them meaningful, and win critical enthusiasm, but also produced angry letters. With the rise of McCarthyism, organized letter-writing became the order of the day.

Meanwhile there were other irritations. Social and psychological problems seldom have neat, clean-cut solutions. The commercials featured products that solved problems of business and pleasure in a minute or less. To a writer like Chayefsky these same problems had complex social and psychological ramifications. These might be fascinating, but they often made the commercials seem fraudulent.

Lower-class settings were another source of exasperation. The enormous success of Paddy Chayefsky's *Marty,* about the love problems of a butcher in the Bronx, inspired a flood of plays about what Chayefsky called "the marvelous world of the ordinary." Sponsors were meanwhile trying to "upgrade" the consumer and persuade him to "move up to Chrysler," and "live better electrically" in a suburban home, with help from "a friend at Chase Manhattan." The sponsors preferred beautiful people in mouth-watering *décor,* to convey what it meant to climb the socio-economic ladder. The commercials looked out of place in Bronx settings. Again the drama undermined the message.[6]

Considering these multiple aggravations, it is easy to understand the reaction of sponsors when in 1955-56 the eight "major" Hollywood studios, which had previously boycotted television, decided to jump on the bandwagon. Led by Warner Brothers, they began to produce for television, while also releasing their backlog of features.

Their chosen form became the episodic series, already successfully exploited by several independent producers—notably in *I Love Lucy* and *Dragnet*. Warner's *Cheyenne*, starring Clint Walker, was followed by a stampede of similar projects. By 1957 there were more than a hundred Hollywood-produced episodic series, with action-adventure leading the pack. Cowboys, detectives, secret agents dominated the action, and thus entered a firm and long-lasting alliance with advertising.[7]

To the sponsor, the business advantages seemed numerous and compelling. Drama moved outdoors into active, glamorous settings. Handsome heroes and heroines set the tone—and some proved willing to do commercials, and even appear at sales meetings and become company spokesmen.

Of even greater importance, the shift to episodic series based on formula reduced policy crises. In the anthology days the writers had, in effect, set the agenda; it was they who decided what people would be talking about next morning in office, school, store, and commuter train. The initiative had now been taken away from the writers. The formula served as a control mechanism. The writer was now asked to think up variations on an approved pattern. Some writers found this a challenge to ingenuity, as well as the basis for a lucrative career. Others—Chayefsky and Vidal among them—moved to other pastures: theater, novel, theatrical film.

The move to filmed episodic series was propelled by still another factor. In 1955 commercial television began in Britain and was also beginning—or about to begin—in scores of other countries. The spread was part of the worldwide surge of American business. The London branch of an American advertising agency, J. Walter Thompson, was credited with having masterminded the lobbying campaign that swung the British Parliament toward commercial television; other countries followed the British example. In country after country, viewers began to see programs and commercials that had already shown their potency in the United States. Action-adventure proved the most transplantable of forms. De-emphasizing dialogue in favor of action, it minimized translating and dubbing problems. Its good-vs.-evil plots could be understood anywhere. The law-and-order stress pleased government and business elements. Within a few years American episodic series were being translated in vast numbers into Spanish (with the dubbing done in Mexico and, temporarily, in Cuba), French (in France), Arabic (in Egypt and, temporarily, in Lebanon), Portuguese (in Brazil), German (in Germany), Chinese (in Hong Kong), Italian (in Italy), Japanese (in Japan). Action-adventure drama, riding the crest of global enterprise, somehow epitomized it. An assembly-line product—"entertainment" packaged for world markets—it helped push other products into world markets.[8]

Sponsors, at home and abroad, were flocking to episodic series for persuasive business reasons, but the transition had implications beyond business. The formulas that tethered writers tethered audiences too. Their imaginations and perceptions, like those of writers, were being reined and fenced in. A look at prevailing formulas will suggest how.

The formulas for cowboy, crime, and secret-agent series are, in spite of surface differences, essentially the same. A central character or characters must catch and/or kill an evil person or persons. A child growing up against this relentless background—hour after hour, year after year—may well sense that the world at large faces few problems that are not solved by catching or killing someone. Things are different in situation comedy, where problems come from misunderstandings involving odd-ball characters; but these have to do with home or office. In the larger society, crises stem from villainous, sometimes psychopathic people. The world seems to be filled with them.

On these programs drama never derives from problems within a central character or characters. The viewer is never asked to look for problems within characters with whom he mainly identifies. The trouble is always someone else—never oneself. Introspection is not encouraged. The pattern has natural appeal for the immature; ceaselessly reenforced, it may help to prolong immaturity. It also holds seeds of paranoia.

That this is not merely a theoretical conclusion is suggested by findings of Dean George Gerbner of the Annenberg School of Communications at the University of Pennsylvania. Interviews with individuals who had, for many years, been action-adventure devotees were compared to similar interviews with others who had not. Action-adventure devotees tended to see their environment in far more threatening terms. Tending to magnify crime statistics, and dangers to their own safety, they saw law-and-order as a dominant issue. This seems to give action-adventure drama a subliminal political dimension. It suggests that law-and-order "entertainment" nurtures law-and-order politics.[9]

In action-adventure the conquest of evil seldom ends with arrest of the villain. More often it involves an action climax. The villain makes a break for it but is finally trapped by heroic and dangerous action. Film has favored such climaxes because only film is capable of them. They have always been impractical in theater, meaningless in radio. Only film can fully exploit what has been called the "pornography of violence." On television it has proved supremely effective as ratings builder, seizing and holding the dial-turner—as an accident or murder stops a crowd. But the constant exploitation of such climaxes may exact a cost. A child may well sense that normal processes of justice are inadequate; that most problems are solved by the physical heroism of a hero. It is violence, society seems to tell him over and over, that solves problems.

That violent dramatic action has influence on behavior is constantly and vigorously denied by television spokesmen as "unproved." Yet researches conducted under the auspices of the U.S. Surgeon General do point to just such a relationship. And the industry spokesmen put themselves in a curious position when they eagerly proclaim that television examples influence our buying habits, hair styles, play, vocabulary, fashions, political choices—but never the way we achieve our goals.

While the social implications of simplistic formula drama have begun to disturb many people including writers, sponsors, advertising agents, most industry spokesmen hew to the line that it is all just "entertainment"—a boon for relaxation and togetherness. And episodic drama remains a dominant dramatic form. Fortunately, it is not the only dramatic form.

Some sponsors have resisted it in favor of the "special." Specials—and groups of related specials—have been with us since the 1950's when Sylvester L. ("Pat") Weaver, Jr., institutionalized them as an antidote to "the robotry of habit-viewing." Specials have ranged widely in subject. The surest audience-getters—and the most expensive for the sponsor—have been major sports events like Super Bowls and World Series. Close behind have been drama and variety specials. Many have been as mechanical and predictable as run-of-the-mill formula series—e.g., *Dean Martin's California Christmas, Perry Como's Hawaiian Holiday, Tennessee Ernie Ford in Moscow*. But occasional drama specials—sometimes in several parts—do serve magnificently the "antidote" function, with work that cuts through assembly line rituals and reminds us of the possibilities of the medium.[10]

Examples of recent years have included *The Autobiography of Miss Jane Pittman*, written by Tracy Keenan Wynn and sponsored by Xerox; and the three-part *Eleanor and Franklin*, dramatized by James Costigan from writings of Joseph Lash and sponsored by IBM. Both won overwhelming critical praise, unprecedented numbers of Emmy awards, and *fairly* good ratings.*

A number of points about these programs are worth noting. Both were of the sort the industry tends to pigeon-hole as "culture" or even "documentary"—and to avoid. Both involved issues considered trouble-making. *The Autobiography of Miss*

---

* *Eleanor and Franklin*, Part I, had a 20.3 rating, and a 30 per cent share-of-audience; Part II had a 24.2 rating, and a 35 per cent share-of-audience. By way of comparison, the season's highest ratings among drama specials went to the two-part *Helter Skelter*, based on the Manson murders and perhaps the most violent program of the season: *Helter Skelter*, Part I, got a 35.2 rating, a 57 per cent share-of-audience; Part II had a 37.5 rating, a 60 per cent share-of-audience. This was surpassed only by the seventh game of the World Series, which had a 39.6 rating, and a 60 per cent share-of-audience. *Variety*, September 22, 1976.

Jane Pittman was about struggles against racial injustice; even though the subject no longer raised the terrors once associated with it, it would probably not have won a place in a network schedule except for the determination of Xerox to sponsor it. *Eleanor and Franklin* touched on an early marital infidelity of Franklin D. Roosevelt.

Each program was wholly sponsored by one sponsor, as in earlier days. In a sense these programs represented a survival, or revival, of anthology drama, or at least of its most essential aspect: each of the works stemmed from the initiative of a writer. Neither was made-to-order piecework. Neither was shaped by a cookie cutter.

At the networks such projects represented a relaxation of the "masters in our own house" policy. The policy was originally born of government pressure following the quiz scandals, but in 1972 the U.S. Department of Justice filed an antitrust suit against the three networks, charging them with monopolizing prime-time "entertainment." Behind this seemingly strange shift was the frequent complaint of independent producers that networks not only controlled schedules, but demanded a financial share in programs they accepted from independents. When the suit was launched, the networks began to retreat from this habit; NBC eventually stipulated, in a consent decree, that it would limit, to two and a half hours per week, prime-time entertainment in which it had a financial interest. The antitrust action also made networks more receptive to independent projects coming to them via sponsors. The relaxation delighted independents. David Susskind of Talent Associates, producers of *Eleanor and Franklin,* summarized it by saying: "For a time, we had only three customers—the heads of the three networks." Sponsors, he felt, at least differ in program preferences. If most sponsors have standardized ideas of "entertainment," a few are mavericks.[11]

A handful of major corporations—IBM, Xerox, Eastman, Mobil, Exxon, and a few others—have favored unusual specials and sole sponsorship of them. There are several reasons for this. Exceptional programs seem a necessary badge—and legitimation—of the exceptional prosperity and power of these companies.

Their status encourages a *noblesse oblige* approach to programming. An image-protection strategy, relating to antitrust perils, has had priority for most of them—a factor also reflected in commercials, particularly those of oil companies.

Companies like IBM and Xerox are motivated by still other factors that set them apart from many sponsors, especially food and drug companies selling through supermarkets. Food and drug companies, dependent on constant and rapid flow of products via supermarket shelves, have generally been most afraid of antagonizing anyone; the thought of protests or boycotts has easily terrified them—as in the blacklist period. Their fears translate themselves into policy timidity, along with stress on ratings and demographics. Thus Procter & Gamble in a memorandum on broadcast policies decreed: "There will be no material that may give offense, either directly or by inference, to any commercial organization of any sort." Colgate instructs its advertising agencies to preview every film in which a Colgate commercial is scheduled to appear; anything not "acceptable" leads to withdrawal of the commercial. Such companies are the steadiest and most profitable customers for the networks, and network policy tends to mirror their requirements—and phobias.[12]

In contrast, IBM, Xerox, and other manufacturers of high-cost products have a very different marketing problem. It involves more sophisticated customers, and carefully considered purchases. An association with "quality" is paramount, as is a "forward-looking image." Some "controversial" topics may even contribute to this, and are less feared than by other sponsors. These companies have occasionally sponsored documentaries.

A Xerox memorandum on television policy states:

> Each program will have an over-purpose—it will not only entertain, it will tend to stretch the mind, to inspire, to stir the conscience and require thought. Our programs should try to advance TV over what it has been. Where possible, we should use our money to lead, not follow.

Such policies—and the conjunction of circumstances behind them—have brought the networks some of their finer moments.

However, networks have not always been eager for the offerings, if the outlook for ratings and share-of-audience seemed doubtful. The brilliant special *The Belle of Amherst*, written by William Luce and starring Julie Harris, was rejected by all networks even though IBM had decided to sponsor it. It was shunted to public television, with underwriting by IBM.[13]

By and large, the continued success of network schedules—especially in financial terms—has kept propelling them in the direction already set. Many executives say that personal preferences would move them in other directions, but that their duty is to mass preferences, as evidenced by quantifiable trends. Such evidence—as in Nielsen ratings—inevitably encourages imitation of current successes. Other favored research techniques do likewise, and may be favored for that reason. Some researchers have taken to testing programs and commercials by skin tests measuring variations in the sweat of the palm; it may be assumed these measure nervous tension, not enlightenment. Another testing system, widely relied on, is that of Preview House in Hollywood. The seats in its auditorium are fitted with dial devices by which a viewer can flick a switch to any of five positions: very dull, dull, normal, good, very good. Audiences are invited in somewhat random fashion to participate in tests of pilot programs. To make sure an assembled group is standard in its reactions and preferences, the procedure has been to start by showing a vintage Magoo short. If an audience reacts in a nonstandard way, findings can be adjusted accordingly. The scores achieved are known in the industry as "Magoos." A pilot is said to have done well if it scores between 5.1 and 6.3 Magoos—according to a study by Roland Flamini in *American Film*.

Writers and directors are generally outraged by the system. Anything unfamiliar, they say, scores low in Magoos. Other writers cooperate with the realities by writing for "the Magoo factor." In a situation comedy, they say, the appearance of a dog or small child can be counted on to make the needle jump. In action-adventure, car chases make grand Magoos, talk doesn't. "If the private eye has to explain something," a writer told Flamini, "he'd better be doing something interesting at the same time, like walking a tight rope over Niagara Falls or screwing his female client." It costs $1500 to test a pilot at Preview House. Executives at networks and sponsoring companies rely on such evidence because it can be cited as a scientific basis for decision, if things go wrong. No one dares cite personal opinion; that would be "elitist." Tests are an instrument of "cultural democracy."[14]

The attachment to quasi-scientific bases for decision occasionally backfires. Some sponsors selecting programs for their youthful demographics have been dismayed to find themselves listed as sponsors supporting violent programs. McDonald's and Burger King found themselves near the top of such lists. They had not set out to buy violence, only youthful demographics. Abdication to machinery may involve such risks. But for reasons of practicality, it remains a basis for program transactions and purchases.[15]

The password is "entertainment"—something stimulating but apparently purposeless, unchallenging. An ABC-TV vice president for programming, Bob Shanks, insists that a program should not move you "too deeply." He explains why:

> Program makers are supposed to devise and produce shows that will attract mass audiences without unduly offending these audiences or too deeply moving them emotionally. Such ruffling, it is thought, will interfere with their ability to receive, recall, and respond to the commercial message. This programming reality is the unwritten, unspoken *gemeinschaft* of all professional members of the television fraternity.*

That programming generally plays a business-supportive role—at least avoiding anything at odds with commercials—is scarcely

---

* Needless to say, not all ABC programming has followed this catastrophic injunction. It was ABC, perhaps encouraged by the huge success of *The Autobiography of Miss Jane Pittman*, that scheduled the eight-part *Roots*, a black family chronicle from Africa via slavery to emancipation. But its powerful content may have underlined Shanks's point. *Variety* commented: "It was a bit disconcerting to cut from the anguished screams of a mother whose oldest son had been enslaved to a blurb for Ben-Gay, for use 'when pain is at its worst.'" *Variety*, Jan. 26, 1977.

noticed by most viewers. What we have tends to seem inevitable.[16]

Some programs are hard to distinguish from commercials. On quiz and game shows both winners and losers are showered with luxury items; the winners have learned to leap and scream as gifts are described and the manufacturers credited; they serve as cheerleaders for the consumption culture. Sometimes they win trips to places like Lake Tahoe; airline and hotel are credited. Daytime serials offer another entree to high-consumption living: here a viewer participates in tense, tangled loves of suburbia, involving beautiful people, mostly professionals. They are well dressed and sit on fine furniture; the designers are credited. The people sometimes go to offices but hardly seem to work. On talk shows the same worlds are recycled. Stars talk about new shows, a new film. They compliment each other on their clothes and looks. A rising night-club act flies in from Las Vegas; the airline gets a credit. Televised football, along with its tense drama, offers a fiesta of dazzling girls, fur coats, strong men; a quota of time-outs is allotted to sponsors as well as teams. Olympic Games are likewise magnificent spectacles sprinkled with handsome commercials, often delivered by sport superstars—for credit cards, deodorants, perfumes, breath mints, sports cars, beer. The games will settle who will do commercials for future games, perhaps for six-figure or seven-figure salaries. Sports champions are also recycled on other programs; they may turn up as dolls merchandized on children's programs. A Saturday morning commercial demonstrates a mechanized boxing ring with two boxers which a boy can manipulate via levers to "make them box"; among available boxers is Muhammed Ali. With levers and pushbuttons he can also launch planes from a Flying Aces Attack Carrier; the commercial tells him: "You've got the power to take command—launch after launch!" For little girls there are girl-things, like Barbie's Dream Boat and Barbie's Town House. The demonstrations alternate with "entertainment" but they are not easy to distinguish. Both lead naturally into the dramas and conflicts and messages of prime time.

While virtually all "entertainment" programs reflect the ethic of consumption, episodic action-adventure series are perhaps its most characteristic expression. Their worldwide applicability, their power to foster useful mythologies, involving unsuspected ideological premises, have made them the ideal instrument of transnational enterprise.

The growth of American business after World War II, at home and abroad, has been an extraordinary political as well as business achievement. In the 1930's political dissent rode high in the United States. In the 1932 presidential election the Socialist Party drew 884,781 votes, more than three times its total in the previous presidential election. To some extent the New Deal defused this radical surge—partly, according to socialists, by appropriating socialist planks like social security and unemployment insurance. The consumer goods explosion after World War II and Korea apparently continued the defusing. Socialism had promised workers a share in the better things of life; the postwar boom seemed ready to confer it. Television proclaimed it as a birthright. Federal housing policy furthered the idea by underwriting the migration to suburbia. The picture window of television showed that everyone could live there; images of poverty were seldom seen through that picture window. Its images were a lesson in living. Soon it was spreading its message in a hundred lands, proclaiming the good life, the age of the consumer.[17]

In view of the traumatic revelations of the 1970's, when Americans learned that the business successes throughout the world had not been solely a product of technical expertise and skillful merchandising, but had involved wide use of bribery and a relationship with the CIA that often made the agency seem like a private police force for multinationals, ready to harass or topple uncooperative regimes, it is interesting to recall the constant mythologizing of covert action in business-sponsored episodic series of two decades. Was there special meaning in the flourishing of spy drama simultaneously with the global push of American business?

Viewers unquestionably thought of all those secret-agent dramas as "entertainment"—as did sponsors. But a closer look at these series, and the circumstances behind them, may further illuminate the elusive meanings of "entertainment."

Spies came early to television. *Foreign Intrigue*, shot on location against European backgrounds, was launched successfully in 1951. It was soon joined by *The Man Called X*, syndicated by Ziv—a company later absorbed by United Artists. Advertisements for the series referred frequently to the newly formed CIA, as though to suggest a link. A CIA trainee, said one advertisement, must learn to kill silently "to protect a vital mission." It also said: "Secret agents have molded our destiny." Soon afterwards came *Secret File U.S.A.*, starring Robert Alda and described by its producers as "semi-documentary"—revealing the "incredible exploits of American Intelligence in the continuing fight for freedom." Another Ziv syndicated series was *I Led Three Lives;* its local sponsor received promotion material proclaiming him a member of "the businessman's crusade" against the communist conspiracy. These various series set the tone: excitement, patriotism, freedom, crusade.[18]

But the greatest eruption of spy series came during the Vietnam War, in a sudden avalanche that included *The Man from U.N.C.L.E., The Girl from U.N.C.L.E., I Spy, Get Smart, The Man Who Never Was, Mission: Impossible, Jericho;* also various police series that suddenly turned into secret-agent series. The millionaire policeman of *Burke's Law* became a millionaire secret agent; *The FBI* began to concentrate on battles against communist agents. Some comedy series, notably *I Dream of Jeannie*, often revolved around espionage. Children's series—*Mr. Terrific, Secret Squirrel, Super 6*, and others—echoed similar themes. Even Tarzan joined the struggle, becoming the champion of emerging African nations against communist conspiracies. All quickly acquired sponsors.

None referred to the wars in Vietnam, Laos, and Cambodia; nor did any television drama series. The whole subject of Vietnam was shunned by drama writers, directors, producers—and by sponsors, though for different reasons. The Vietnam buildup years—1964-66—were a boom time. They created, according to U.S. Labor Department statistics, a million new jobs during this period, with ripples of prosperity throughout the economy. Significantly, over half the Federal tax revenue was going into the war, and more than half of that was going directly to the Amer-

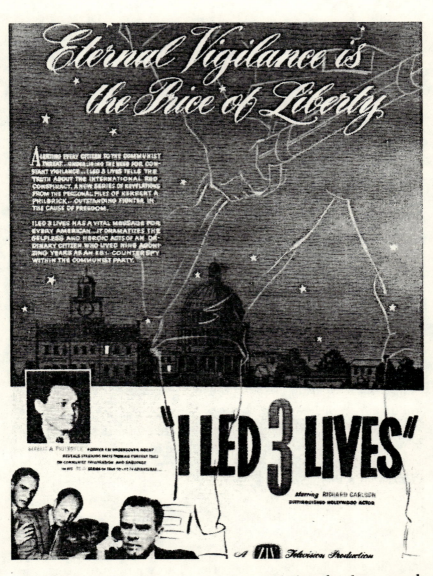

THE SECRET AGENT: Excitement, patriotism, freedom, crusade. (*Wisconsin Center for Theatre Research.*)

ican corporations which were the chief government suppliers. On the list of the hundred largest government suppliers, over half were companies heavily involved in broadcasting—as sponsors, broadcasters, or manufacturers. None wished to proclaim the relationship on television—it would have been "controversial." Nor did they wish to feature anything anti-war—that would have been even more "controversial." Exciting "entertainment" provided the escape route—seemingly unrelated yet subtly supportive of what was being done.

As "entertainment" the spy, drama had high credentials. Handsome men and sexy women fitted the formula. And the new group of spy series had other plus values. Before his Vietnam escalation, President Johnson had given historic impetus to Negro rights with the Civil Rights Act of 1964. Television was under strong pressure to admit blacks to meaningful participation. It became suddenly fashionable to have a *group* of heroes, one of whom was black. On the *Mission: Impossible* team it was Barney, the most skillful technician of the group; he was the one who could defuse time-bombs. *I Spy* won praise on similar grounds; its two spies, a white and a black, played by Robert Culp and Bill Cosby, worked together in friendly, total equality. The appearance of blacks in a context unrelated to "the Negro problem" was in itself a breakthrough. Thus these spy series won praise for liberalism.

But meanwhile the drama could have meaning only if viewers accepted, consciously or unconsciously, its underlying premise: that "we" faced enemies so evil and so clever that "the intricate means used to defeat them are necessary." So said the instructions to writers of *Mission: Impossible*. Thus the plots served as continual rationale for covert warfare. They also rationalized government secrecy and official lies. On each program the secret mission was assigned via a tape recording that would quickly "self-destruct." The agents were told: "Should you . . . be caught or killed, the Secretary will disavow any knowledge of your actions." At a time when Assistant Secretary of Defense Arthur Sylvester was proclaiming the right of government to lie in an emergency, the program seemed to endorse the idea.[19]

The enemy was generally organized in fiendish undercover

groups with names like KAOS—on *Get Smart*.* The countries involved were sometimes identified as "iron curtain countries" or "people's republics," without specific names—a procedure that avoided diplomatic protests. But Cuba, East Germany, or China, unrepresented in Washington, could be mentioned in any way whatever. In an *I Spy* episode ("Weight of the World") the Red Chinese were depicted as planning to drop bubonic plague bacteria in the water supply of a large American city. In a *Man from U.N.C.L.E.* episode ("Her Master's Voice Affair"), about a prominent girls' school where daughters of American leaders were enrolled, the girls had been "programmed," via a Red Chinese plot, to annihilate their famous fathers. At a time when the Administration was justifying the Vietnam War as necessary to contain Chinese "hordes" who would otherwise sweep down from the north, and was picturing the North Vietnamese as Chinese puppets, such inventive plots made their contribution to paranoia. Paranoia was, indeed, the underlying theme of the action-adventure drama of the period. Americans seemed to be surrounded, at home and abroad and even in outer space, by fiendish enemies who must be combated by the weapons and tactics they were expected to use on us, if given the chance.[20]

Examined by a stranger from another planet, this "entertainment" might give the impression that it was part of a vast conspiracy to prepare the population—especially its youth—for an American Armageddon against enemies. But there was no conspiracy: there were merely parallel decisions by many producers and sponsors to do something that was timely, popular, and—above all—*not* controversial. What was needed was "entertainment."

From the vantage of any culture, entertainment of almost any other culture can be seen as propaganda. One's own cannot. Pre-

---

* Curiously, it turned out there *was* an Operation CHAOS—a CIA project for keeping dossiers on thousands of Americans via illegal wiretaps and mail interceptions. It involved names of 300,000 people, indexed by computer. It was officially halted in 1974. *Intelligence Activities and the Rights of Americans* (Washington, D.C., GPO, 1976), pp. 99–102.

cisely because the same underlying premises constantly reappear, they tend to be accepted as natural elements.

With the revelations of the 1970's, spy drama subsided, and the pendulum swung back to policemen and detectives. Events had brought a slight shift to the evolving mythology.

The huge block of programming known as entertainment has here been described as reflecting the dominance of sponsors. Many television executives would agree, and see no apology needed. Entertainment and advertising—these are seen as a combination that serves public and sponsor alike—and is profitable.

The awareness that television has become the main transmitter of the culture, a principal conditioner of millions of lives, involves them in mixed emotions. It places on the medium a burden that most of its entrepreneurs never sought nor wanted. Yet it is there, and troublesome.

"Public service" seems to be required of them—as licensees and users of publicly owned channels. It involves subject matter that often intrudes disruptively on the world dedicated to the sponsor. The problem is to minimize its disruptions, and keep it reasonably contained.

"Don't you understand? This is *life*, this is what is happening. We *can't* switch to another channel." *Drawing by Rob't. Day;* © *1970 The New Yorker Magazine, Inc.*

> Private enterprise and private investment are being
> aroused to their responsibilities—as they have
> without result a hundred times before.
>
> JOHN KENNETH GALBRAITH

THE SATRAPIES—"public service"

When our lawmakers stipulated—in 1927 and again in 1934—that the holder of a broadcasting license must serve the public interest, convenience, and necessity, they were pursuing a strategy followed in the writing of the Constitution. Framing a charter for developments they could not foresee, they relied on open-ended phrases that could gain meaning from later history, case by case. Inevitably, the strategy has produced conflicts over interpretation.

"I suggest that a program in which a large part of the audience is interested," said Frank Stanton in 1960 as president of CBS, Inc., "is by that very fact a program in the public interest." To hold otherwise, he suggested, was to be an elitist and not a believer in "cultural democracy." The Stanton interpretation was attractive to licensees; it seemed to sanction anything that might prove profitable. It could even be used, if one were so inclined, to encompass pornography.[1]

Other broadcasters have held that advertising, because it keeps the wheels of industry turning, is of the essence of public service and should in itself be considered justification for a license. One broadcaster, Gordon McLendon, proposed a radio station devoted solely to classified advertising, and actually got FCC approval. The project was not a success, however.[2]

The FCC has had a long history of conforming to industry rationales, but on most occasions has been slightly more demanding in interpreting "the public interest." However, even its modest demands have been protested by industry lobbyists.

A key point in many FCC decisions has been that democracy requires a citizenry that understands decisions facing it. To this end, a station is expected to provide adequate coverage of "issues of public importance." In doing so, it is expected to air "conflicting views" on the issues. This FCC doctrine, formally approved by Congress in 1959, became known as the "Fairness Doctrine." Challenged in court by various sectors of the industry, it was upheld by the U.S. Supreme Court in 1969. Growing public reliance on television for ideas on "what's going on in the world" seems to many observers to give the doctrine increasing importance, in spite of industry opposition.

Network and station practice has often concentrated on avoiding programming that might generate complaints under the Fairness Doctrine. With almost all time becoming salable and increasing in market value, "reply time" has seemed to some broadcasters a problem to be avoided at all cost. Some have made this a keystone of policy. Strip-mining was a crucial issue in 1976, so a West Virginia station avoided any mention of it—and was then chastised by an FCC review board. The FCC's point was that the Fairness Doctrine was not just a warning against unfairness; it also involved an affirmative obligation to cover "issues of public importance."

Broadcasting magazine, generally considered an unofficial voice of the industry, upbraided the FCC in an angry editorial. The FCC, said *Broadcasting,* was forcing broadcasters to "carry the kind of programming that generates fairness complaints." Elements in the industry were determined to continue efforts to eliminate the Fairness Doctrine.[3]

Meanwhile the implications for broadcasters were clear. License protection seems to require a body of programming, troublesome and sometimes costly, that many broadcasters would prefer to do without: news, documentaries, discussion programs, public service messages—all material that tends to evoke unsolved dilemmas and failures of our society. The problem, as many television executives see it, is to keep this body of programming small, and integrate it as smoothly as possible into the sponsor-world.

That it is small—even minuscule—can hardly be doubted. CBS anchorman Walter Cronkite, one of the most respected of network newsmen, complains of the "hypercompression we are forced to exert to fit 100 pounds of news into the one-pound sack that we are given to fill every night." The result, says Cronkite, falls far short of the information "that a citizen would need to intelligently exercise his franchise in this democracy." The resulting "distortion," he feels, could "lead to disaster."[4]

It is extraordinary—though many Americans have unquestionably come to take it for granted—that world news does not even have a foothold in network prime time. Network newscasts are offered as an *hors d'oeuvre* to the main fare of the evening. Each network carries a half-hour of world and national news but does not offer it in "network time." Instead it offers it in the earlier period long earmarked as "station time." Most affiliates feel obliged to carry it; they could not otherwise provide a plausible program of world news. But they resent their dependence on it, for they receive only a fraction of what the program earns—far less than what a local program would yield. And when network leaders advance the idea of lengthening these network newscasts to one hour, most affiliates protest furiously.

The early-evening network newscasts began as 15-minute programs, which were extended to half-hour length in 1963. Even this extension brought protest. Edward W. Barrett, former network executive who had become Dean of Journalism at Columbia University, attended a 1964 broadcasting convention and heard a broadcaster talking about his station. Asked with what network it was affiliated, the man answered: "NBC, damn it."

"Why do you say it that way?"

· "Well, they're ruining it with all this damned news and documentary stuff. . . . We lose audiences every time we have to put that stuff in place of entertainment. Take that nonsense of extending the Huntley-Brinkley program from fifteen minutes to a full half-hour. That alone costs us way over $100,000."[5]

If affiliates tend toward this attitude, network news departments have also gathered strength and influence—despite the limits within which they work. Riding the crest of network prosperity and power, and an indispensable element in legitimizing that power, network newsmen have become the elite of journalism. Some become superstars, often attracting more attention than the national leaders whose activities they are "covering." In special events, when they have a chance to stretch their talents, some show brilliance. Their fame—and lecture fees—eclipse those of Senators and Governors. At the same time many, like Cronkite, are painfully conscious of the simplistic nature of what they convey in nightly newscasts. Internally they press for news of greater depth and complexity—but they do so against large odds.

The inadequacies are not only a matter of time restrictions, although they begin there. On a half-hour newscast, the 23 minutes devoted to news provide information that can fit easily on one page of a newspaper. The items of major impact are those built around film, which can provide active, fascinating moments, but may yield little comprehension. Popular notions notwithstanding, the camera evades the roots of problems while focusing on surface results. Vietnam War coverage brought endless shots that conveyed the general hellishness of war, but gave no hint of what it was about. As Eric Sevareid lamented after a 1966 trip to Vietnam, "The facts didn't yield to the equipment."

As arbiter of news value, the camera inevitably produces distortions. Each network maintains camera crews in half a dozen American cities and in nine or ten foreign cities—which thus become "the" major news centers. Events they film are usually chosen hours before they happen, so that crews can be sent there and get ready. In other words, they are planned events—often "pseudo-events" created for the camera: dedications, award ceremonies, cornerstone layings, press conferences, parades, demonstrations: the dramaturgy of current history. Main exceptions are catastrophes that last long enough for camera crews to get there—fires, floods, wrecks. Choosing cities where permanent camera crews are to be placed involves a selectivity that may have bizarre aspects. For years Africa was "covered" from Rome. Until 1965 Indochina was "covered" from Jakarta or Tokyo, although the United Sates had been playing a military role in the area for well over a decade. The work of regular crews can be supplemented with footage from "stringers" who send material unsolicited, and are paid for what is used; but their role is minimal. Footage from regular crews pours in daily and has the inside track.[6]

The dependence on camera events, pseudo-events, gives enormous power to those in a position to create such events. No network dares ignore a White House rose garden "scenario" or a military "photo opportunity." Thus, in regard to current happenings, the arrangers tend to set the agenda for national discussion, directing our attention *to* some events, some problems—and, far more significantly, *away from* others. By this process, as we have seen, Americans can be kept oblivious even to a war, as in Laos and Cambodia. In such cases, the ability of the Defense Department and CIA to influence the deployment of television news units can prove especially dangerous. It is not surprising that many international crises have caught the nation by surprise. Americans were unprepared for Vietnam, the Bay of Pigs, Angola, the Chilean crisis, the Korean scandals. Concerning all these events there had been advance reports and warnings in print, but these tended to remain shadowy while the camera crews, with their sequences in living color, were spotlighting more readily available occurrences.

Almost all the shadowy crises involved American multinational corporations. Miniaturized news made for minimal public agitation over their involvements, and may well have been television's most notable contribution to the sponsor-world, even though not so intended.

Most local news, meanwhile, has merged almost wholly into sponsored "entertainment." During the 1970's many stations hired consultants specializing in the raising of newscast ratings, to provide a basis for increasing the advertising rates. The process, as described by David Halberstam, begins with selection of anchor people for "their smiles and their masculinity and femininity." One consultant group was reported to be using "galvanic skin response tests" to measure emotional reactions of selected viewers to on-the-air reporters. Concentration on filmed action sequences—fires, accidents, arrests—has become standard strategy, with items generally limited to 15 or 30 seconds. One local news executive, Robert Schaefer of KNXT, Los Angeles, was quoted as stating: "The average viewer has an attention span of eight seconds." He felt news strategy must be guided accordingly. News consultants have generally been successful in raising ratings and, in consequence, time charges. The *Wall Street Journal*, surveying local news, found a widespread feeling that it had become "pure entertainment" and that the process was "chipping away at the credibility of all TV journalists."[7]

The profitability of local newscasts is enhanced by terms of the NAB Television Code. The code places limits on the number of interruptions permitted in most programs; thus a 30-minute variety program may have two interruptions if in prime time, four interruptions at other times. But on news programs there are no limits. The official explanation: "News, weather, sports and special event programs are exempt from the interruption standard. This is in recognition of the nature of such programming and the fact that they contain natural breaks." A kaleidoscope of "action items" followed by "natural breaks" is the formula for much local news.[8]

The selection of news has become so standardized that rival newscasts often present similar items in identical sequence. Television executives see this as demonstrating the spread of professionalism. A different view was expressed by the writer Jack Richardson in *Harper's;* he saw the nightly news as a species of ritual, designed to provide "a stylized assurance that there is stability and sameness in the world on which the tribe can depend." It enables the viewer to make "a comfortable covenant with reality."

He used to fret, he explains, over what seemed the "carefully crafted emptiness on the screen." But then:

. . . sometime during the many reportorial litanies of the Vietnam War, in which a network shaman stood in the standard
sacramental rice paddy and intoned the dogma that war is an
unpleasant experience, I became enlightened. I realized that I was
not supposed to be receiving from such broadcasts either startling
facts or probing explanations; instead, I was being offered a display of sanctified movements and words which turned reality
into a tidy, predictable companion. War, the secular world's
highest moral dilemma, gradually was purged of all human intrigue and responsibility and became a comfortably vague condition of nature. I and my fellow citizens could look upon the
worst techniques of slaughter and, in lieu of any evidence that
human intelligence and choice were behind them, could feel that
our obligations to human suffering had been discharged simply
by our observing it regularly and by our feeling, until the commercial, a deep and righteous melancholy.[9]

The ritual nature of news programming emphasizes again the
manner in which the political process has been compressed into
meaninglessness. A major campaign speech may be represented
by a filmed item of a few seconds, balanced against a filmed segment of similar length by an opposing candidate. The segments,
necessarily out of context, are chosen for some colorful or
provocative aspect, which is then seen as "the campaign." Candidates in recent years have constantly been criticized for campaigning superficially. The superficiality may be in the ex-
cerpting rather than the campaigning. The candidate driven to
30-second "commercials" to supplement such "coverage" can
hardly repair the damage. Whether on network or locally, the
burgeoning of sponsored "entertainment" and the squeeze on
news have helped create a system in which enormously compli-
cated issues are, in the words of Halberstam, "brutalized" and
"trivialized." Cronkite is harsher. Addressing the Radio Television News Directors Association, he said:

You will recognize in what I am saying an indictment of what
you and I are doing every blessed day of our lives. I'm afraid
we compress so well as to almost defy the viewer and listener to
understand what we say. We now have a communication problem of immense dimensions partly of our own making.[10]

All this puts a huge burden on forms of programming that are presumed to add perspective and detail on "what's going on in the world"—discussion programs, documentaries, public service messages.

Discussion programs, largely following press-conference formats, have proved congenial to broadcast management. They are inexpensive. Built on an adversary formula, they offer minimal Fairness Doctrine hazards. In providing a coveted platform, they cement relations with government and industry leaders. Pronouncements made on the program may become the basis for newspaper stories—a factor regarded by many as the chief value of the programs. At the same time, scheduled in Sunday "cultural ghetto" hours, they offer minimal disruption to the prosperity of television. Scheduled as they are, they reach a small audience, and the smallness of the audience demonstrates the necessity of scheduling them where they are. The discussions can be enlightening to the news-initiated, but are generally meaningless to most viewers, and avoided by them. They do little to repair the over-all deficiency of television journalism.

The greatest opportunity to counteract the deficiency is in the television documentary. Documentaries have, on numerous occasions, illuminated aspects of the society seldom spotlighted on the tube. Network spokesmen cite this as a special function of the documentary. The Murrow-Friendly *See It Now* series offers a precedent that has achieved almost legendary status. Each of the network news departments includes dedicated documentarists determined to carry on the tradition. Yet the tradition has been tragically eroded. Network policy, riding the mounting profitability of television time, has contributed to the erosion.

The most serious—and dangerous—part of this policy has been its monopolistic aspect. As noted earlier, the documentary revival prodded into being by the 1959 quiz scandals was followed almost at once by a decision, on the part of each network, to schedule only its own documentaries. In response to protests from the Writers Guild of America, NBC explained that this was necessary to assure "objective, fair, and responsible presentation" of issues. CBS made a similar statement, citing the need for "standards." So did ABC, although its documentary achievements had been almost nonexistent. Some categories of documentaries, such as travelogues and nature films, won exemption from the network policy, but NBC explained that any program that might be "opinion-influencing" would have to be done by the network itself.* With some exceptions, the three networks have followed this policy. Opinion-influencing was to have network supervision.[11]

In the backwash of the quiz furor, the policy had some plausibility. The problem, at the moment, seemed to be to insulate programming from irresponsible fly-by-night production firms and sponsor pressure on them. This, along with the fact that network production was still equated with the luster of Edward R. Murrow, helps explain why the monopoly decision went unchallenged at first—except by independent documentarists. To them it seemed clear that the networks, having accepted the necessity of maintaining documentary units, wanted to corner the limited sponsorship funds that might be available for documentaries.

The policy has had wide repercussions in the documentary field. Network exposure for a documentary has become an almost essential step toward rentals and sales to universities, colleges, schools, libraries, film societies. The monopoly over nationally televised documentaries has thus tended to confer dominance also over other channels of distribution.

The policy has meanwhile had serious impact on the network documentary itself. For almost two decades the popular connotations of "documentary" have been shaped by the routine network version of the genre. This has been heavily dominated by narration—often, on-camera narration by a network newsman—which charts a course purporting to be "objective." It often introduces statements of opinion, balanced by opposing statements of opinion. Reuven Frank, former president of NBC News, has used the expression "fairness filler" to describe material introduced for this purpose. The pretension is that the narrator,

---

* The assumption that travelogues and nature films are not "opinion-influencing" is, of course, questionable.

walking a tightrope between opposing biases, represents reasoned judgment, objective truth. But the truth is not always equidistant between opposing biases. The "on the one hand . . . on the other hand" structure of numerous network documentaries has hastened the decline of the genre. Pedestrian, often pretentious in its stance, it has kept audiences at bay and provided a rationale for reducing further the time allotted to documentaries.[12]

Network spokesmen say the Fairness Doctrine necessitates the balancing act. Unfortunately, the FCC has on at least one occasion given credibility to this notion. When the 1972 NBC documentary *Pensions: The Broken Promise*—about fraudulent pension plans—brought a complaint under the Fairness Doctrine, the FCC ordered NBC to do another program about *good* pension plans. The order was voided by litigation, but illustrates the network view.[13]

Yet the heart of the problem lies in the skimpiness of public affairs programming. When a complex issue is so seldom examined on the tube, a single treatment acquires exaggerated importance—particularly when it makes the impossible claim of objectivity. Fairness Doctrine problems yield readily to ample programming originating from diverse viewpoints; they cannot possibly be solved by "fairness filler," dispensed by a documentary oligopoly.

That pretended objectivity is the death of documentary is clear to most network documentarists. When network documentaries have had memorable impact, it has been on isolated occasions when they took a stand on a crucial issue, and presented compelling evidence. So it was in the case of the Murrow-Friendly *See It Now* programs of 1953-54 on McCarthyism (for which Senator McCarthy received reply time); it was so also in the case of the 1960 *CBS Reports* program on migratory labor, *Harvest of Shame*, a David Lowe production narrated by Murrow.

It was so also for the 1969 NBC documentary on chemical-biological warfare, *CBW: The Secrets of Secrecy*. Proceeding without help from the U.S. Defense Department, which refused to cooperate, NBC explored the mysterious death of thousands of sheep in Utah in 1968 and its relation to activities at the nearby Dugway Proving Ground. The documentary horrified viewers including Congressman Richard D. McCarthy of Buffalo, New York, who instigated congressional hearings that brought to light activities clearly at odds with proclaimed national policy. Amid the resulting indignation, the White House announced that President Nixon was ending biological-warfare experiments and had ordered the destruction of all existing stocks of biological weapons. The sequence of events was a notable tribute to a carefully researched, deeply moving documentary, which won a well-deserved Alfred I. du Pont-Columbia University Award.*

In 1971 CBS scored a similar triumph with *The Selling of the Pentagon,* written and directed by Peter Davis, and spotlighting the vast—partly illegal—expenditure of public funds to promote militarism. The program brought furious protest from the defense establishment, and criticism of editing methods, but no contradiction of its central revelations. CBS confidently repeated the telecast, gave air time to the criticisms, answered them, and won a Peabody and other awards. The Pentagon, even while protesting, withdrew some of the more jingoistic—and shoddy—propaganda films it had been circulating.[14]

If these programs had stunning impact, it was partly because they were so thoroughly at odds with the booster atmosphere pervading most programming. To some, this was their special glory. If documentaries did not serve as corrective—or at least as supplement—to salesmanship-saturated hours of "entertainment" and "commercials," what function did they serve?

But viewers happily addicted to prime-time values were likely to react differently. Disruptions like *CBW: The Secrets of Secrecy* and *The Selling of the Pentagon* seemed unsettling and

---

* Its achievement was not dimmed by the fact that the publicized presidential order was quietly circumvented, as the Senate committee on intelligence operations learned years later. Army officials secretly transferred to the CIA enough shellfish toxin to equip assassination teams with tens of thousands of lethal darts. It represented a third of the total world production of the toxin. *Foreign and Military Intelligence* (Washington, D.C.: GPO, 1976), pp. 362-63.

even "subversive" to some. Network executives who saw merchandising as the sanctified mission of television—as well as its blessed source of wealth—tended to share the feeling. Few major sponsors wanted to associate themselves with attacks on the military-industrial-political complex—of which many were a part. They almost never protested such programs—they merely ignored them as sponsorship possibilities. The protests—the pressure—came from network executives, including sales executives, who were determined to put network documentaries, if such things were really necessary, on a profit-making basis.

The search for topics that might win sponsor dollars has helped to hasten the network documentary further toward oblivion. Over the years it has yielded such projects as *A Bird's Eye View of Scotland, Barry Goldwater's Arizona, An Essay on Women, An Essay on Hotels, Gauguin's Tahiti,* and *Mr. Rooney Goes to Dinner*—a CBS program on "how Americans eat when they dine out, where they go and why."

"Most network documentary producers," the long-time ABC documentarist Richard Hubert told *Variety* in 1969, "are working on shows that don't get anyone mad." At that time ABC procedure called for staff members to write synopses of proposed documentaries; portfolios of these synopses were then given to salesmen to discuss with potential sponsors. No work was done on a documentary until a tentative commitment had been made. The companies willing to consider documentary proposals included the aerospace company North American Rockwell. The procedure resulted in Rockwell sponsoring *The View From Space,* a program using NASA footage and plugging for continuation of the space program. Commercial and program were hard to distinguish. The same was true of *Blondes Have More Fun,* an ABC documentary sponsored by Clairol.

CBS News has generally shown far greater integrity in its documentary projects, but during the 1960's was guilty of similar lapses of journalistic ethics. It presented a moonshot documentary sponsored by Hughes Aircraft, maker of much of the equipment involved. It also presented *The Lot of the Policeman,* with extensive footage of police department use of computerized communication; this was sponsored by IBM.[15]

If sponsored "documentaries" of this sort involve an element of news corruption, the failure to find sponsorship may also corrupt—perhaps in a more dangerous way because the process can remain unseen. The early 1970's saw rising concern over the environment, impelled by many factors: mounting water and air pollution; ecological disasters inflicted on Vietnam; unsolved problems of atomic waste disposal; and finally the 1969 moon landing with its stress on our "life support system," the talk of "spaceship earth," and the awed contemplation of our world by the astronauts from the void of space. At this juncture NBC announced a weekly ecology series, *In' Which We Live*, launched in May 1970—scheduled Sunday afternoons, narrated by Edwin Newman. It would depict various environmental hazards.

In late June the series was abruptly ended without announcement. Its writer and director, Robert J. Northshield—an ornithologist by avocation—was queried by a reporter about the sudden termination, and said bitterly: "I guess they noticed that all the ecological problems have been solved so there's no need for the show." A network salesman, asked the same question, said that the sale of a few more spots could have saved the program. Reuven Frank, NBC News president, denied that the lag in sponsor support had anything to do with the cancellation. "We were told to cut our budget. . . . Every once in a while there are budget emergencies." The only way to do it, said Frank, was to cancel the series.[16] The reason for the sudden budget cut, at a time of enormous RCA-NBC prosperity, was not explained.*

The custom at NBC has been to assign to the news division, usually once a year, an allotment of specific periods for documentaries or news specials. The allotment has sometimes been cut back later. CBS has evolved a more flexible system. When CBS News completes a documentary, it is turned over to the

---

* *Broadcasting*, Mar. 16, 1970, reported that ecology was the "hottest topic" for programs *and* commercials and that Atlantic Richfield, Chevron, Coca Cola, General Motors, International Paper, Phillips Petroleum, Standard Oil of New Jersey, and Western Electric were among sponsors producing ecology commercials. Since their message was one of reassurance, they apparently did not regard an NBC documentary series focusing on problems as a suitable setting.

CBS Television Network for scheduling. Once it is scheduled and announced, network salesmen offer its commercial slots to advertisers via a brief descriptive paragraph. Prospective sponsors are not invited to preview the program, and CBS News will make no further changes.

The procedure is meant to insulate programming from sponsor influence but cannot accomplish this. The network presents a preview of any controversial program via cable to its affiliates several days before telecast, so that affiliates can decide whether to carry it. Affiliates are free to invite anyone—sponsors and others—to sit in on these closed-circuit previews. Networks also hold press previews. The previewing may lead to last-minute sponsor withdrawals.

The CBS documentary *The Guns of Autumn*, written and directed by Irv Drasnin, was scheduled for September 5, 1976, on the eve of the hunting season. By late August the six minutes allotted to commercials were sold. But the announcement of the program had made the National Rifle Association apprehensive; it alerted its one million members, warning them that their "right to bear arms" might be jeopardized if the program turned out to be "anti-hunting." When CBS arranged its coast-to-coast closed-circuit preview for affiliates, gun-club members arranged to sit in and soon unloosed a flood of letters and phone calls on scheduled sponsors as well as on CBS. More than 20,000 letters were sent. All sponsors except the Block Drug Company, which was represented by two 30-second spots, withdrew their commercials. The gaps were plugged with the filler used for such emergencies—"public service announcements," mainly from the Advertising Council.*

The sponsor withdrawals did not affect the program, but clearly created intra-industry pressures. Sponsored glorifications of hunting—annual events on many stations—would appear again. Films like *The Guns of Autumn*, in which various groups of hunters were followed—with their consent—with camera and

---

* Mr. Leonard Block of the Block Drug Company explained why he stood firm. He had never felt happy about having knuckled under to Laurence Johnson in 1950. "It doesn't pay to give in to those fellows." Telephone interview, Sept. 1976.

tape recorder, would not be likely to appear again. The National Rifle Association, guardian of the $2 billion-a-year industry based on hunting, had demonstrated its clout—and advertisers, their readiness to respect it.[17]

Working amid such pressures, it is perhaps remarkable that network documentary units achieve what they do. The most formidable impediment is not censorship, but self-censorship. Its monuments are proposals not budgeted, ideas never proposed.

The units include some of the highest paid and most talented documentarists of today. Handsome budgets await plausible projects. Because these artists occasionally achieve what they want, they tend to rationalize their monopoly hold over a unique channel into the minds of millions. Intramurally, they press their own fitful struggles against restrictions.

In recent years the only weekly documentary series with a foothold in prime time has been the CBS *60 Minutes*, presenting on each program a miscellany of reports. It is, in its way, a remarkable success story. Though often buffeted around the schedule, it has built a following and shown, to the surprise of some network executives, a persistent and rising demand for "reality programming." In 1975 its 30-second slots were still offered at "bargain prices"—running from $18,000 to $27,000. Two years later the network was asking at least $30,000, and as much as $50,000 during mid-winter months. The program was beginning to outpoint *The Wonderful World of Disney*.

The series does not pretend to do "objective" surveys; instead, its newsmen report on their personal investigations. The series has been credited with carrying on the Edward R. Murrow tradition, but it does not really resemble *See It Now*. It seldom tackles complex issues; it seems to abhor complexity. It looks for situations that can be understood almost instantly. "The trick in TV," says its producer Don Hewitt, "is to grab the viewer by the throat." He prefers to "shine light in dark corners, and if people are doing things in dark corners they shouldn't be doing, well all we did is shine a light." This focus on individual malefactors characterizes many of the items. "We'll show you documented abuses practiced by unethical debt collectors," says Dan Rather at the start of a program, grabbing viewers. But the focus often suggests that we really do live in a good guy/bad guy world, as the action-adventure series would have it. And the series structure, dominated by superstar reporters, likewise seems to echo the world of fiction. Mike Wallace has specialized in a relentless style of interview that recalls Jack Webb of *Dragnet* grilling a suspect. The series occasionally uses entrapment—the hidden camera—in *Candid Camera* fashion.

60 Minutes has provided a small opening for outsiders—a loophole in the monopoly policy. But it buys *footage*—usually at $1000 a minute—rather than films. For the outsider this may involve destruction of his film. Thus CBS rejected a Frank Mankiewicz film based on his visit to Fidel Castro, but used six minutes of it on *60 Minutes*, reprocessing the material to feature Dan Rather. In a sense, use of the material wipes out a principal CBS rationale for its policy, for the footage was in no sense made "under the supervision and control" of CBS.

The *60 Minutes* success formula involves both assets and liabilities. Lively and topical, produced with *élan*, sometimes vigorously investigative, it settles for relatively superficial triumphs. It has been aptly called "pop doc."[18]

But the most serious aspect of network documentary remains its exclusion of the completed works of numerous other documentarists, American and foreign. Network spokesmen readily—and correctly—assail governmental restrictions on freedom of communication; but nothing has been more restrictive, more blatantly monopolistic, than the network decree barring from access to network lines any opinion-influencing documentary that is not its own.

During the early Vietnam War years this policy constituted *de facto* national censorship, though privately operated. It eliminated from consideration Vietnam documentaries made by Canadian, British, Japanese, and other units that would have given American viewers a very different picture than they received from network productions.[19]

When the U.S. Department of Justice filed its 1972 antitrust suit against the networks for monopolizing "prime-time entertainment," it explained that documentaries were not included in the charge. When asked why such material—potentially significant—was exempted, the Justice Department explained that news was a sensitive area on which government hesitated to intrude. But the First Amendment, in enjoining the Federal government from "abridging" press freedom, was not intended to clear the way for private abridgments. The government has moved resolutely against such abridgments in Associated Press vs. U.S., U.S. vs. Paramount et al., and other cases.[20]

Documentary, though potentially powerful, remains a small and largely neutralized fragment of network television, one that can scarcely rival the formative influence of "entertainment" and "commercials." On the local level, some commercial stations maintain documentary units, and a few have done notable work. But their output is far outnumbered by "free" business-sponsored documentaries—a field still led by Modern Talking Picture Service, rivaled only by Association-Sterling. According to Modern, 95 per cent of American stations continue to use its films—documentaries and other types, subtly commercial or propagandistic. They involve many major sponsors, and some 75,000 television bookings annually. They include films sponsored by foreign countries: South Africa has in recent years spent more than $100,000 annually subsidizing distribution of its free films through Association-Sterling—to stations, schools, churches, groups.

A Modern Talking Picture Service brochure tells its sponsors: "Documentaries concerned with matters of national interest do extremely well since stations can often use them as public service programming in fulfilling FCC requirements." Modern also distributes business-sponsored "public service announcements" as well as "newsclips" for insertion in local newscasts. The sponsor is identified on the cassette, not necessarily on the air.[21]

This business-subsidized distribution has been so successful that federal agencies and non-profit groups have adopted the system. The Federal Energy Administration, to get its film on the energy crisis on the tube, has followed the example of various oil companies and subsidizes its distribution via Modern. The U.S. Office of Education does likewise with films on environmental education and other topics. The Save the Children Federation and the Salvation Army are other Modern "clients."

Free Film

Modern TV, television division of Modern Talking Picture Service, has advertised its "free" (i.e. sponsored) programming items regularly in *Broadcasting*.

All this reflects the pressure placed on the non-profit world by the burgeoning of commercial sponsorship. On the networks, access by non-profit groups and government agencies has tended to become restricted to "public service announcements"—"PSA's"—now generally associated with the Advertising Council.

Since its formation during World War II, the Advertising Council has generally been treated as a sacred institution. Every President has issued eulogies of it—generally drafted by the Council. The Council itself proclaims its services in dazzling statistics and with unrestrained satisfaction. After its first television spot campaigns in 1950, it said it had achieved "267,506,000 home impressions" on behalf of various causes. That claim would look puny by 1974, when it said it made "46,126,120,000 home impressions" for the year. A council spokesman concedes this is a "ballpark figure." The Council also reported that its projects had already used $7 billion dollars' worth of media time and space in the service of the nation.

An early leader in Council affairs was Charles E. Wilson, former president of General Electric, who said: "Through the Advertising Council, American business supports more causes, solves more problems and serves more people than is possible through any other single organization." C. W. Cook, chairman of General Foods, said: "The Advertising Council is America's showcase to the world."[22]

Most Council campaigns involve messages to which few people could object. They urge people to vote, drive carefully, give blood, avoid drug abuse, support the Red Cross, prevent forest fires. The Council's television spots, produced under advertising agency supervision, are handsomely mounted. Most are built around slogans, sometimes tending toward cuteness. People are asked to support education—with "dollars for scholars"; to save gasoline—"don't be fuelish"; to buy U.S. government bonds— "take stock in America." A campaign for the elderly used the slogan "gray liberation."

The campaigns have a pervasive innocuousness that is apparently intentional. Programmers look on the television spots as useful fillers that can be relied on to be well-produced and cause no arguments, while winning "brownie points" with the FCC. They plug up unsold gaps such as those on *The Guns of Autumn;* most are seen in less desirable periods.*

How much is accomplished by the sloganeering is difficult to assess. Claims are made in puzzling terms. An early Advertising Council brochure said its safety campaigns had "helped bring about" a 40 per cent reduction in fatal traffic accidents. There was no indication of the period of time involved; the brochure was undated. If it referred to the World War II period, gasoline rationing and the unavailability of new cars may have "helped." In 1967 the Advertising Council claimed to have "helped save more than 600,000 lives on the nation's highways in 20 years." The Council could apparently tell how many people would have died but for its safety messages.

While the Advertising Council has generally been treated with deference, objections have occasionally erupted. In a 1955 union bulletin, a United Auto Workers spokesman commented:

> Now the Advertising Council has announced that it's going to put on a national advertising campaign to support anti-delinquency programs. This is wonderful, and good-hearted people are inclined to applaud this fine public-spirited action, but then you look at the directors of the Advertising Council, you find that they are the big shots . . . who stand foursquare against

---

* Sometimes producing curious juxtapositions. In a WCBS-TV documentary on the life of models, the young women—all earning $60 and up per hour—stressed that no schooling was necessary. The unsold commercial slots were allocated to Advertising Council spots, including: "Give to the college of your choice." Another urged viewers to help the Boy Scouts "build America's heritage." WCBS-TV, New York, July 28, 1964.

federal aid to education, against a federal housing program, and against city improvements that would tend to cut the breeding ground out from under juvenile delinquency.[23]

Anti-pollution spots have recently been attacked on similar grounds. At a time of public alarm over water, air, and other forms of pollution, to a large extent of industrial origin, the Advertising Council launched an "anti-pollution campaign" that urged viewers to clean up after picnics and stop littering highways. The slogan was: "People start pollution. People can stop it." The Council seemed intent on redefining "pollution" as a purely personal transgression. "Next time you see someone polluting, point it out." One spot showed an Indian with a tear in his eye, observing litter by a highway. "It's a crying shame," was the caption. Nonreturnable bottles and cans went unmentioned.[24]

The "anti-drug-abuse" spots brought similar comment. Former FCC commissioner Nicholas Johnson commented that while the industry takes bows for combating drugs, it also takes the leading role in promoting pill-popping to soothe you, pick you up, or help you sleep. It had become, he thought, the nation's "chief pusher" of the drug habit.

Such criticisms depict the Advertising Council spots as a smokescreen of words and images, diverting attention while real fires burn. One of the Advertising Council's own slogans provides a succinct expression of this view: "Youth needs your help this summer. Not a lot of yak."

The Advertising Council consists of representatives of advertisers, advertising agencies, and media. They provide the operating budget for the Council office and staff, but not for its campaigns. A committee of Council members decides the campaigns, on the basis of proposals from groups and government agencies. It also lists causes which it "approves" and recommends to the media, but for which no campaign materials are produced. A broadly based Public Policy Committee, which meets twice a year, is invited to make suggestions and review accomplishments, but is largely ornamental. It makes no decisions.

Though Advertising Council campaigns give a public impres-

PUBLIC SERVICE MESSAGE, 1966-67. Radio Free Europe, organized, financed, and controlled by the Central Intelligence Agency but publicly denying any connection ("Radio Free Europe is a private American enterprise; it depends on voluntary subscriptions") appeals for "truth dollars" through Advertising Council television spots, radio announcements, car cards, etc. Fund appeal brought minimal return but this was apparently not the real purpose. Actual purpose: to fortify the "private enterprise" deception and quash rumors about a CIA connection.

sion of being eleemosynary, they are not. An organization asking for a campaign on behalf of its cause is expected to provide a campaign budget of $100,000 to $300,000 for materials and expenses. Thus it makes a sizable investment. Many do so because it now seems the only entree to public attention.

Each campaign is assigned to an advertising agency, which writes and supervises production of material including television spots—usually filmed in a New York or Hollywood studio, and made in various lengths. The agency contributes staff services but is reimbursed for expenses, sometimes including trips to Hollywood, plus overhead. Most agency staff members are eager for assignment to Advertising Council projects, which seem to give them a coveted sense of service.

Many applicant groups are eliminated from Advertising Council consideration by the financial requirements. Some are rejected on the ground that they are "controversial." The Council will not divulge which applicants were rejected on this ground. However, the Washington-based Center for Growth Alternatives, suggesting a campaign on the theme, "We can't grow on like this," said it received no encouragement. The National Organization of Women, wanting a campaign to amend the stereotyped image of the women's movement, was at first rejected but later accepted.

A 1976-77 campaign on economics, presumably non-controversial, did raise heated public controversy. Its theme was "The American Economic System . . . And Your Part In It." It urged the public to send for a booklet on the subject, described as "a rich source of useful information," designed to correct public misconceptions. The project had received funds from the U.S. Department of Commerce—which, according to an indignant statement by Representative Benjamin Rosenthal of New York, chairman of the consumer subcommittee of the House committee on government operations, "took $239,000 earmarked for the creation of jobs and minority business opportunities and turned that money over to the Advertising Council to produce an economic-understanding booklet that reflected the views of the Nixon-Ford administration." A number of economists condemned the booklet for "bland misrepresentation," "smooth Madison Avenue language," "soothing words."

Meanwhile a Public Media Center, based in San Francisco and backed by a coalition of groups calling itself Americans for a Working Economy—including many prominent organizations*— prepared its own spots, also offering a booklet. "It raises some questions," said the narrator of the spots, "about our economic system—unemployment, inflation, things like that . . . it should get people talking, which is just what we want it to do." The

---

* American Federation of State, County, and Municipal Employees, Consumer Federation of America, Environmental Action, Exploratory Project for Economic Alternatives, Friends of the Earth, International Association of Machinists, National Education Association, National Organization of Women, Scientists' Institute for Public Information, United Auto Workers Union, and U.S. Conference of Mayors.

promotional emphasis was: "The worst thing we can do about our economic problems is cover them up."

Various parallel challenges now converged on the broadcasting industry. A People's Bicentennial Commission demanded time for its spots on numerous issues including "monopolistic practices . . . industrial pollution . . . multinational corporations. . . ." A Citizens Communication Center and a Committee for Open Media wanted a policy of access for Free Speech Messages on diverse topics—a plan already in effect at stations in San Francisco and several other cities. They argued that PSA's were "an appropriate forum for the ventilation of issues" and an "appropriate means for satisfying some of the licensee's obligations under the Fairness Doctrine." All these movements challenged the business dominance of PSA's.[25]

ABC-TV and CBS-TV, alarmed at the rising tide, declined to run the Advertising Council's economic-understanding spots until the booklet-promotion was eliminated. As revised, the spots merely urged viewers to go to the library and read about economics. Now satisfactorily innocuous, the spots received ABC-TV and CBS-TV exposure. But the protesting groups had made clear that the *access* issue would continue to harry the industry. A number of groups received time for their spots—yet nothing comparable to the Advertising Council distribution.

Groups included in the Advertising Council lists of "approved" causes have found the listing valuable when asking local stations for time. Groups not so listed have found it a handicap; it provides stations with a convenient basis for saying "no." Thus the Advertising Council lists have tended to create a roster of "approved" causes. How this has affected action on the local level was graphically revealed in a 1963 interview by John E. Hill, public service director at KTRK-TV, Houston. Describing his job as "guarding the ears of our community against brash and sometimes dishonest requests for free time," he explained:

We have developed here a questionnaire which we send out to all agencies that are not approved by the Advertising Council, and if they are successful in filling out this questionnaire to our satisfaction, we give them free time. To date, nobody's been able to, I might add.[26]

At networks, 80 per cent of the PSA's have tended to be Advertising Council spots. At some stations the percentage has been higher; at others, lower.

The decades since mid-century—television network decades—have witnessed the rise of increasingly intractable problems at home and complex and perilous involvements abroad. Network attention to these matters—via "public service" programming of various kinds—has meanwhile been squeezed into an inadequacy that haunts its own leaders. Yet the public, beguiled by what it sees through the picture window, depends on it.

The commercial-network absorption in other matters would seem to pose a historic challenge and opportunity for public television, the "alternative" system. Many in the system have, in fact, seen this as one of their chief missions and labored to fulfill it. The final days of NET represented a surge in that direction—cut short by the traumatic reorganization of the system. But the effort was bound to resume. In 1976 the *MacNeil-Lehrer Report* began to give an indication of the potentialities of television journalism. Though generally limited to interview techniques, it unpeeled the multiple layers of issues in highly revealing ways far removed from the simplistic capsules of network newscasts. Fascinating but pioneering work, it would take time to develop its skills and its audience. Also in 1976 the Public Broadcasting Service made Friday evenings a public affairs night encompassing its admired—if cautious and sober—*Washington Week in Review* and *Wall Street Week* as well as a *Documentary Showcase* offering work from many sources, American and foreign. Here and elsewhere in the schedule, public television stations began to show documentaries long ignored by commercial television—in some cases, shunned by public television itself in its traumatized days: *I. F. Stone's Weekly*, film portrait of an American dissenter by a young Canadian documentarist, Jerry Bruck, Jr.; *Sad Song of Yellow Skin*, by Michael Rubbo, a young Australian working for the National Film Board of Canada, depicting the impact of the Vietnam War on Saigon life in a way untouched by network documentaries; *Waiting for Fidel*, the same documentarist's interim report on Cuba; *Antonia*, film portrait by Judy Collins and Jill Godmilow of the Dutch conductor Antonia Brico and her struggles in a world dominated by male maestros; *Compañero*, the life and murder of Chilean folk singer Victor Jara, narrated by his English widow; *Carnivore*, informative and urbane film essay by John Beyer, Iowa documentarist, on the human species and the meat industry it supports; *End of the Game*, unforgettable portrait by Robin Lehman of African wildlife, and threats facing it; *Birth Without Violence*, French close-up of a new approach to childbirth, by Frederick Leboyer and Pierre-Marie Goulet; and *Plain Speaking*, words of Harry Truman brilliantly reenacted by Ed Flanders, produced by David Susskind. Some public television stations were also showing episodes from *The World in Action*, the remarkable documentary series of Granada television.[27]

For independents long faced with entrenched barriers and discouragements, the new policies stirred hope. But economic and other obstacles remained. On public television the documentary was not immune to the squeeze it experienced elsewhere. During the reorganization push, the Nixon White House had pressed the system to stay away from "public affairs." Public television, it was indicated, should focus elsewhere. As the system looked increasingly to underwriters for survival, they too deflected effort "elsewhere." Most would not assist "public affairs" programs—a reluctance to some extent abetted by PBS, which was always anxious to avoid conjunctions of sponsor and subject matter that might *look* like sponsor influence, whether or not there was any.

But the corporations *would* support "culture." By the mid-1970's 74 per cent of programming supported by corporate underwriters was classified as "culture." For public television "cultural programming" became the dominant feature of prime time—and for sponsors, a significant sphere of influence.

"That's Mr. Panasovich, dear. Mr. Panasovich was made possible by a grant from Mobil Oil." *Drawing by Stan Hunt; © 1975 The New Yorker Magazine, Inc.*

> The aging society develops elaborate defenses
> against new ideas.
>
> JOHN W. GARDNER

SPHERE OF INFLUENCE—"culture"

"Culture," like "entertainment," is a term used for a strategic purpose rather than to convey a precise meaning. In the case of public television, "culture" has come to mean the safe area the system is urged to focus on to keep it free of the pitfalls of "public affairs."

Public television has won a growing following in recent years through a number of high-quality—sometimes brilliant—prime-time series: *The Forsyte Saga, War and Peace, Tom Brown's Schooldays, Vanity Fair, Cousin Bette, Jude the Obscure, Cakes and Ale, Upstairs, Downstairs, Shoulder to Shoulder, The Six Wives of Henry VIII, Civilization, The Tribal Eye, The Ascent of Man, The Adams Chronicles, The Pallisers, Poldark,* and others, as well as specials of similar excellence, including many concerts. Major underwriting by global corporations was involved in all these projects. Their value to public television has been inestimable. They have given it a sense of a beginning renaissance. Audiences have had reason to be grateful.

All have had one aspect in common. They focused on matters removed, in time or place or both, from pressing concerns of the American scene. Many television executives have come to view "culture" in precisely these antiquarian terms. In a sense, it is a throwback to a time when "culture" meant Europe, and artists went to Europe for training and apprenticeship. Most artists thought that this attitude had vanished, but public television has tended to revive it.

None of the dictionary definitions of "culture" justify this exclusion of the here and now, and of "public affairs." One dictionary definition calls culture "the sum total of ways of living built up by a group of human beings, which is transmitted from one generation to another." Another defines culture as "a particular state or stage of civilization, as in the case of a certain nation or period: *Greek culture*." As understood in public television, American civilization, here and now, is excluded from consideration.[1]

There is irony in this. Commercial television drama deals almost wholly with the here and now, as processed via advertising budgets. These have virtually taken charge of the shaping of modern American culture, and its transmission to the future. For public television, by some unspoken consensus of which its executives may not even be conscious, the here and now is out of bounds as a focus for "cultural programming."

Illumination of the past *is* essential: the past, as "prologue to present," needs better and wider understanding. And it is conceivable that the current surge of antiquarian interest will trigger a reawakening in the arts—in the way that the rediscovery of Greek and Roman classics via the printing press helped trigger the Renaissance centuries ago. But at the moment the current scene is grotesquely missing from the continuing survey of "culture." Culture has come to mean "other cultures."

Economic factors have probably contributed to this. Acquisition of already completed foreign series is less costly than the funding of new ventures. But the quest for the noncontroversial—the safely splendid—contributes to the push. It has tended to create on public television a fascinating past safely removed from the modern American culture of commercial television.

A new dictionary describes culture as "the ideas, customs, skills, arts, etc., of a given people in a given period; civilization."[2] The arts are men's efforts to understand and cope with their environment. Many of the works presented as cultural classics on public television today were not written in an antiquarian spirit; they were the deeply felt responses of their writers to the world in which they lived. It was so with *Vanity Fair*, *The Pallisers*, *War and Peace*, *Cousin Bette*, *Jude the Obscure*, *The Forsyte Saga*, *Cakes and Ale*. Television awaits precisely such visions and interpretations of our world. At the moment they are shunted elsewhere—mainly to the printed page. "The book," said Daniel J. Boorstin at his inauguration as Librarian of Congress, "remains our symbol and our resource for the unimagined question and the unwelcome answer." It is a comment with tragic implications for television, the medium of the time.[3]

It has been suggested in these pages that sponsors—mainly global corporations that form the large majority of leading network sponsors—dominate our programming far more extensively than most viewers suppose.

Their influence over it is spearheaded by "commercials"—the "focal point of creative effort"; protected by "entertainment" designed to fit sponsor needs; bordered by a fringe of successfully neutralized "public service" elements; and by a buffer zone of approved "culture."

Few viewers know what may be missing from the picture window, for their idea of the world is increasingly formed by that window.

As the ability to read declines—as it seems to be doing with alarming rapidity—dependence on the picture window will continue to increase.

The apparatus of commercial television comprises a huge selling machine, based in the United States but reaching into more than a hundred other countries. It sells products but also a way of life, a view of man himself, a vision of the future.

What kind of future is it selling us? Where is it leading us? What outlook does it offer? To what choices is it already committing us? What are its implications for future generations?

THREE

PROSPECT

"How about changing seats? I've viewed everything from the same angle for twenty-three years." *Drawing by Joe Mirachi;* © *1977 The New Yorker Magazine, Inc.*

> The government of an exclusive company of merchants is, perhaps, the worst of all governments for any country whatever.

> ADAM SMITH (1776)

PROBLEM: SUCCESS

Television, a bright world in the middle of the home, has had comparable impact wherever it has won a place. Viewing habits have grown similarly in dissimilar societies. A six-hour stint is normal in Rio de Janeiro, Leningrad, Osaka, Chicago. The Hungarian writer Iván Boldizsár likens the television set to a strange new animal that has come to live with us. "We cannot domesticate it—it domesticates us."

He also describes television as creating "a second reality" that blurs "the first reality."[1]

There can be no doubt that business dominance of the "second reality" in the United States—through the "American system"—has spread it here more rapidly and spectacularly than could have happened under other arrangements. Also, without question, the system has achieved amazing successes for its custodians and sponsors. The long-time president of the National Association of Broadcasters, Vincent T. Wasilewski, has called

American television "the most successful and universally accepted business enterprise in history." Economist John Kenneth
Galbraith, writing from a different vantage, finds that modern
industry "could not exist in its present form without it." And
according to *Advertising Age*, the television years have brought
"the most dizzying leap forward in American history . . . revo-
lutionizing everything from sales pitches to politics."[2]

Statistics help to fill out the story. Americans appear to be
spending some $20 billion a year on sleeping pills, stomach set-
tlers, headache tablets, deodorants, mouthwashes, shampoos, cos-
metics, and other "personal care" items; some $30 billion a year
on canned and bottled drinks, alcoholic and non-alcoholic; and
more than $200 billion a year on the purchase, care, and feeding
of their automobiles—at least 500 per cent more than in 1950. In
fact, Americans—scarcely 5 per cent of the world's population—
are consuming the globe's resources at a rate approximating that
of the rest of the world combined.[3]

All this raises the question of how much more of such success
we—the nation, the world—can afford.

THE MEDIUM AND THE BIOSPHERE

The squandering of resources only begins the problem. The
consumption binge which television has done so much to push
has been fouling air, water, roads, streets, fields, and forests—a
trend we failed or declined to recognize until almost irreversi-
ble. It has given us garbage statistics as staggering as our consumption statistics, and closely related to them. Each year Americans junk at least 7 million cars, discard some 30 billion bottles
and 50 billion cans, and throw away more than 30 million tons
of paper. Behind such statistics lies environmental ravage. Destruction of forests throughout much of the globe outpaces re-
forestation. Tropical rain forests are reported disappearing at
the rate of 50 acres a minute, day and night.[4]

But to keep the binge going our energy companies—leading
sponsors and media owners among them—have plunged us
deeply into atomic energy, bequeathing to posterity new kinds

of waste that will threaten life for hundreds of thousands of years—a problem for which no solution is in sight and which television has, until recently, tended to ignore or smother with "fairness filler." Man is among the endangered species.

American television is not only American, but multinational. Sending its programs, mythology, and salesmanship into more than a hundred countries, it offers its salvation-through-consumption message—welcomed by many groups and creating enclaves of high consumption even within wastelands of poverty. In poor societies the drive to divert scarce resources and funds into the unnecessary-made-necessary naturally meets resistance and even indignation—and yet presses on. If it should achieve success comparable to that on the home front, it could quickly push the planet to catastrophe.

Though we seem to be careening in the direction of disaster, a commercial television system is unlikely to do other than try to keep us moving. All its built-in incentives are to find solutions in *more,* not *less.* Growth rate, productivity, are its trusted passwords. It believes in them, associating them with such values as freedom and democracy.

If the dangers were always inherent in a system built on salesmanship, there are reasons why the system grows more dangerous. We noted that in earlier decades much network time—including prime time—remained unsold and that some was used for non-profit groups and purposes. With alternative views now reduced to battling for an occasional "public service announcement" or "free speech message"—a platform not unlike a corner of Hyde Park—the business domination increases, permeating the system. And the present time-sale system, essentially a continuing auction, gives domination increasingly to global corporations, whose ability to pay sets the scale.

Our broadcasting companies have generally been thought of as "media"—neutral entities dedicated to "communication" and able to mediate not only between their audiences and the world but also between conflicting interests, commercial and noncommercial. The terminology persists but without corresponding reality. Aided by policies and regulations that have turned station-selling, like time-selling, into an auction, our networks and major station owners have become, or have been absorbed by, huge conglomerates, in many cases with global interests. Our main media are themselves big-league sponsors. Along with the networks, the leading owners of groups of stations—Capital Cities, Cox Broadcasting, General Electric, General Tire & Rubber, Kaiser Industries, Metromedia, Taft Broadcasting, Westinghouse, Wometco—are all deeply involved in other businesses. The involvements include weapons production, aerospace manufacture, atomic energy, aviation, radar, uranium mining, police surveillance systems, computer systems, newspaper publishing, book publishing, cable television, theaters, amusement parks, toy manufacture, medical equipment, medical textbooks, soft drink bottling plants, vending machines, mobile homes, real estate. The words "conflict of interest" are often mentioned in newscasts, but almost never in reference to the overwhelming conflict of interest within television. And media leaders are virtually never seen on the tube, facing probing questions such as politicians must occasionally face.[5]

Significantly, stations owned by the National Broadcasting Company are encouraged by headquarters to air station editorials on diverse subjects, but *not* on broadcasting. On this topic reply time is not to be risked, even locally. It is by ukase a non-issue.[6]

What is true of networks and stations is equally true of dominant production companies. The Paramount, Universal, MGM, Warner, and United Artists studios have become units within conglomerates, with wide-ranging stakes.

The symbiotic growth of American television and global enterprise has made them so interrelated that they cannot be thought of as separate. They are essentially the same phenomenon. Preceded far and wide by military advisers, lobbyists, equipment salesmen, advertising specialists, merchandising experts, and telefilm salesmen as advance agents, the enterprise penetrates much of the non-socialist world. Television is simply its most visible portion.

There are many dangers in the symbiotic relationship. One of the most serious is its connection with one of the most explosive issues of our time—unemployment, both in America and abroad.

This connection is seldom discussed—for reasons that are compelling and clear.

THE NEW LIBERATION

The business boom of the post-World War II years is essentially a new phase of the Industrial Revolution, stemming from the rise of electronics and its offspring the computer. Television is an aspect of this surge and its mightiest promotional tool.

In earlier phases of the Industrial Revolution, machinery replaced much heavy labor; in the present phase it replaces "blue collar" and "white collar" workers alike, and at an accelerating pace. And that is its essential mission—eliminating much of the human element from the production and distribution of goods, to increase productivity and profit.

Business leaders prefer to say it differently. They prefer to say that automation *liberates* people for other kinds of work—new products, new markets. There is enough truth in this to have won it some acceptance and endless repetition. That is understandable: the rationale comforts business leaders including media leaders, and offers a glimmer of hope to the displaced. But the new products are obviously not catching up with the displacement. More workers are being "liberated" for unemployment than for work in new employment—other than army service.

On a global scale, multinational corporations are clearly hastening the displacement process—through automation, huge economies of scale, and other factors. Their ability to shift assembly lines from country to country helps them minimize and depress labor costs. And since global conglomerates are constantly buying from themselves, they can arrange prices to minimize tax obligations, shifting them wherever governments are at the moment most amenable. This gives them blackmail power over innumerable governments, whose bargaining position weakens as the companies grow.

The authors of *Global Reach*—Richard J. Barnet and Ronald E. Müller—make it clear that these advantages are widening the gap between large and small business, between have and have-not nations, and between rich and poor people on all continents. They are tending to "Latin-Americanize" the United States itself: into rich enclaves in wastelands of poverty.[7]

Far from relying on accelerated big-business enterprise to close the unemployment gap, we must in due time face the idea that the world's necessities—and many of its luxuries—can now be produced by a fraction of its competent adults. That the huge implications of this simple fact have almost totally escaped attention from commercial television need not surprise us. Its incentives deflect it in an opposite direction.

Meanwhile the stress on new products, new markets, brings us back to the nub of our gathering crisis. Consumption patterns pushed via television, involving an avalanche of the needless made necessary, also drain resources and pollute the environment at a more devastating rate than any necessities. Television-promoted convenience foods, packaged for mass distribution and long shelf-life, involve hosts of preservatives, texturizers, and dyes, some of which have proved irritants and health hazards; in some cases, substitutes have been found which have subsequently proved to be more hazardous. Spectacular packaging designed for on-the-tube and point-of-purchase selling power uses quantities of paper that later inundate sidewalk, backlot, and field. It also uses quantities of plastics that clog drains and rivers, while the manufacture of packaging—and numerous other products—has involved such genetically risky chemicals as polychlorinated biphenyls—"PCBs"—that wash into seas and are found in accumulating quantities in fish and wildlife, even to the penguins of Antarctica. It has also involved polyvinyl chloride, considered a contributor to cancer. Some paper manufacture has used mercury, associated with birth defects; its presence in rivers and seas has made some fish dangerous to eat and has further increased our dependence on factory-processed foods. Factory-processing increasingly preempts harvests of sea, farm, orchard. The chemicals accumulate while life patterns built around shopping centers, suburbs, and commuting traffic increasingly subjugate us to the automobile and its contributions to the chemical miasma. Of the hundreds of chemicals constantly released to our environment, many are introduced with little knowledge of their ultimate effect. Their very pervasiveness and slow, cumulative action protect the polluters: a medical crisis can almost never be linked to a specific cause. Cancer, which may take a decade or two to develop, is virtually litigation-proof.[8]

But we do know that most cancers are now ascribed to environmental factors; also, that 7 per cent of American babies—200,000 a year—are being born with abnormalities, ranging from defects of internal organs to physical deformities, and that the March of Dimes considers 20 per cent of those abnormalities to be environmentally caused. Clearly there are troubles here that our society hesitates to confront.[9]

Unfortunately, we tend to acquire a vested interest in each step in the direction of disaster. Every success in foisting a new product on a hopeful public—whether junk food or drink, electric toothbrush, supersonic plane, breathmint, weapon system, vaginal spray, dial-matic coffeemaker, luxury car, shower massager, stomach settler, snowmobile, air-conditioned stadium—is described as public "demand" calling for more energy production and justifying more pollution, in a spiral of growing momentum.

Perhaps the most fateful legacy of the spiral, reflecting the links between global enterprise and the military, has been the plunge into atomic energy.

GENIE FROM THE TUBE

The power of the atom ended World War II. For all its horror it was widely welcomed for the peace it brought. And it put the United States, almost unscarred by the war, in a position of extraordinary worldwide prestige and power. Only the Soviet Union seemed a remotely possible contender. The situation seemed to many people to assure a long peace, with American power as its principal guarantor.

To strengthen the guarantee, the United States maintained farflung bases—virtually ringing the Soviet Union—and continued the development of atomic weapons. Russian development of similar weapons, and the rise of a communist regime in China, brought increased American stress on "security." In this spirit the Advertising Council in 1952 "sponsored" a telecast of a Yucca Flat, Nevada, bomb test, linking it to promotion of a Ground Observer Corps.

Radiation effects of nuclear weapons were discussed in detail in some print media, but avoided on the air. The first film footage of the Hiroshima and Nagasaki devastation, shot by Japanese cameramen and subsequently confiscated by the occupation, was declared SECRET by the Defense Department and withheld from the public for almost a quarter of a century. It was first seen on television in 1970.[10]

In the 1950's emphasis shifted from weapons-testing to "the peaceful atom." The Atomic Energy Commission was put in charge of its promotion *and* regulation—a linkage of duties that proved to have built-in conflicts.

Frame from 1952 Advertising Council spot proclaiming its "sponsorship" of Yucca Flat atomic test. The Council urged home owners to build atomic-war radiation shelters.

The promotion focused on the better life—to be ushered in by virtually unlimited electric energy, which would be clean, safe, and available at negligible cost, according to AEC forecasts. But other factors were also involved. The shift to atomic energy would assure the military of vast, continuing supplies of fissionable material and weapons—to be furnished to it by the AEC, and provided for in the AEC budget.[11]

AEC regulations barred cameramen, other than U.S. Army Signal Corps cameramen, from all nuclear installations. Such regulations were accepted at the time as necessary to national security.

During the early 1950's the Signal Corps cameramen compiled a body of film footage—more than 100,000 feet, in 35 mm.—on atomic energy installations, available to producers and broadcasters—"only with AEC permission." Producers were asked to submit scripts showing use to be made of the footage.[12]

By this control over access, along with script review, the AEC held firm supervision for many years over documentaries on atomic energy. A documentary on the NBC 1954-55 series *American Inventory* was made under the AEC arrangements. So were numerous documentaries made for school, club, and church use, including a series on *The Magic of the Atom* produced in 1954-55 by Handel Films. The U.S. Chamber of Commerce joined the campaign in 1957 with the television film *The Atom Comes to Town*. Others joining the campaign were General Electric and Westinghouse—giants which had helped launch the broadcasting era and were now also emerging as leaders in atomic energy equipment. GE sponsored the 1953 animated film *A Is For Atom*, distributed free for many years, and the 1954 documentary *The Atom Goes to Sea*, showing GE engineers working with AEC and the U.S. Navy in designing machinery for atomic-powered submarines. Westinghouse contributed a number of films including the 1964 *Operating Experience—Yankee*, on the development of a Massachusetts nuclear plant.

But the AEC itself became the chief fountainhead of films promoting atomic energy. During the 1950's and 1960's it released more than a hundred such films, almost all given free to television stations. At least twenty appeared on educational stations via the National Educational Television program service. The films had titles like *Opportunity Unlimited* (1962, about "friendly atoms in industry"), *The Atom and Eve* (1966, "how nuclear power has come of age"), *Atomic Power Today* (1967, "dependable service . . . many safeguards"), *Guardian of the Atom* (1967, "the role of the AEC . . . in developing the peaceful uses and national security uses of the atom"), *Go Fission* (1969, "about careers in the atomic field"). Almost all described atomic energy as safe, clean, cheap, and absolutely necessary to meet surging energy "demands"—demands which were meanwhile being manufactured via television and other media.[13]

The 1960's witnessed many mergers in the energy field, with the major oil companies acquiring coal, gas, and uranium reserves. By the early 1970's 45 per cent of American uranium reserves were controlled by oil companies. They became increasingly involved in atomic energy promotion, on and off the air.[14]

Throughout these years—cold war and Vietnam War years—television fiction was mythologizing the harnessing of the atom. Superman often faced enemies armed with atomic weapons, but quickly swallowed a pill that made him immune; radiation presented no peril to the champion of the American Way. And a child sending 15 cents and a Kix boxtop to *The Lone Ranger*, sponsored by General Mills, could acquire an "atomic bomb ring," which apparently bestowed secret superpower.[15] Plots involving United States atomic scientists, and fiendish enemy schemes to kidnap them, were favorites in children's series, live and animated. American ability to solve all scientific problems was inherent in all such mythologizing.

The AEC constantly predicted a rapid shift to atomic generation of electricity, but it actually began very slowly. The utilities held back until Congress enacted the 1957 Price-Anderson Act, relieving the companies of major insurance risks. With the main risks shifted to the public, atomic energy gathered momentum during the 1960's.

Until the end of that decade, nothing seen or heard on television could lead viewers to think that atomic energy involved risks of any serious kind. Documentaries and public service messages had come overwhelmingly—perhaps exclusively—from those who had a stake in promoting the industry.

But the Price-Anderson enactment implied that large risks existed, and during the 1960's these risks received increasing discussion in newsletters such as the *Bulletin of the Atomic Scientists*, and later in bulletins of environmental groups.

These groups became aware that fail-safe systems designed to avert catastrophe, in case of a break in a major cooling pipe, had been tested only in small-scale models and that all such tests had actually failed. The AEC had proceeded anyway on the basis of computer projections—involving some assumptions that later proved invalid, such as that metals would hold their shape.[16]

Readers of environmental bulletins also became aware of innumerable shutdowns and equipment failures, generally unmentioned on television. The Vermont Yankee plant had 17 major shutdowns in its first 19 months of operation because of safety violations, fuel rods buckling, and other accidents and malfunctions—followed later by spillage of low-level radioactive wastes in the Connecticut River. The absence of catastrophic accident was often cited by AEC spokesmen as a demonstration of safety and reliability, but this scarcely reassured environmentalists.[17]

The environmentalists also became aware that the AEC, in the opinion of many atomic scientists, was consistently understating the carcinogenic effects of low-level radiation, and was firmly suppressing dissenting views within the atomic community. Its promotional zeal was seen to be submerging its regulatory function.

Perhaps the most serious of all issues, virtually unmentioned in the early promotional barrage, was that of radioactive wastes—some low-level and slow-acting, some high-level and rapidly lethal. They represented a bequest to future generations, and would be with mankind—if it survived—for at least a quarter of a million years. The immorality of the policy shocked environmental groups, and began to alarm many others.

During the 1950's thousands of barrels of radioactive wastes had been dumped into the Atlantic and Pacific oceans, but such dumpings were forbidden when barrels were found to be leaking. Several reprocessing and burial sites were designated within the United States, but leakage from containers to surrounding areas proved a persistent problem. The atomic energy plants were eventually ordered to keep their wastes on-site, pending a permanent solution. The wastes accumulated rapidly.

The late 1960's produced an apparent solution: the AEC announced that quantities of the wastes would be embedded in an abandoned Kansas salt mine. The inert salts were expected to shield mankind forever from dangerous radiation. The 1969 AEC film *Project Salt Vault*—free to all television stations—proclaimed the good news. But further study of the site showed that water seepage would inevitably disperse the radioactivity, and the State of Kansas soon forced abandonment of the plan. The setback was noted briefly on the ABC-TV evening newscast of February 8, 1972; it went unmentioned on the CBS-TV and NBC-TV evening newscasts.[18]

But CBS-TV and NBC-TV did find time on January 14 for another "historic" AEC announcement: at Rogersville, Tennessee, the Federal government would help to establish a commercial "breeder" reactor—one that would make "more nuclear fuel that it uses." Walter Cronkite, with a lift in his voice, quoted President Nixon as calling it "the best hope for meeting the nation's needs in economical, clean energy." This news item, which lasted just over a minute, did not mention that here, too, the unsolved radioactive waste problem would exist; nor that the supposed advantage of the "breeder," its production of vast quantities of plutonium, would in fact involve new perils, due to the fact that it could readily be made into bombs—as published information had already made clear.[19]

Within television news units, many newsmen were increasingly troubled over the medium's failure to report and examine the issues. As in early stages of the Vietnam War, the medium had served largely as transmission belt for official and corporate promotion, closely coordinated. It was an easy role to slip into: at what point does one begin to challenge an apparently solid official and corporate alignment? But many newsmen—particularly documentarists—pressed for an opportunity to probe the issues.

Early in 1975 a statement signed by thirty-two Congressmen

and addressed to broadcasters sounded a similar note. The statement began:

> Dear Broadcaster:
>
> We are deeply concerned over the imbalance on the public airwaves created by many years and millions of dollars worth of government and industry promotion of nuclear power. Consequently, we are appealing to the nation's broadcasters to take affirmative action to assure that the public is fully and fairly exposed to all sides of this crucial issue. . . .[20]

The Atomic Energy Commission had been dissolved late in 1974. Its regulatory function was assigned to a Nuclear Regulatory Commission (NRC), the development function to an Energy Research and Development Administration (ERDA). As they began work, the industry entered troubled days. Early in 1976 three General Electric engineering officials, all of whom had spent years working in atomic energy, resigned in the conviction that it represented a threat "to all life on this planet"— as one of them, Gregory Minor, expressed it. All three men had struggled with private doubts and become convinced that nuclear power had to be halted. In the same year a government safety inspector at the Consolidated Edison plant at Indian Point near New York City resigned, calling the plant "almost an accident waiting to happen." He urged that the plant be closed. Three utilities were meanwhile suing Westinghouse for reneging on commitments to supply enriched uranium for many years at $9.50 a pound. The market price had risen to over $40 a pound; Westinghouse, calling itself a victim of price conspiracy, planned to sue its suppliers. The company's survival was thought by some observers to be in jeopardy. A number of utilities were canceling orders for nuclear plants. The dream of "cheap" electric power from the atom seemed increasingly illusory. Plant repair costs were growing, citizen opposition mounting.[21]

Industry promotion continued, but with a rising counterpoint of questions and challenges. On public television skepticism found dramatic expression in two programs on the science series *Nova*, from WGBH, Boston. One concerned a twenty-year-old chemistry student who, using only published information, had undertaken to design an atom bomb. The resulting design was shown to a nuclear physicist, who concluded that the bomb would explode with a force of 1000 tons of TNT. In *The Plutonium Connection*, produced by John Angier in 1975, the *Nova* series recounted these events, underscoring the use that terrorists could make of a small quantity of plutonium. Early in 1977 *Nova* contributed *Incident at Brown's Ferry*, produced and written by Robert Richter—a detailed anatomy of an accident that had caused $150 million worth of damage at an Alabama nuclear complex. The program ended with a quotation from Albert Einstein: ". . . to the village square we must carry the facts of atomic energy . . . from there must come America's voice."[22]

Meanwhile the San Francisco–based Public Media Center, in association with Friends of the Earth, was having some success in distributing 30-second and 60-second spots on the theme "Nuclear Power Is a Terrible Way To Go." One of the spots was narrated by Ralph Nader.[23]

But to the nuclear establishment the most devastating blow was a 1977 NBC documentary—*Danger: Radioactive Waste*, produced and written by Joan Konner. Virtually the first examination of the nuclear waste impasse offered to American viewers, it provided glimpses of the Hanford atomic graveyard—"industrial park" in officialese—575 square miles in Washington State near the Columbia River, operated by Atlantic Richfield under government contract, where 55 million gallons of high-level waste from the military program lay buried, with quantities of obsolete radioactive equipment and more accumulating, all stored in ways considered unsatisfactory, temporary, potentially disastrous, waiting for a solution. The nation had created, the documentary suggested, a "radioactive monster with no cage to keep it in."[24]

Coming from NBC, subsidiary of RCA—"a key element in our defense structure," Lyndon Johnson had once called it—the documentary had especially strong impact. It broadened the base of the spreading revolt against atomic energy. Was the uprising too late to matter? General Electric, Westinghouse, and others had negotiated many foreign reactor sales. Nuclear know-how, processes, and wastes were accumulating worldwide.[25]

And with billions of dollars of investments and orders at stake, the equipment makers were determined to press the battle. For this purpose they had organized the Atomic Industrial Forum, which began to replace the AEC as chief propagandist for the industry, defending its record, exuding confidence that all problems would be solved, and castigating critics. It attacked, with vitriolic rhetoric, such expressions of dissent as the *Nova* and NBC programs. And it raised a war chest to fight resolutions introduced by environmental groups in several 1976 state elections. In California alone, the campaign to defeat an anti-nuclear resolution received $150,000 from General Electric, $90,000 from Westinghouse, lesser sums from Atlantic Richfield, Bank of America, General Motors, Kaiser Industries, U.S. Steel. Contributions came also from dozens of utilities, including many out-of-state companies.[26] The total receipts far exceeded funds available to anti-nuclear groups.

The war chest financed a barrage of television spots which helped to defeat the California resolution. Arguments used by the Atomic Industrial Forum in all this campaigning included one theme of particular significance.

JOBS WANTED

The attack on atomic energy, said the Forum in its six-page protest to NBC, would "jeopardize the economy" and deepen the unemployment crisis. The campaign spots made similar use of the unemployment issue. One spot featured a college student:

> STUDENT: Hello, I'm Kathy Higley. I'm majoring in physical chemistry at Reed College, and I operate our research nuclear reactor. A lot of students like myself will soon be out of school looking for jobs. Our energy supply is very important to us. No energy—no jobs. Please join me and vote "no" on measure 9. It would ban further development of nuclear power, a clean and safe energy source. Vote "no" on 9, and beat the ban.[27]

On the same grounds, the state AFL-CIO joined forces with the Atomic Industrial Forum in the campaign.

That the unemployed, pervasive product of the new Industrial Revolution, should be coopted to carry it further, was ironic and tragic. Services for which many of them were qualified—in education, health, conservation, social work, the arts—were reduced and even starved because the wealth of the society was channeled into the unneeded, the wasteful, the damaging. All this stressed the need not for atomic energy, but for a far more basic revision of economic arrangements, and the communication system interlocked with them.

The historian-philosopher Arnold Toynbee, in *Surviving the Future*, offered a long-range view of the dilemma and its implications. He felt it inevitable that a small minority of mankind would be able to produce, with technology, the products needed by all. Then what of the vast "unemployed" majority? He saw the nightmare possibility—"if we do not take care"—that they might be destined to live in shantytowns, "subsisting on an inadequate dole which would be given them by the productive minority, who would themselves live in fear of being massacred by the resentful unemployed majority."

To forestall such a nightmare, Toynbee saw active steps needed. The unemployed majority would have to be given more than a mere dole by the "productive" minority. They would have to be "subsidized generously, tactfully, and in a creative way." He went on:

> We shall have to share out the fruits of technology among the whole of mankind. The notion that the direct and immediate producers of the fruits of technology have a proprietary right to these fruits will have to be forgotten. After all, who is the producer? Man is a social animal, and the immediate producer has been helped to produce by the whole structure of society, beginning with his own education. So it is not reasonable that he should claim to have a proprietary right in his product, and under the new conditions of automation, this will certainly not make any sense at all.

But such a realignment requires a wide transformation of attitudes. And here Toynbee's comments touched on communication media and their role in shaping ideas and mythologies. He saw automation producing a "second Renaissance" provided we view the displaced not as stigmatized, but as freed for activities that serve and enrich our society. "We shall have to overcome the feeling that it is almost disgraceful to be unemployed in the technical sense of not being employed on work for which one is paid a salary. The Buddha and Jesus were unemployed in this sense—that is, in economic terms." Toynbee conceded that in the present world they might be considered "unproductive economically and therefore unsatisfactory."

Thus the electronic phase of the Industrial Revolution seemed to Toynbee to offer a choice of possibilities—a second Renaissance or, on the other hand, "a parasitic society which, like the urban proletariat in the Roman Empire, lives for 'bread and circuses' and turns savage if it is not given to them."[28]

Bread and circuses—to some observers, welfare and television seemed modern equivalents, pacifiers of empire, protectors of power and privilege.

THE CIRCUSES

If television has assumed this role, it is not the result of a struggle between good guys and bad guys. If it were, it would be easy to solve, like problems in televisionland. But it is not such a problem.

The sponsor who thinks in terms of maximizing sales and profits is doing his duty. If he habitually made business decisions in a spirit of philanthropy, or to aid favorite causes, his stockholders might reasonably object. He may himself be a lover of nature, and contribute to the Sierra Club and Audubon Society, but in business decisions his eye is on sales and profits. If he senses an ultimate conflict between his interests, he prefers not to think about it.

The advertising agency executive who recommends programs and time-slots in terms of audience size and demographic targets is likewise doing his job. He may earnestly welcome a chance to write Advertising Council spots about pollution, and feel he is really doing something about that problem, but such concerns

AND CIRCUSES. A nighttime sports event draws fifty thousand people to a stadium; some drive fifty miles or more to join the crowd—a huge audience for the Goodyear blimp. The event uses enough electric power to light a city for a week. The blimp, equipped with television camera with zoom lens, is also part of the machinery that brings the circus to millions of viewers—an audience for which sponsors are ready to pay at least $100,000 per minute to push sales of luxury cars, gasoline, beer, airplane travel, cosmetics, etc. Goodyear, the network, *et al.* meanwhile proclaim their devotion to conservation. *Don't be fuelish.*

stay in a separate compartment from his basic business decisions. If not, he would soon be forced out.

The network sales executive who favors programs that advertising agencies will recommend to sponsors is performing his task. He may himself make a donation to a public television station and admire some of its meaty programs, but his job depends on sales to sponsors.

The problem—the folly—is not in any of these, but in a system that has made the center of national attention a market item, for sale at auction prices. The system has put the leadership of our society on the auction block.

When was such a decision made? As we have seen, the "American system of broadcasting" was never really adopted. Neither in 1927 nor in 1934—when our basic broadcasting laws were written—did the people's representatives in Congress assembled decide that the air should be a commercial commodity. They *seemed*, with their emphasis on "the public interest," to decide the opposite. But they placed few restraints on future developments. The rest of the story, as we have seen, was a gradual take-over by business, which was soon accepted as a *fait accompli* and almost a fact of nature.

The business elements included electronic companies that had risen to importance in World War I, and had then launched the first broadcasting boom. They remained dominant in broadcasting, particularly in network broadcasting.

The evolution of an advertising-based system gave broadcasters a special relationship to major manufacturers of mass-produced, mass-distributed products, who became increasingly dependent on broadcasting as its power spread. They thrived together, even during Depression years.

The government-sponsored, war-related beginnings of the electronics industry were almost forgotten during the Depression. The early New Deal years were marked by hostility between big business and government. But war rumblings in Europe, Africa, and Asia brought a new surge of military contracts, and began to foster a closely knit military-industrial-political complex. Military dependence on electronics and its offshoot the computer, and subsequently on atomic energy, increased the power of the alignment and its influence over legislators and regulators.

After the war it experienced a global boom, with help from American aid programs. These programs, always projected in humanitarian terms, functioned as export subsidies. After the Marshall Plan all aid programs were "tied aid," requiring that funds—or credits—be used to purchase American goods and services. Often the recipient nation was required to accept military aid with other aid, producing a continuing dependence on American weapons, parts, services. Thus "foreign aid"—enthusiastically backed by conservative legislators, to the puzzlement of some observers who thought it was philanthropy—became a program by which the American taxpayer subsidized the global reach of the multinationals, and at the same time fostered their close relationship with military hegemony.

Many companies invested their foreign earnings in foreign branches and mergers, being encouraged to do so by tax policies, low wages, access to raw materials, new markets. American television rode the crest of the foreign expansion. It lobbied for the American system—often with success—and soon sold its programs on all continents, often sponsored by subsidiaries or affiliates of American sponsors. Many of the countries had dictatorial regimes, which needed circuses. In much of the world, American-style television became a way of life.[29]

EMPIRES

In his book *Empire and Communications* the Canadian scholar Harold A. Innis traced the role of media from ancient times, and concluded that major empires have tended to be dominated by media monopolies. Technical circumstances surrounding a new medium have often helped determine which elements of society rose to control.

The completeness of a communication monopoly could, however, become a liability. It could encourage new media, or old media in new forms, to rise on the fringes of society, representing other social elements and bringing a shift in power—which might eventually lead to a new monopoly.

Thus the church monopoly of knowledge in the Middle Ages, based on scarcity of parchment and the skills of monastic copyists, was undermined by the advent of paper. Ample supplies of paper encouraged the development of printing, which spread new information and ideas, including heresies. The chain reactions echoed through centuries, as old heresies became new orthodoxies.[30]

The scarcity of broadcasting channels and the control of them have proved key instruments of modern power. Their leverage over thought, aspiration, and action have served to concentrate economic power, and political power with it.

Yet intimations of change are at hand. They revolve around new developments—CATV, or cable television; satellites; laser beams; cassettes; videodiscs; home facsimile printouts; optical fiber. Singly or jointly, they are seen likely to upset current patterns of influence. The view is reenforced by dissatisfactions, not only with media but with power structures behind them. In developing countries the dissatisfied call for "decolonization of information," an end to one-way traffic in television programming. At home dissent is especially associated with educational, consumerist, environmental groups. Their view: "If environment is a fad, it's going to be our last fad."[31]

Among technicians, speculations revolve around optical fiber. Laser beams, which normally take a straight line, can follow a curved path through these mysterious glass fibers, and can carry innumerable streams of communication in both directions, vastly exceeding the capacity of coaxial cables. The picture of a nation of homes and businesses linked by an optical-fiber network— made from cheap, plentiful silicon—stirs visions of a greatly changed telecommunications system. Replacing the cable in today's cable television, such a system could also encompass the telephone service, and at the same time make it a two-way, sight-and-sound service. Corporations could hold interbranch meetings in which executives would see each other in split-screen arrangements. Much office work could be done at home, with occasional face-to-face communication with the office via the telescreen. The insanity of rush-hour traffic might pass into history. The home viewer, via computer pushbuttons, could have access not only to current television programs but to a choice of other resources: classic films or research data might be summoned from an electronic archive. The home receiver could have a facsimile printout adjunct: newspapers, tax forms, letters might arrive in this way. The system could produce the teleshopper, tuning to displays of available merchandise and ordering and paying by pushbutton; payment could simply be deducted electronically from one's bank balance. It could also produce the telecourse, with each lesson summoned in turn from a computer-controlled repository, climaxed by the final exam. Question after question would appear on the screen, to be answered by pushbutton; a grade would at once be recorded in an electronic data bank.[32]

Most telecommunications futurists assume that some of the available choices would be free while others would involve payment. But most prognostications avoid details of the flow of finance and of control, and concentrate on the visions.

To some educators, the two-way aspect seems all-important. Using such terms as "interactive communication" and "citizen feedback," they foresee a system that would be democratizing, liberating. They see the homes of a whole neighborhood joined electronically in planning and discussion, fostering a new "community ethos." On national issues, the country could be polled by pushbutton.[33]

It should be remembered that every step in modern media history—telephone, phonograph, motion picture, radio, television, satellite—stirred similar euphoric predictions. All were expected to usher in an age of enlightenment. All were seen as fulfilling the promise of democracy. Possible benefits were always easier to envisage than misuses and corruptions, and still are. Yet cautions are in order.

In the early 1930's, when it was reported that Nazi Germany and Soviet Russia were developing wired-radio systems, they were at once interpreted in the United States as instruments of control. Why, when we move toward a wired system, do we see it as democratizing and liberating? Does a multiplicity of choices guarantee a meaningful contest of ideas? How meaningful is pushbutton participation?

Is it conceivable that the teleshopper, telestudent, televoter of the futurist scenarios may feel more alienated than ever? Do they really want to stay home—out of the way—at the end of a glass wire?

The dangers as well as advantages of a wired system became apparent with the very first such system, the telegraph. As its wires spread, its monopoly implications became clear.

By the 1870's Western Union, having absorbed smaller companies, stretched its web of wires over most of the country. As the only such system, it could charge monopoly rates, but its leadership found other—even more lucrative—formulas for wealth and power. Representative Charles A. Sumner of California charged in 1875 that sudden changes in market prices were repeatedly withheld from San Francisco until insiders had made a killing. Control of the flow of information could yield bonanzas.

To break the control, bills for a government telegraph service linking the nation's post offices—to create an alternative channel of communication—were introduced in Congress almost annually during the 1870's. But Western Union had potent weapons to use against such efforts. Congressmen friendly to Western Union received unlimited supplies of "franks"—forms providing free telegraph service—to keep in touch with constituents and to use in election campaigns. And newspapers, having become totally dependent on Western Union service for speedy national and international news, felt under strong pressure to go along with the monopolistic status quo. Newspapers backing postal telegraph proposals were said to have had disastrous interruptions of service. Under Jay Gould, who also controlled railroads, Western Union power seems to have been used ruthlessly.

With the invention of the telephone in 1876 the monopoly position of the telegraph began to erode: information had an alternative route. Western Union tried to smash the competition with patent litigation, but failed to do so, and the telephone thrived.

By the 1900's AT&T was so wealthy that it could, with one $30 million check, buy control of Western Union. But the nation had learned to fear a communication monopoly, and the sale was halted by antitrust action. The two wire systems remained as competitive elements, along with another rival, Postal Telegraph. This was a private company formed in 1882, having no connection with the postal system; it merely called itself "postal" because the word had acquired an anti-monopoly ring. It became active in communication systems abroad, and eventually metamorphosed into ITT—International Telephone & Telegraph Company.[34]

Meanwhile still another instant-information route had become available: wireless, which led to radio, television, and the whole world of electronics, including the computer. They helped such new giants as RCA and IBM rise to power. They also led to satellites and COMSAT, in which we find AT&T, ITT, RCA, and Western Union International as *partners*. Have they ceased to be competitors?

Now comes a development by which the services of all of these may reach home and office through one glass-fiber system. Is it Utopia, or are we back to "square one"—in monopoly terms?

Who will be the gatekeepers of the evolving system? Who will man the control points? Will the multiplicity of choices provide diversity, or only seem to? Who will decide what will be stored in the electronic archives and information banks available to pushbuttons? Our history teaches us that these are crucial questions.

Underlying them all is another: what role will sponsorship—and the financial control it involves—play in the system to come? Will it be a diminishing role, as many assume?

At a workshop session of the Association of National Advertisers, Richard Pinkham, chairman of the executive committee of the Ted Bates advertising agency, was sure it would not be so. The home audience would be more fragmented: viewers would have more alternatives. But so would sponsors. He urged sponsors to take up the new possibilities early, and with "ingenuity and guts." He reminded them of the huge benefits that had accrued to Texaco when, at the dawn of television, it bought the hour between 8 and 9 p.m. Tuesday nights on NBC-TV for Milton Berle, and kept "that golden time period" for five years.

Will there be opportunities like that staring you in the face as CATV and satellite transmission emerge?

Will there be opportunities for your company to own its own programming, tailor-made to attract precisely your target audience no matter how small, protected from the escalation of network costs, providing in-show star commercials and generating the gratitude factor we all lost when we went to scatter? I'll bet the answer is yes.

How much thought have you given to the marketing potential of two-way communication? What should your company do to get there first? At least one of our clients is already experimenting with techniques to exploit this kind of one-to-one contact with the consumer in her living room. Are you working on it?

What will facsimile printout from the television set do for you? Should you start now to devise a sponsored woman's page or crossword puzzle or sports section? Will you be able to devise a TV commercial with printed recipes and perhaps a coupon? Here's a medium which will combine the news impact of newspapers with the visual demonstrations of television. It could be a blockbuster combination.

Are sponsored videodiscs a possibility?

Have you thought of using CATV's low rates to buy time for your sales force to demonstrate your product or show its possibilities on the counter or announced a special cents-off promotion? Should you start now to train them as television salesmen?

How will you harness worldwide satellite-to-home transmission to your international marketing challenge? Will universal sponsorship become available? . . .

The opportunities, thought Pinkham, were immense.[35]

FRINGE MEDIUM

Amid the think-tank fever, what would become of public television—the system legislated into being in 1967, on the basis of a Carnegie commission manifesto?

The Carnegie document, surveying American television, concluded that society has communication needs which could not be met by an advertising-based system. These needs were felt to call for a "public" television service channeling a different set of motives, a system through which Americans would "know themselves, their communities, and their world in richer ways." The commission termed it "a civilized voice in a civilized community."

In its first decade this "public" system, linked by a Public Broadcasting Service and receiving Federal funds through a Corporation for Public Broadcasting, has made important strides in the hoped-for direction. It has broken away from rigid formulas of commercial-network drama, documentary, and children's programming. It has opened new worlds for many viewers through its imported programs; its extended coverage of events, like the Watergate hearings; its arts festivals; its unhurried and often lucid news analyses. Its audience has grown.

Yet its outlook is clouded. Many of its affiliates are UHF stations with shaky reception. Some areas of the country remain unreached. Worst of all is the system's financial status, which affects its equipment and staffing, and limits program plans.

A key element in the Carnegie manifesto was its financial recommendation. To assure the independence of the system, it was to have an automatic source of revenue such as a dedicated tax on electronic equipment. Several alternative tax bases were suggested. The dedicated tax was meant to parallel, to some extent, arrangements in effect in Britain and Japan, both of which have effective, well-financed non-commercial systems based on license fees—systems existing side by side with their commercial systems, and holding large audiences.

The reasons for the Carnegie stipulation were clear. To fulfill its purpose, the system had to be independent not only of sponsor domination but also of pressures involved in constant confrontations with congressional committees over appropriations and policies.[36]

Congress did not follow the recommendation. Congressmen ensured their hold over the system by making it dependent on periodic appropriations. Many were unwilling for it to have the independence recommended by the Carnegie commission. So the system was kept on a short tether, harried by uncertainties—making long-range planning difficult. Legislation of the Nixon period compounded the squeeze by requiring matching funds—two and a half dollars to be raised for every dollar provided in Federal funds. This has virtually pushed the system into the arms of the corporate sponsor and also into endless subscription drives—which may meet increasing resistance as the sponsor's role expands.

The relationship to Congress has dark aspects. The National Association of Broadcasters is considered one of the most powerful lobbies, rivaled only by the armaments lobby, with which it has an overlapping constituency. There have long been special reasons for the effectiveness of the broadcasting lobby. Some Congressmen—or their families—have had a financial interest in commercial broadcasting. The Lyndon Johnson family was a prominent example: it virtually leaped to multimillionnaire status through broadcasting, beginning with a modest invest-ment in a radio station. When in 1952 it acquired a television channel—one of the first allotted after the freeze—the station be-came profitable even before it reached the air. "AUSTIN'S BRING-ING IN A GUSHER," read a *Broadcasting* magazine headline. The station was in Mrs. Johnson's name, but Senator Johnson took a hand in management. And sponsors seemed anxious to do busi-ness with stations owned by the family of Senator—later Vice President—later President—Johnson.[37]

Other links bind Congress and commercial broadcasters. Many Congressmen have regularly received free radio or tele-vision time—except during election campaigns—from stations in their areas to "keep in touch with their constituents"—a rough equivalent of the Western Union "franks" of other days. For Congressman and stations alike, the ties yield benefits. His door is open; on problems relating to commercial broadcasting, the Congressman is kept constantly aware of industry views and desires.

Whatever attitudes and fears were involved, the financial status inflicted on public television has done much to sabotage the original plan. At most stations major program proposals are drawn up, then held in abeyance while fund raisers seek under-writing. The sponsor's nod is awaited.

In the wired system envisaged for the future, where will pub-lic television fit? Will it thrive or be drowned out? Will its de-pendence on sponsors increase? Will it become—more than now—a link in the world of merchandising?

Adam Smith, who published *The Wealth of Nations* the year Jefferson drafted the Declaration of Independence, is regarded by many businessmen as a patron saint of free enterprise. He saw national wealth springing primarily from the merchant's exercise of self-interest—or rather, from the competitive impact of many self-interests. Thus he gave self-interest an almost theological sanction.

But there is more to Adam Smith. He observed that the merchant is so perceptive in discerning his self-interest that he is often credited with large wisdom and given a role of authority. But this seemed to Smith a mistake. The merchant's alertness to his own interest is likely to blind him to "the public interest," thought Smith. Merchants should therefore not have monopolistic or governmental power. It would produce "the worst of all governments for any country whatever."[38]

The sponsor, the merchant, has been living at the summit of our communication system. He has had things largely his way, and we are in trouble. He himself is aware of it. Impending change is in the air.

When the role of commercialized television is questioned or criticized, its defenders often condemn the criticism as a call for "government control." The call here is nothing of the sort. It is against the pervasive control that now exists, in which industry and government are closely linked. The call is for an alternative voice, one that can provide "the unimagined question and the unwelcome answer."

Public television has won a place on the fringe of our society. If it is to be a strong voice, one that can help new relationships and priorities to evolve from our dilemmas—a "civilized voice in a civilized community"—the Carnegie commission has made clear the most essential needs.

From present upheavals and impasses, new institutions will evolve. What sort of society will they tend to create? Decisions made about media will help to determine.

While we make our media, our media make us.

RISE

1. Statistically, the explosion of broadcasting can be traced in the monthly issues of the *Radio Service Bulletin*, published by the U.S. Department of Commerce from 1915 to 1934. The social impact and euphoria are tellingly reflected in the magazine *Radio Broadcast*, published monthly, 1922-30, by Doubleday, Page, in Garden City, N.Y. The most revealing personal accounts of the period may be found in the celebrated Oral History Collection—the first such project—launched by Alan Nevins at Columbia University in the late 1940's. In 1950, in association with Broadcast Pioneers, it began a long series of interviews with participants in the upheaval; most of the interviews were conducted by Frank Ernest Hill. They are available both at Special Collections, Columbia University, N.Y., and at the Broadcast Pioneers library in Washington, D.C. Individual interviews among them will be cited in subsequent notes as "Broadcast Pioneers reminiscences"; Barnouw, Erik, *A Tower in Babel* (New York: Oxford University Press, 1966), first volume of the three-volume *History of Broadcasting in the United States*, drew on seventy of these reminiscences.
2. For the role of the U.S. Navy in the development of radio see Schubert, Paul, *The Electric Word: The Rise of Radio* (New York: Macmillan, 1928) and *History of Communications—Electronics in the U.S. Navy*

(Washington, D.C.: GPO, 1963). For the adventures of the "hams" and their guerilla warfare with the Navy see the Broadcast Pioneers reminiscences of Everett L. Bragdon, Edgar Felix, Edgar S. Love, and Stanley R. Manning. Biographies important to an understanding of the period are Fessenden, Helen M., *Fessenden: Builder of Tomorrows* (New York: Coward-McCann, 1940); Lessing, Lawrence, *Man of High Fidelity: Edwin H. Armstrong* (Philadelphia: Lippincott, 1956), and Lee de Forest's autobiography, *Father of Radio* (Chicago: Wilcox & Follett, 1950).

3. All these predictions can be found in the very first issue of *Radio Broadcast* (May 1922). For the corporate maneuvers of the period, see two volumes by Archer, Gleason L., *History of Radio: To 1926* (New York: American Historical Society, 1938), and *Big Business and Radio* (New York: American Historical Company, 1939); see also Landry, Robert J., *This Fascinating Radio Business* (Indianapolis: Bobbs-Merrill, 1946).

4. For the role of Herbert Hoover in the broadcasting boom, both as Secretary of Commerce and as President, see Barnouw, Erik, *A Tower in Babel* (New York: Oxford University Press, 1966). The various Washington Radio Conferences were discussed in detail in issues of *Radio Broadcast,* 1922-25.

5. Banning, William Peck, *Commercial Broadcasting Pioneer: The WEAF Experiment 1922-26* (Cambridge, Mass.: Harvard University Press, 1946), is in the nature of an AT&T corporate review of its plunge into "toll" broadcasting. For a less formal—and often more revealing—account see the Broadcast Pioneers reminiscence of AT&T executive Lloyd Espenschied.

6. The full text of the first sponsored message will be found in Archer, *History of Radio.* This first "commercial" had a prophetic ring. Urging listeners to flee the city for the suburbs, it foreshadowed the crucial role played by the electronic media and their sponsors in glorifying suburbia. In this continual promotion, they may well have furthered the decay of the central cities, the erosion of the cities' tax bases, and the associated problems that began to plague the nation in the 1950's. The first Queensboro commercial included the following: "I wish to thank those within sound of my voice for the broadcasting opportunity afforded me to urge this vast radio audience to seek the recreation and the daily comfort of the home removed from the congested part of the city, right at the boundaries of God's great outdoors, and within a few miles by subway from the business section of Manhattan. . . . The cry of the heart is for more living room, more chance to unfold, more opportunity to get near the Mother Earth, to play, to romp, to plant, and to dig. Let me enjoin upon you as you value your health and your hopes and your home happiness, get away from the solid masses of brick, where the meager opening admitting a slant of sunlight is mockingly called a light shaft, and where children grow up starved for

a run over a patch of grass and the sight of a tree. Apartments in congested parts of the city have proved failures. The word neighbor is an expression of peculiar irony—a daily joke. . . . The fact is, however, that apartment homes on the tenant-ownership plan can be secured by . . ."

7. The early business trials of WEAF are vividly told in the Broadcast Pioneers reminiscences of Edgar Felix, William Harkness, and Mark Woods (later president of the American Broadcasting Company), all participants in the AT&T venture. Woods relates that every dollar of income was, for a time, a struggle. When any of the salesmen made a sale—even of a single program—"it was almost like a Christmas holiday." Woods, "Reminiscences," p. 10.

8. The quotation is from a quaint textbook that has become a museum piece among broadcasting business texts: Felix, Edgar A., *Using Radio in Sales Promotion: a book for advertisers, station managers and broadcasting artists* (New York: McGraw-Hill, 1927). Almost puritanical in his policy pronouncements, Felix felt that such words as *company* and *corporation* "must, of course, be omitted" in crediting a sponsor. *The Kodak Chorus* would be an acceptable reference; *The Eastman Company Chorus* would not be. Too crass.

9. The Herculean behind-the-scenes battle between AT&T and the "radio group" (GE, Westinghouse, RCA) remained largely unknown until 1938, when David Sarnoff made his files on the struggle available to Archer, who had just published his *History of Radio*. As a result Archer's subsequent volume, *Big Business and Radio* (New York: American Historical Company, 1939), covered virtually the same period as his first, but added a detailed account of the battle of the titans, largely from an RCA vantage.

10. *The Radio Act of 1927. An Act for the Regulation of Radio Communications, and for Other Purposes.* Public Law No. 632, Feb. 23, 1927, 69th Cong., 2nd sess. The famous "public interest" phrase has puzzling variants. In the 1927 radio law it is sometimes "public convenience, interest, or necessity," sometimes "public interest, convenience, or necessity"; later, in the 1934 law, it becomes "public interest, convenience and necessity." Sometimes "public interest" is used by itself. The significance of the variations remains unclear.

11. For the Aylesworth statement see *Federal Radio Commissioners: Hearing, Before a Subcommittee on Interstate Commerce, U.S. Senate, 72nd Cong., 2nd sess.* (Washington, D.C.: GPO, 1928), p. 219. When Aylesworth was chosen for the NBC presidency he was totally new to broadcasting, but had won the favor of NBC's owners because of his work as managing director of the National Electric Light Association, which represented private power companies and propagandized against public power. He had constantly urged private utilities to step up their propaganda activities, pointing out that the costs could be passed on to the customers—as Aylesworth put it, "the public pays." See Gruening,

Ernest, *The Public Pays: A Study of Power Propaganda* (New York: Vanguard, 1931, 1964). The author, who took his title from Aylesworth's phrase, later became a U.S. Senator from Alaska.

12. *Broadcasting*, Jan. 15, 1933. Minutes of earlier meetings of NBC's Cabinet-like Advisory Council of "distinguished citizens" were printed in cloth-bound, numbered, limited editions. In each copy were printed such words as:

> Only 30 Copies Printed
> This is No. 19
> For the Personal Use of
> Hon. Elihu Root

The practice was soon abandoned. The existence of the Advisory Council was gradually forgotten.

13. Carson, Gerald, *The Roguish World of Doctor Brinkley* (New York: Holt, Rinehart & Winston, 1960), provides a fine introduction to the rise of radio quackery. For its glossier network counterparts, see *The Voice of Experience* (New York: Dodd, Mead, 1933), and *Stranger Than Fiction* (New York: Dodd, Mead, 1934), both by "The Voice of Experience," the pseudonym of M. Sayle Taylor. The drug commercials, all delivered by Taylor, do not appear in the books.

14. Possibly the most notable example was CBS's stylishly designed brochure, *You Do What You're Told*, printed as though meant as a coffee-table conversation piece. Conceding that its thesis "flicks the pride . . . without which none of us can live," it went on to ask questions. When the dentist says, "Open your mouth," you open, don't you? When your wife says, "Tuck her in tight," you tuck, don't you? So too with "don't go yet"—"shake hands with Jim Brown"—"come right in." The point was, said CBS, that voices of affection and authority were involved in these cases, as in broadcasting—a fact that set broadcasting apart from other media. Where such voices come into play, said the brochure:

> Seven times
> Eight times
> Nine times out of ten
> People do what they're told.

Such brochures, largely by Paul Kesten, were considered potent in winning new sponsors for CBS—and for radio in general.

The "a little child shall lead them" advertisement is quoted in Seldes, Gilbert, *The Public Arts* (New York: Simon & Schuster, 1956), p. 252.

15. Quoted in Payne, George Henry, *The Federal Communications Act: Lecture at Harvard University School of Business Administration* (New York: Ritz Tower, 1935), p. 29.

16. Frost, S. E., Jr., *Education's Own Stations: The History of Broadcast*

Licenses Issued to Educational Institutions (Chicago: University of Chicago Press, 1937), offers a careful documentation of the educational disenchantment with American radio, as regulated by the Federal commissions. For additional details see Tyler, Tracy F. (ed.), *Radio as a Cultural Agency: Proceedings of a National Conference on the Use of Radio as a Cultural Agency in a Democracy* (Washington, D.C.: National Committee on Education by Radio, 1934).

17. Herring, E. Pendleton, "Politics and Radio Regulation," *Harvard Business Review*, Jan. 1935.

18. *Federal Communications Commission: Hearings Before the Committee on Interstate Commerce, U.S. Senate, 73rd Cong., 2nd sess., on S. 2910* (Washington, D.C.: GPO, 1935).

19. The Rorty quotations are from Rorty, James, *Our Master's Voice: Advertising* (New York: John Day, 1934). See pp. 32-33, 70-72, 270.

20. *Broadcasting*, May 15, 1934.

21. For further light on the Wagner-Hatfield battle see *Congressional Record*, vol. 78, pp. 8829-36; also *Education on the Air: Yearbook of the Institute for Education by Radio, 1936* (Columbus, Ohio: Institute for Education by Radio, 1936).

22. To promote the new "cooperative" era, the FCC appointed a Federal Radio Education Committee, which issued pamphlets on such topics as *Local Cooperative Broadcasting, College Radio Workshops,* and *Public Service Broadcasting,* all by Leonard Power; also *The Groups Tune In,* by Frank Ernest Hill, and *Forums on the Air,* by Paul M. Sheats.

23. For a summary of the career of Boake Carter and his relations with sponsors, see Culbert, David Holbrook, *News for Everyman: Radio and Foreign Affairs in Thirties America* (Westport, Conn.: Greenwood Press, 1976), pp. 34-66.

24. For the Senate hearings on munitions profits see *Munitions Industry: Report of the Special Committee on Investigation of the Munition Industry.* U.S. Senate, 74th Cong., 2nd sess. (Washington, D.C.: GPO, 1936); for the du Pont statistics, see vol. 3, pp. 20-22. Arthur Miller's career as *Cavalcade of America* "utility writer" is discussed in his Columbia University oral history reminiscence, recorded 1959.

25. "Ballad for Americans" by John Latouche and Earl Robinson (Robbins Music Corporation, 1939) had a curious political history. Written for the Federal Theater musical *Sing for Your Supper* shortly before the Federal Theater was abolished by Congress, the song was rescued from oblivion by the Paul Robeson performance on *The Pursuit of Happiness,* and was so widely acclaimed that CBS soon repeated it, and *Broadcasting* magazine called it "an American epic." It was chosen as featured song for the Republican National Convention of 1940, but was subsequently—and absurdly—considered "leftist." See also the Norman Corwin interview in the Columbia University oral history collection.

26. The Kaltenborn account of the Klauber persuasions is in the Broadcast

Pioneers reminiscences recorded by Kaltenborn in 1950. The policy dispute is also discussed in *Radio Daily*, Sept. 16, 1943.

27. For various Donald Nelson and Guy Helvering statements see *Broadcasting*, Oct. 5, Nov. 16, 1942. "All-time" network sales records are cited in *Broadcasting*, Aug. 24, 1942. Senator Truman's misgivings are quoted in *The New York Times*, Sept. 18, 1943 ("Truman Hits Ads Using 'Public' Cash") and in *Common Sense*, Dec. 1943 ("Advertising Rides the War").

28. The brochure *This Is an Army Hitler Forgot!* is available in the Broadcast Pioneers Library, Washington, D.C. For Secretary of Commerce Jesse Jones's eulogy of "the great information industry . . . essential ingredient of a free society," see *Advertising Age*, July 6, 1942.

29. Swing, Raymond, *Good Evening! A Professional Memoir* (New York: Harcourt, Brace, 1964), pp. 222-23.

30. Several companies were in the business of arranging "plants," usually charging a client $250 for network mention of a brand name, with a $100 payoff going to a writer or director. One such company, Promotions Unlimited, claimed that Paper-Mate Pens, Life Savers, and Tabasco Sauce were among those "using this type of promotion." See "Free Loading on the Air: Big Trade in Shady Deals," in *Broadcasting*, May 21, 1956. Another company, Allied Public Relations Associates, which listed National Potato Chip Institute among its clients, wrote to the Writers Guild of America for help in expanding its list of cooperating writers: "We realize that the subject is an extremely sensitive one, but there have been many instances in the last twelve months where writers have found extremely compatible situations, and in nowise have found that they have compromised their integrity." Files, Writers Guild of America, East, Mar. 20, 1956. Disc jockeys were wooed on a more generous scale, with cash and/or other benefits. Rock Records of Nashville, offering disc jockeys resort-hotel vacations for themselves and their families, used a subtle approach: "We do not have it in mind to try to buy spins and plays from you, but to try to give you a little something in return for the plays you will naturally give us." Quoted, *Variety*, Sept. 3, 1958.

31. See *Red Channels: The Report of Communist Influence in Radio and Television* (New York: American Business Consultants, 1950). For an analysis of the blacklist mania and its impact see Miller, Merle, *The Judges and the Judged* (Garden City, N.Y.: Doubleday, 1952); Cogley, John, *Report on Blacklisting*, 2 vols. (Fund for the Republic, 1956); Kanfer, Stanley, *A Journal of the Plague Years* (New York: Atheneum, 1973); Rovere, Richard H., *Senator Joe McCarthy* (Cleveland: World, 1960).

32. For the early struggles of educational television see Powell, John Walker, *Channels of Learning: The Story of Educational Television* (Washington, D.C.: Public Affairs Press, 1962); Schramm, Wilbur (ed.), *The Impact of Educational Television* (Urbana: University of Illinois Press, 1960).

33. See the chapters "Warner Brothers Presents" and "Telefilms" in Barnouw, Erik, *The Image Empire* (New York: Oxford University Press, 1970), final volume of the 3-volume *History of Broadcasting in the United States*. By 1958-59 the *Television Market List* issued periodically by the Writers Guild of America, West, for the information of its members, listed 69 filmed action-adventure series—out of a total of 103 series inviting writer contributions. Most of the remaining series were filmed situation-comedy ("sitcom") series. Files, Writers Guild of America, West. The period brought an early eruption of protest against "television violence." See "Let's Get Rid of Tele-Violence," *Reader's Digest*, Apr. 1956.

34. *Sponsor*, July 12, 1954.

35. *Television Network Program Procurement: Report of the Committee on Interstate and Foreign Commerce, House of Representatives, 88th Cong. 1st sess.* (Washington, D.C.: GPO, 1963), p. 394.

36. The *modus operandi* of Laurence A. Johnson in his pressures on sponsors and networks was first spotlighted in the second volume of Cogley, John, *Report on Blacklisting* (The Fund for the Republic, 1956). It was further illuminated in the successful libel action by John Henry Faulk against Johnson and others, as related in Faulk, John Henry, *Fear On Trial* (New York: Simon & Schuster, 1964), and Nizer, Louis, *The Jury Returns* (Garden City, N.Y.: Doubleday, 1966). The sudden death of Laurence Johnson came near the climax of the trial and its unprecedented award to John Henry Faulk.

37. The case is discussed in *The Relation of the Writer to Television* (Santa Barbara, Calif.: Center for the Study of Democratic Institutions, 1960).

38. *Sponsor*, Nov. 11, 1955. The author is indebted to Fred W. Friendly for his detailed reminiscences relating to *See It Now*. Interview, Jan. 1976.

39. *The Opportunity for Sponsored Films: How To Make Your Program Successful* (New York: Modern Talking Picture Service, 1956). This promotion brochure stated: "Sponsored motion pictures are used by almost all stations to fill 'sustaining' or unsold time. . . . THE PAYOFF? Your share of more than 100,000,000 TV viewers." According to the brochure, stations were using "an average of five hours of sponsored films each week."

40. *Report of the Attorney General to the President*, Dec. 30, 1959. Quoted, *Television Network Program Procurement: Report of the Committee on Interstate and Foreign Commerce, House of Representatives, 88th Congress, 1st session* (Washington, D.C.: GPO, 1963), p. 365.

41. Ibid. pp. 370-71. The questioning was mainly by Ashbrook Bryant, who conducted the FCC's study of "network program procurement."

42. Ibid. p. 372.

43. Ibid. p. 391. One tobacco company, R. J. Reynolds, assumed somewhat similar rights in connection with newscasts it sponsored. On the

NBC-TV series *Camel News Caravan*, featuring John Cameron Swayze, there was a "gentleman's agreement" to avoid shots of famous people with cigars—unless it was Winston Churchill, to whom the sponsor conceded special status.

44. For the full Van Doren disclosure ("I would give almost everything I have to reverse the course of my life in the last three years. . . .") see *The New York Times*, Nov. 3, 1959. See *Broadcasting*, Nov. 9, 1959, for testimony about sponsor instructions to producers.

45. The policy pronouncements were made in reply to protests from the Writers Guild of America. The network letters were dated Mar. 25 (ABC), Mar. 29 (CBS), and Mar. 31 (NBC), 1960.

46. *Television Network Program Procurement*, p. 335.

47. *Broadcasting*, May 16, 1960.

48. *Broadcasting*, Apr. 19, 1954. The author is indebted to Robert B. Hudson and James Day for details of NET history.

49. The KTCA-TV crisis was reported in *Variety* ("MPLS Does a Burn") Sept. 25, 1957. The *Wall Street Journal* attack on WGBH-TV was dated Jan. 8, 1957, and was answered in the Feb. 4, 1957, issue by President Nathan M. Pusey of Harvard. He stated that Harvard and WGBH-TV, in accepting the $44,000 programming grant from the John Hancock Life Insurance Company, stipulated "that the project shall involve no direct or exclusive benefit accruing to the donor."

50. Mighty struggles were involved in the efforts to establish non-commercial outlets in New York, Washington, and Los Angeles. The New York struggle, aided by skillful bureaucratic maneuvers by FCC Chairman Newton Minow, is told in Boekemeier, Barbara, *The Genesis of WNDT: A Noncommercial Station on a Commercial Channel*, Columbia University master's essay, 1973. The collapse of the first Los Angeles station was a bizarre tragicomedy. Established at the University of Southern California, it depended almost entirely on the largesse of one man, Captain Allan Hancock, a member of the university's board of trustees. An ardent violinist, he participated in a Hancock string quartet featured by the station. When he later disagreed with a decision of the university on an unrelated matter, he withdrew from its board, ended his bequests to the station, and went elsewhere with his quartet.

51. After seeing a preview, Cleveland Amory, writing in *Saturday Review*, called the film "so moving it will make you first ashamed, then angry, and finally utterly determined to make everyone you know see it." In the *New Yorker* Michael Arlen, referring to "all those scenes of bombed towns and villages, of leveled huts, and craters, and silent children," commented that "even if Saint Peter himself, and all the other admirals, should one day explain and make meaningful these scenes, these facts of life, it seems that they are indeed facts of life and that it is better to glimpse them now, even through prejudiced eyes, than not at all." Opponents were indignant over the showing of "enemy" propaganda.

52. For the Carnegie proposals see *Public Television: A Program for Action* (New York: Bantam, 1967). For some telling close-ups of President Johnson as broadcaster and image manager see Davie, Michael, *LBJ: A Foreign Observer's Viewpoint* (New York: Ballantine, 1967) and Goldman, Eric F., *The Tragedy of Lyndon Johnson* (New York: Knopf, 1969).

53. Letter to the author from Paul Kaufman, Nov. 11, 1970. According to Kaufman, who produced the panel discussion that followed the film, the U.S. State Department refused to provide a spokesman to participate in it, and expressed outrage that the film was scheduled.

54. Mobil's commitment in 1970-71 of more than a million dollars for the support of *Masterpiece Theater* raised corporate underwriting to new levels. Herbert Schmertz, vice president for public affairs at Mobil, later explained: "I think it would be naïve to deny that there is a link between the popular acclaim for *Masterpiece Theater* and our other profitable operations of our business. As a commercial company, we are concerned not only with day-to-day money-making but with the climate of opinion in which we can continue to operate successfully. . . . Our cultural broadcasting, like our institutional advertising in *The New York Times* and other newspapers, is designed to help us gain the understanding and support of important segments of the public." Quoted, *Access* (Washington, D.C.: National Citizens Committee for Broadcasting), Mar. 22, 1976.

55. For details on the WNET-TV flip-chart see *The New York Times*, Mar. 5, 1975. The quoted comments were made by Richard D. Depew, director of corporate underwriting for WNET-TV and previously media vice president at the Fuller & Smith & Ross advertising agency—part of the migration from commercial to "non-commercial" television.

56. See *National Program Funding Standards and Practices*, an expanding loose-leaf "blue book" of do's and don'ts maintained by the Public Broadcasting Service legal staff. Its compilers were constantly confronted with new problems and the need for new pronouncements, inevitably followed by new frustrations. In 1976 they issued a revised policy statement on sporting events, which included the following guideline: "Sponsors of the event (e.g., the XYZ Tennis Tournament), as opposed to underwriters, shall be mentioned only in the program title. Any on-air mention of the sponsor other than in the program title must be specifically cleared with PBS." Shortly afterwards PBS broadcast an Almaden Tennis Tournament featuring champions of former years. The broadcast tournament concluded on Nov. 21, 1976, with the awarding of the prize—by an Almaden official who commented: "These old champions seem to improve with age—like our fine Almaden wines." The drift to commercialism was difficult to stem.

57. For a notable exposition of spot-buying practices see Brown, Les, *Televi$ion: The Business Behind the Box* (New York: Harcourt Brace Jovanovich, 1971).

58. *Where the Girls Are* (New York: CBS, 1970). The cover of this bro-

chure, a "product wheel," was detachable so that an advertising executive could keep it "close at hand for repeated reference."

59. *Green Acres* and *The Virginian* also seem to have succumbed from
demographic failings.

60. Interview, Harry Way, Mar. 26, 1976. The subject of "assurances" has
seldom been discussed openly. But see "Webs Charge What Traffic
Will Bear in '77-'78," *Variety*, Mar. 2, 1977.

61. *Trends in Public Attitudes Toward Television and Other Mass Media,
1959-1974: A Report by the Roper Organization, Inc.* (New York:
Television Information Office, 1975), p. 21.

DOMAIN The inner fortress—the "commercial"

1. Inaugurated in 1960, the annual TV Commercials Film Festivals draw
entries by the thousands, in several dozen categories. Besides winning
Clio Awards, entries are eligible for election to a Commercial Classics
Hall of Fame. Reels of each year's award winners are available for
rental from the Clio organization, based in New York.

2. For the Screen Actors Guild statistics see Raddatz, Leslie, "The Hours
Are Short and the Green Is Long," *TV Guide*, Sept. 21, 1974.

3. See esp. Galbraith, John Kenneth, *Economics and the Public Purpose*
(New York: Houghton Mifflin, 1973).

4. Quoted, Sampson, Anthony, *The Sovereign State of ITT* (New York:
Stein & Day, 1973), p. 74.

5. The Texaco and Mobil commercials quoted here were both used repeatedly during 1976.

6. See "How ITT Improved Its Image," *The New York Times*, Apr. 18,
1975; also *Advertising Age*, Aug. 23, 1976. For the scheduling of ITT
commercials on network newscasts—44 times in six months—see the
monthly indexes of the Vanderbilt University Television News Archive.

7. The Courtney Brown eulogy to multinationals is quoted in Barnet,
Richard J., and Ronald E. Müller, *Global Reach* (New York: Simon &
Schuster, 1974), along with numerous other "rhapsodic" rationales for
planetary enterprise. The authors tell us: "The managers of the world's
corporate giants proclaim their faith that where conquest has failed,
business can succeed." The book examines their methods and successes,
and their cost to society.

8. Quoted, *New Republic*, May 25, 1974.

9. See "Ad Controls: Road to Truth or Invitation to Disaster?" *Broadcasting*, May 1, 1972.

10. *Time*, Oct. 12, 1962.

11. *Variety*, Oct. 13, 1965; *Broadcasting*, Jan. 19, 1976.

12. *The New York Times*, Dec. 11, 1964.

13. Supporting the ACT position, Dr. Richard I. Feinbloom of the Har-

vard Medical School wrote (Nov. 22, 1971): "To children, normally impulsive, advertisements for appealing things demand immediate gratification. An advertisement to a child has the quality of an order, not a suggestion. The child lacks the ability to set priorities, to determine relative importance, and to reject some directives as inappropriate. . . . Because of the nature of children, I believe that all advertising for children is inherently deceptive and should be banned." Action for Children's Television noted with satisfaction that Canada's radio-television commission banned all television advertising directed to children on the CBC network effective Jan. 1, 1975. In the United States, industry opposition to such ideas was far more strenuous.

14. *Washington Post*, Feb. 8, 1977.
15. The tricky release was issued by the NAB's Television Information Office Mar. 22, 1971.
16. Green, Timothy, *The Universal Eye: The World of Television* (New York: Stein & Day, 1972), p. 73. Also Paulu, Burton, *Radio and Television Broadcasting on the European Continent* (Minneapolis: University of Minnesota Press, 1967).

The outer defenses—"entertainment"

1. See Lonney, Gerald, "The Ecology of Childhood," in *Action for Children's Television* (New York: Avon, 1971), p. 55. A symposium on the effect on children of television programming and advertising.
2. Schramm, Wilbur, with Jack Lyle and Edwin Parker, *Television in the Lives of Our Children* (Palo Alto: Stanford University Press, 1961).
3. *Trends in Public Atttitudes Toward Television and Other Mass Media 1959-1974: A Report by the Roper Organization, Inc.* (New York: Television Information Office, 1975), pp. 3-6.
4. The 1972 testimony of television writer David W. Rintels before the Senate subcommittee on constitutional rights concerning his work for the series *The FBI* is worth noting. "I was offered a job writing on the series; when I asked them which case they wanted me to adapt, they told me to come up with a story of my own invention—no case needed. . . . It doesn't always work this way. . . . Sometimes the shows are in fact based on real cases. But in many cases the story is not only not 'based on' or 'inspired by' real FBI cases, it is invented solely by the writer and/or producer, and inevitably the details are fabricated from beginning to end. . . . I was asked to write another episode of *The FBI* on a subject of my choice at about the time—five or six years ago—when four little black girls were killed by a bomb in a Birmingham church. It had been announced that the FBI was involving itself in the case and I told the producer I wanted to write a fictionalized account of it. The producer checked with the sponsor, the Ford Motor Company, and with the FBI—every proposed show is cleared sequen-

tially through the producing company, QM; the Federal Bureau of Investigation; the network, ABC; and the sponsor, Ford; and any of the four can veto any show for any reason, which it need not disclose—and reported back that they would be delighted to have me write about a church bombing subject only to these stipulations: the church must be in the North, there could be no Negroes involved, and the bombing could have nothing to do with civil rights. . . . If you want to do a kidnapping, great; communist espionage, wonderful; organized crime, marvelous; civil rights, never." Testimony of this sort, and information about the FBI's own persistent violations of law and illegal harassments of minority groups, have been reported in print but seldom "dramatized" in prime time. Under these circumstances, they have clearly been unable to puncture or even deflate the long-sponsored, TV-nurtured legend. Crowds still line up at the J. Edgar Hoover building.

5. For Dec. 1-7, 1954, the Videodex rating service listed *Studio One, Philco-Goodyear Playhouse, Kraft Theater,* and *Ford Theater* among its top ten. *Ford Theater* was on film, Hollywood-produced. The other series were "live" New York productions.

6. Possibly the most telling expression of the advertising agency view was embodied in a letter from an agency to Elmer Rice, who had proposed a series of telecasts based on his Pulitzer Prize play *Street Scene.* "We know of no advertiser or advertising agency of any importance in this country who would knowingly allow the products which he is trying to advertise to the public to become associated with the squalor . . . and general 'down' character . . . of *Street Scene.*" The letter continued: "On the contrary, it is the general policy of advertisers to glamorize their products, the people who buy them, and the whole American social and economic scene. . . . The American consuming public as presented by the advertising industry today is middle class, not lower class; happy in general, not miserable or frustrated. . . ." Quoted, *Theatre Arts,* Nov. 1959.

7. Dr. Ernest Dichter, a psychological consultant who gave advertisers gratifying rationales for their campaigns, explained that most people feel a great hopelessness about the world's problems, but that westerns help to mitigate this feeling. In westerns "the good people are rewarded and the bad people are punished. There are no loose ends left. . . . The orderly completion of a western gives the viewer a feeling of security that life itself cannot offer." Quoted, *Broadcasting,* Sept. 2, 1957. On another occasion he ascribed a somewhat similar role to consumer goods. In our culture, he wrote in his periodical, *Motivations* (Croton, N.Y.: Motivational Publications), "psychological demands are being made upon the family today which it cannot fulfill. There is a gap between human need and the capacity of the family institution to fill that need." This gap, he wrote, is being filled in part by acquisition of consumer goods. *Motivations,* Sept. 1957. Dr. Dichter constantly gave advertisers a sense of destiny about their role, both as merchandisers

and as sponsors. Consumer goods and hero/villain drama both offered "security," and their alliance presumably held important social values.

8. The extraordinarily rapid expansion—and Americanization—of television throughout the world was stimulated by the formation in 1959 of a television division of the Motion Picture Export Association, and in 1960 of a Television Program Export Association representing the networks. Both lobbied effectively for the "American system" of television, based on advertising—as did the United States Information Agency. New nations were constantly urged to launch television on this basis as a necessary instrument of "development." From a central studio, it was argued, the classrooms of a whole nation could learn physics, chemistry, and all their practical applications, and move into a new era. And advertising would pay for it all. Robert E. Button, deputy director of the Voice of America, made a television-promotion tour of a number of developing nations in 1956 and came back in a state of euphoria. "If I ever saw anything that would lick the communists on their own front, this is it," he said. *The New York Times*, Feb. 26, 1956. In some countries, the launching of commercial television was done by a consortium of interests. A group of set manufacturers, advertisers, and program distributors could virtually guarantee success. For writings illuminating the worldwide spread of commercial television see Dizard, Wilson, *Television: A World View* (Syracuse, N.Y.: Syracuse University Press, 1966); Wilson, H. H., *Pressure Group: The Campaign for Commercial Television in England* (New Brunswick, N.J.: Rutgers University Press, 1961); Braddon, Russell, *Roy Thomson of Fleet Street* (London: Fontana, 1968); Green, Timothy, *The Universal Eye* (New York: Stein & Day, 1972); also a 1958 report by the Foote, Cone & Belding advertising agency, analyzing foreign television opportunities for its clients, published in *Sponsor*, Apr. 5, 1958.

9. Gerbner, George, and Larry Gross, "The Scary World of TV's Heavy Viewer," *Psychology Today*, Apr. 1976.

10. For the early history of specials—originally called "spectaculars"—see Barnouw, Erik, *The Image Empire* (New York: Oxford University Press, 1970), pp. 60-61. For some enlightening observations on the scheduling of specials see Brown, Les, *Television: The Business Behind the Box* (New York: Harcourt Brace Jovanovich, 1971), pp. 182-204.

11. Interview, David Susskind, Nov. 1976.

12. The Procter & Gamble policy statement is quoted in Green, Timothy, *The Universal Eye: The World of Television* (New York: Stein & Day, 1972), pp. 28-29.

13. Interview, Charles Francis, Nov. 1976. *The Belle of Amherst* was scheduled to be broadcast on PBS Dec. 29, 1976, with two subsequent repeats, with IBM underwriting.

14. Flamini, Roland, "Television and the Magoo Factor," *American Film*, May 1976.

15. During 1976 the National Citizens Committee for Broadcasting, headed

by former FCC commissioner Nicholas Johnson, began the practice of listing sponsors "according to the amount of violence they sponsored in prime time." See NCCB's newsletter, *Media Watch*, Mar. 1976, and subsequent issues; see Aug.–Sept. issue for rosters of advertisers sponsoring "least" and "most" violence.

16. The quotation is from *The Cool Fire: How To Make It in Television* (New York: Norton, 1976), p. 98, by ABC-TV vice president Bob Shanks, who also describes television as "a massage, a 'there, there,' a need, an addiction, a psychic fortress—a friend." Ibid. p. 78. That programming should be business-supportive is generally taken for granted by sponsors and their agents; they find little reason to verbalize this except when their expectations are jolted. When Bumble Bee seafoods decided to withdraw their advertising from CBS-TV, the agency explained: "Advertisers select television stations as hospitable vehicles for their messages. Our client, quite reasonably, feels that CBS has destroyed the hospitality of its affiliates for advertising from Bumble Bee, as well as all seafoods." The company had objected to a CBS News report of a Senate hearing on seafood canning practices, and their contribution to pollution. *The New York Times*, Mar. 7, 1972.

17. The trend is reflected in the globalization of American advertising agencies. By 1976 the J. Walter Thompson, McCann-Erickson, Ogilvy & Mather, SSC&B, Ted Bates, and Compton agencies—all among top U.S. agencies and perennial leaders in television billings—earned more abroad than in the United States. J. Walter Thompson had 23 U.S. offices, 35 abroad; Ogilvy & Mather had 5 U.S. offices, 49 abroad; Ted Bates had 5 U.S. offices, 28 abroad. *Advertising Age*, Mar. 14, 1977. For U.S. domination of program schedules see "The U.S. as TV Programmer to the World," *Broadcasting*, Apr. 18, 1977. For financial aspects see "Global Prices for TV Films," *Variety*, Apr. 20, 1977. For critical comment on "TV's one-way traffic" see *Intermedia* (London, Eng.: International Broadcast Institute), No. 3, 1973.

18. *Broadcasting*, Nov. 9, 1953; *Sponsor*, Apr. 19, 1954.

19. The quotations are from a 6-page mimeographed document, *Writing "Mission: Impossible,"* prepared at the start of the series for participating writers. It referred to the spy unit as the IMF—"impossible missions force"—a term later dropped, perhaps because of confusion with International Monetary Fund. Excerpts from the document: "The tape message contains the problem. An enemy or criminal plot is in existence; the IMF must counter it. The situation must be of enough importance and difficulty that only the IMF could do it. The villains (as here and later portrayed) are so black, and so clever that the intricate means used to defeat them are necessary. Very commonly, but not inevitably, the mission is to retrieve a valuable item or man, and/or to discredit (eliminate) the villain or villains. . . . We avoid names of actual countries as well as mythical Balkan kingdoms by being vague. This is not a concern at early stages of writing: use real names if it's easier."

20. See the chapter "Paranoid Pictures Presents," in Barnouw, Erik, *The Image Empire* (New York, Oxford University Press, 1970), pp. 260-71.

The satrapies—"public service"

1. The Stanton quotation is from his FCC testimony, *Television Network Program Procurement: Report of the Committee on Interstate and Foreign Commerce, 88th Congress, 1st session* (Washington, D.C.: GPO, 1963), pp. 330-31.
2. For the McLendon proposal see *Broadcasting*, Dec. 27, 1965.
3. Ibid. July 26, 1976.
4. Ibid. Dec. 20, 1976.
5. *Columbia Journalism Review*, Spring 1964.
6. See Epstein, Edward Jay, *News From Nowhere: Television and the News* (New York: Random House, 1973), for an analysis of built-in limitations and distortions. See also the valuable *Survey of Broadcast Journalism* series, a project of the Alfred I. du Pont–Columbia University awards (New York: Grosset & Dunlap, 1968-69, 1969-70, 1970-71; Thomas Y. Crowell, 1971-72, 1972-73, etc.); and Arlen, Michael J., *Living Room War* (New York: Viking, 1969). For the comments by Eric Sevareid see *Congressional Record*, vol. 112, pp. 14125-6.
7. *Wall Street Journal*, Oct. 15, 1976. One of the leading news consulting firms, Frank N. Magid Associates, advised radio station WMAQ, Chicago: "In terms of news . . . ratings are improved not when listeners are told what they should know, but what they want to hear." Quoted by Ron Powers, *Philadelphia Inquirer*, June 14, 1977.
8. The explanation is quoted from *Code News*, Mar. 1, 1968, the monthly publication of the NAB Code Authority. The NAB Television Code, XIV, 3 (f), states: "News, weather, sports and special events programs are exempt from the interruption standard because of the nature of such programs." *Broadcasting Yearbook 1976* (Washington, D.C.: Broadcasting Publications).
9. Richardson, Jack, "Six O'Clock Prayers: TV News as Pop Religion," *Harper's*, Dec. 1975.
10. *Broadcasting*, Dec. 20, 1976.
11. The statements were in letters dated Mar. 25 (ABC), Mar. 29 (CBS), and Mar. 31 (NBC), 1960. Files, Writers Guild of America, East.
12. Reuven Frank's phrase "fairness filler" is quoted in Knoll, Steve, "Fair or Foul," *New Republic*, Aug. 31, 1974. For the problems of the documentarist in television see Yellin, David G., *Special: Fred Freed and the Television Documentary* (New York: Macmillan, 1972); and the chapter "Promoter" in Barnouw, Erik, *Documentary: A History of the Non-fiction Film* (New York: Oxford University Press, 1974), pp. 213-28.

13. For various stages of the litigation see *The New York Times*, Sept. 28, 1974; *Broadcasting*, Nov. 10, 1975, Jan. 19, 1976.

14. The script for *The Selling of the Pentagon* is in Barrett, Marvin (ed.), *Survey of Broadcast Journalism 1970-1971: A State of Siege* (New York: Grosset & Dunlap, 1971), pp. 151-71. Among films quietly withdrawn from circulation by the Defense Department after the *Selling of the Pentagon* telecasts were *Red Nightmare*, narrated by Jack Webb; *A Nation Builds*, narrated by John Wayne; *Road to the Wall*, narrated by James Cagney; *The Eagle's Talon*, narrated by Walter Cronkite. New York *Post*, July 28, 1971.

15. Sponsor control of documentaries has been the subject of several important *exposés* in *Variety*; see esp. the issues of June 22, 1966; July 2, 1969; Sept. 3, 1969. The last mentioned, in an article by Steve Knoll, gave details of ABC procedures in securing sponsor support. It precipitated a policy review. For *Blondes Have More Fun* see MacNeil, Robert, *The People Machine* (New York: Harper & Row, 1968), p. 80.

16. Interview, Reuven Frank, Dec. 1975. For the sudden emergence of ecology as the "hottest new program topic" for shows and commercials see *Broadcasting*, Mar. 16, 1970. For the equally sudden demise of *In Which We Live*, and diverse explanations of it, see *The New York Times*, June 25, 1970.

17. What apparently spurred the National Rifle Association into action was an item in the June 28, 1975, issue of *TV Guide*, which read, in its entirety: "*The Guns of Autumn* will be a CBS documentary about hunting to be seen sometime around Labor Day. You'll get an extraordinarily graphic look at what hunting really is, says CBS vice president Bill Leonard. It's 50% from the animals' point of view." Letters from hunting-club leaders, alerted by the NRA, began almost immediately. They came from people who had not seen the film, but assumed the worst. The president of the National Shooting Sports Foundation wrote: "We are so certain that CBS will be abusing its privileges as a network in this broadcast that, without seeing it, we hereby make formal application for a viewing copy, with an eye to analysis and protest to the FCC for equal time treatment." Letters threatening boycotts included one with this warning: "A coalition of concerned millions when threatened by a capricious act could be difficult to handle, especially when an advertising client's products are suddenly involved." A number of such letters were quoted by CBS News in a follow-up broadcast, *Echoes of "The Guns of Autumn*," telecast Sept. 28, 1975. Commercials withdrawn from *The Guns of Autumn* after letters, phone calls, and telegrams from gun-club members included those for Lanacane, Grecian Formula, Odor-Eaters, Aqua-Tech, Lenox Air Conditioning, Williams Lectric Shave, Datsun, Mr. Coffee.

18. For the increasing commercial success of *60 Minutes* see Brown, Les, "Ad Rates To Rise on '60 Minutes,'" *The New York Times*, June 26, 1976. For a history and analysis of the series see Zito, Stephen, "Inside 'Sixty Minutes,'" *American Film*, Dec. 1976–Jan. 1977.

19. See Barnouw, Erik, *Documentary: A History of the Non-fiction Film* (New York: Oxford University Press, 1974), pp. 268-87, for an international look at films on Vietnam.

20. Associated Press *vs.* United States, 326 U.S. 1 (1944); United States *vs.* Paramount *et al.*, 334 U.S. 131 (1948).

21. See the following Modern Talking Picture Service promotion pieces: *What Television Stations Want from Sponsored Films* (1972), *The Television Audience* (1975), *Modern TV Spots* (1975), and *Projecting the Corporate Image* (undated). Both Modern and Association-Sterling include a number of foreign countries among their sponsors, and must therefore register as foreign agents with the U.S. Department of Justice at its foreign agents registration office. Contracts and earning data are on file there, and available for public scrutiny. The 1965 agreement of Sterling (before merger of Sterling and Association Films) with the Republic of China (Taiwan) news service guaranteed the sponsor 440 U.S. bookings, including 193 telecasts, of its film *The Face of Free China*.

22. Interviews, Advertising Council, Dec. 1975. The statement by C. W. Cook was quoted in *Advertising Age*, Nov. 21, 1973. The statistics are from annual reports of the Advertising Council.

23. Broadcast of Aug. 5, 1955, in daily UAW-sponsored radio series *Eye Opener* over CKLW, Windsor, Ont., quoted in union bulletin dated Nov. 14, 1955, mailed to schools in the United States (Detroit, UAW-CIO).

24. *Access* magazine (Washington, D.C.: National Citizens Committee for Broadcasting) points out that the "people start pollution, people can stop it" campaign was financed by Keep America Beautiful, Inc., presumably a non-profit educational organization. Its board members were reported by *Access* to include Thomas F. Baker and Sidney P. Mudd of the National Soft Drink Association; Henry B. King of the U.S. Brewers Association; William F. May of the American Can Company; Earle G. Ingels of Kerr Glass Manufacturers Institute; S. L. Goldsmith, Jr., of the Aluminum Associates; Victor A. Bonomo of Pepsi Cola; Donald R. Keough of Coca Cola; Roger Powers, former public relations director for U.S. Brewers, serving as president of Keep America Beautiful, Inc. *Access* felt that the nature of the campaign was "not surprising." See "The Ad Council: Gatekeepers for PSA's," *Access*, May 17, 1976. The 1974-75 Advertising Council annual report listed W. Howard Chase of American Can Company as "volunteer coordinator" of the Advertising Council anti-pollution campaign.

25. For the furor over the "economics-education" campaign of the Advertising Council see *Access*, May 17, 1976; *The New York Times*, May 17, 1976; *Washington Post*, July 23, 1976; *Advertising Age*, July 19, 26, Sept. 27, Aug. 2, 1976. See *Access is Fairness*, the lengthy petition filed with the FCC Aug. 12, 1974, by the Citizens Communication Center and the Committee for Open Media, for their experiences relating to Free Speech Messages.

26. Hill, John E., Broadcast Pioneers oral history interview, p. 5 of transcript.
27. The persistent determination of David Susskind to win television exposure for the uncensored reminiscences of Harry S. Truman, and the equally strong determination of networks, sponsors, and underwriters to have nothing to do with them ("wouldn't touch them with a 10-foot pole" was a frequent refrain) form an extraordinary television saga. Truman reminisced on film in 1962, but the "documentaries" were rejected by all networks, since they had not produced them, and no sponsor could be found to finance syndication. Excerpts from the films were sold to other producers, and the films scrapped. But Merle Miller, who had been associated with the documentary project, had kept audio tapes of all Truman's reminiscences during the making of the films, and these became the basis of his book *Plain Speaking*, a best seller throughout much of the world. Susskind, who owned the audio tapes, then commissioned and produced a 90-minute script consisting of verbatim excerpts of the Truman comments, which were brilliantly performed by actor Ed Flanders and offered to networks and sponsors as "entertainment"—to circumvent the network policy on "documentaries." (The Flanders special should not be confused with the more strident, less authentic theatrical film starring Howard Whitmore.) All networks, and many sponsors, rejected the 90-minute special both in script form and as taped at WQED, Pittsburgh. The PBS telecast was finally made possible by private donations to WQED—from 32 different donors—plus a grant from the Corporation for Public Broadcasting. See *Washington Post*, June 6, Oct. 5, 1976; *The New York Times*, Oct. 10, 1976. Sponsor readiness to participate in filmed Richard Nixon reminiscences, and NBC eagerness to contract with Gerald Ford for unspecified documentaries, contrast sharply with their flat rejection of reminiscences by the 33rd President.

Sphere of influence—"culture"

1. *The American College Dictionary* (New York: Random House, 1965).
2. *Webster's New World Dictionary of the American Language* (New York and Cleveland: World Publishing Company, 1970).
3. Inaugural comments of Daniel J. Boorstin, Nov. 12, 1975, as Librarian of Congress.

PROSPECT

1. Smithsonian Institution, International Conference, Sept. 30, 1976.
2. "Advertising: 1776–1976," *Advertising Age*, Apr. 19, 1976.

3. Cole, Lamont, "In Unison," in *Earth Day: The Beginning* (New York: Bantam, 1970), p. 27.

4. See "Waste of Resources Called Peril to Man," *The New York Times*, Dec. 1, 1976.

5. Bunce, Richard, *Television in the Corporate Interest* (New York: Praeger, 1976) offers an impressive and disturbing analysis of the enormous conflict of interest. His chapter on "The Conglomerate Complex" quotes an American Broadcasting Company advertisement, pridefully citing its diverse involvements: "When you go out to the movies in Tucson, you're watching ABC. Or in Chicago. Or Houston. Or Jacksonville. Because ABC owns the largest chain of motion picture theaters in the world. When you play a top ten record, you're watching ABC. Because ABC is one of the largest producers of records in the world. When you're learning all about high-lysine corn in *Prairie Farmer*, you're watching ABC. When you ride in a glass-bottom boat . . . or talk to the porpoises at Marine World, you're watching ABC. . . . There's a lot more to American Broadcasting Companies than broadcasting. We're not quite as simple as ABC." Bunce applies this rhetorical formula to various media corporations that are also conglomerates and shows that we are, in innumerable facets of our lives, constantly "watching" not only ABC but also CBS, RCA, and multiple-station owners AVCO, Capital Cities, Cox, General Electric, General Tire and Rubber, Kaiser Industries, Metromedia, Storer, Taft, Westinghouse, Wometco.

6. *Manual on Editorializing* (New York: NBC, 1971), p. 3. The version was still in effect in 1976. RCA seldom intrudes visibly into NBC affairs, but employees have been kept aware of the RCA-NBC connection. One personnel orientation booklet stated: "RCA is a major figure in maintaining the United States defense posture. There is hardly an area of national defense in which one or another of RCA's operating divisions has not played a key role." Quoted in Green, Timothy, *The Universal Eye* (New York: Stein & Day, 1972), p. 20.

7. Barnet, Richard J., and Ronald E. Müller, *Global Reach* (New York: Simon & Schuster, 1974), pp. 213-53.

8. See *Environmental Science and Technology*, Vol. 10, no. 13, for data suggesting that 90 per cent of all cancers are caused by environmental factors.

9. For the March of Dimes assessment see *Washington Post*, Aug. 7, 1976.

10. See Barnouw, Erik, "How a University's Film Branch Released Long-Secret A-Bomb Pic," *Variety*, Jan. 5, 1972.

11. This aspect of the AEC budget, involving more than $1 billion annually, was never widely understood. At the formation of the Energy Research and Development Administration, taking over some of the functions of AEC, the subject was discussed in "Ford May Back Continued Free Atom Weapons for Pentagon From Agency," *The New York Times*, Dec. 22, 1975.

12. *Information Sheet: Atomic Energy Commission Stock Film Footage* (Washington, D.C., U.S. Atomic Energy Commission, 1952).

13. *TV Free Film Source Book* (New York: Broadcast Information Bureau, 1974).

14. For the uranium statistics see Ridgeway, James, *The Last Play: The Struggle To Monopolize the World's Energy Resources* (New York: New American Library, 1974), p. 52.

15. *Sponsor*, May 1947.

16. *Public Interest Report: Nuclear Power Plants* (Los Angeles: Environmental Education Group, 1974) mentions a series of tests of the emergency core cooling system by Aerojet Nuclear Company, using model reactors: "All six tests of the model system failed."

17. There is a voluminous literature questioning the safety of nuclear power plants. For an introduction: Curtis, Richard, and Elizabeth Hogan, *Perils of the Peaceful Atom: The Myth of Safe Nuclear Power Plants* (New York: Ballantine, 1969); Gofman, John W., and Arthur R. Tamplin, *Poisoned Power: The Case Against Nuclear Power* (Emmaus, Pa.: Rodale, 1971); Clark, Wilson, *Energy for Survival: The Alternative to Extinction* (Garden City, N.Y.: Anchor, 1974; Nader, Ralph, and John Abbotts, *The Menace of Atomic Energy* (New York: Norton, 1977). The Nobel laureate in physics, Dr. Hannes Alfven, observes that the nuclear industry requires a level of perfection in which "no acts of God can be permitted."

18. Vanderbilt University Television News Archive, index for Feb. 1972.

19. *CBS Evening News With Walter Cronkite*, Jan. 14, 1972. Vanderbilt University Television News Archive.

20. Dated Feb. 10, 1975, organized by Rep. Benjamin S. Rosenthal of New York.

21. See "Hope for Cheap Power From Atom Fading," *The New York Times*, Nov. 16, 1975; "3 Engineers Quit G.E. Reactor Division and Volunteer in Antinuclear Movement," *The New York Times*, Feb. 3, 1976; "Westinghouse Survival Seen in Jeopardy," *Washington Post*, Feb. 11, 1977.

22. "Incident at Brown's Ferry," written and directed by Robert Richter for *Nova* series, WGBH, Boston. First transmission, PBS, Feb. 23, 1977.

23. For a summary of this "PSA" campaign see "The Unselling of Nuclear Power," *Access*, Mar. 10, 1975.

24. "Danger: Radioactive Waste," written, directed, and produced by Joan Konner. Jan. 26, 1977.

25. Increased sales of nuclear plants abroad appear to have been encouraged during the Nixon and Ford administrations to combat the balance-of-payments problem. They involved generous support via the Export-Import Bank, which helped finance 80 per cent of the foreign purchases of nuclear power plants, usually for 15-year terms. *The New York Times*, Aug. 17, 1975.

26. "Nuclear (Ad) Warfare Heats Up in California," *Advertising Age*, May 31, 1976.

27. Quoted, *Nova* series, *op. cit.*, PBS, Feb. 23, 1977.
28. Toynbee, Arnold, *Surviving the Future* (London, Eng.: Oxford University Press, 1971), pp. 94-96.
29. Green, Timothy, *The Universal Eye: The World of Television* (New York: Stein & Day, 1972); Schiller, Herbert I., *Communications and American Empire* (New York: Kelley, 1969).
30. Innis, Harold A., *Empire and Communications* (Oxford, Eng.: Clarendon Press, 1960).
31. Hayes, Denis, in *Earth Day: The Beginning* (New York: Bantam, 1970), p. xi.
32. "So You Think TV Is Hot Stuff? Just You Wait," *Smithsonian* magazine, July 1976.
33. Pool, Ithiel de Sola, *Talking Back: Feedback and Cable Technology* (Cambridge, Mass.: MIT Press, 1973); Barnett, Harold J., and Edward Greenberg, *A Proposal for Wired City Television* (Rand Corporation, 1967).
34. Harlow, Alvin F., *Old Wires and New Waves: The History of the Telegraph, Telephone, and Wireless* (New York: Appleton-Century, 1936); Sampson, Anthony, *The Sovereign State of ITT* (New York: Stein & Day, 1973).
35. *Broadcasting*, Mar. 1, 1976.
36. *Public Television: A Program for Action. The Report and Recommendations of the Carnegie Commission on Educational Television* (New York: Bantam, 1967).
37. *Broadcasting*, Oct. 27, 1952; Davie, Michael, *LBJ: A Foreign Observer's Viewpoint* (New York: Ballantine, 1967).
38. Smith, Adam, *An Inquiry Into the Nature and Causes of the Wealth of Nations* (New York: Modern Library, 1937), p. 537.

INDEX

A Is For Atom, animated film, 163
ABC, *see* American Broadcasting
  Company
Action for Children's Television,
  8, 91-95, 194-95
Adams, Evangeline, 26
Adams Chronicles, The, series, 66,
  149
Adventure, series, 45
Advertising Age, magazine, 93*n.*,
  156
Advertising Council, origin, 39-40;
  later history, 67. 74, 136, 140-46,
  162
AEC, *see* Atomic Energy Commis-
  sion
Africa, 86, 114, 117, 127, 139, 147
Age of Kings, An, series, 61
Alcoa, 51-52, 66
Alda, Robert, 117
Ali, Muhammed, 115
Allis Chalmers, 39

Amahl and the Night Visitors, television opera, 45
*America's Town Meeting of the
  Air,* series, 31, 45
American Broadcasting Company:
  and Hollywood studios, 46;
  shared sponsorships, 47; docu-
  mentaries, 56, 134, 200; views on
  "entertainment," 114, 196, 198;
  policies on "PSA's," 145-46; con-
  glomerate status, 203
American Business Consultants,
  44
American Express Company, 16
American Federation of State,
  County, and Municipal Em-
  ployees, 144*n.*
American Film, magazine, 113
American Inventory, series, 163
American Medical Association, 25
American School of the Air, series,
  31, 45

American Society of Composers, Authors, and Publishers, 19-20, 24

American Telephone and Telegraph Company: in early radio, 10-21, 24-25, 29; history, 53, 177-79, 186-87

American Tobacco, 25

Americans for a Working Economy, 144

Amm-i-dent, 48

Ampico Hour, series, 24

Angier, John, 168

Angola, 127

Annenberg School of Communications, 109

anthology series, 105-7

antitrust moves, 20-21, 51-53, 84, 112

Antonia, documentary, 147

A & P Gypsies, series, 17

Arbitron, ratings, 69

Arco, *see* Atlantic-Richfield

Armstrong, Edwin H., 10

ASCAP, *see* American Society of Composers, Authors, and Publishers

Ascent of Man, The, series, 149

Associated Press, 139

Association of National Advertisers, 47, 178

Association-Sterling, 139

Atlantic Refining Company, 39

Atlantic-Richfield, 66, 135n., 168

Atom Comes to Town, The, documentary, 163

Atom and Eve, The, documentary, 164

Atom Goes to Sea, The, documentary, 163

atomic energy, 88, 161-70, 203-5

Atomic Energy Commission, 162-67, 169, 203-4

Atomic Industrial Forum, 169

Atomic Power Today, documentary, 164

auction, in fund drives, 59

audimeter, 70

Autobiography of Miss Jane Pittman, The, special, 110-11, 114n.

Avon, 67

Aylesworth, Merlin H., 23-25, 187-88

Baby Ruth, 92n.

Bachelor's Party, drama, 106

"Ballad for Americans," 36, 189

Bank of America, 169

Banzhaf, John, III, 87-88

Barbie, 115

Barnet, Richard J., 159

Barrett, Edward W., 125

Barry Goldwater's Arizona, documentary, 134

Bate, Fred, 35

Batten, Barton, Durstine & Osborn, advertising agency, 29; representing du Pont, 34-35, 49; U.S. Steel, 49-51

Behind the Lines, series, 65

Bell & Howell, 56

Belle of Amherst, The, special, 113

Benét, Stephen Vincent, 35

Ben-Gay, 114n.

Benny, Jack, 33, 35

Bergen, Edgar, 33

Berkeley, Busby, 81

Berle, Milton, 178

Beyer, John, 147

Big Blue Marble, The, series, 85-86

Big Wheels, 92n.

Bird's Eye View of Scotland, documentary, 134

Birth Without Violence, documentary, 147

Black Journal, series, 63

blacklists, 44, 48-49, 112, 136n.

blacks: treatment in drama, 34, 50-

51, 110-11, 114*n.*, 119, 196; as talent, 36, 50*n.*, 63, 69, 119, 189; in commercials, 50*n.*, 80
Bliven, Bruce, 17
Block Drug Company, 48-49, 136
Blondes Have More Fun, documentary, 134
Boldizsár, Iván, 155
Book, Albert C., 80
Boorstin, Daniel, quoted, 151
Boston Symphony, 39
Brazil, 108
Brenner, Thomas E., 29
Brinkley, David, 126
Brinkley, "Dr." John R., 25
Britain: control of cables, 11; television programs from, 61, 66, 147; 149-51; start of commercial television, 107-8; U.S. network barriers against British documentaries, 138-39; set licenses, 180
British Airways, 80
Broadcast Pioneers, 185
Broadcasting magazine, 30, 58, 60, 124, 135*n.*, 140, 181
Brown, Courtney, 87
Browning King, 17-18; Browning King Orchestra, photo, 18
Bruck, Jerry, Jr., 146
Bulletin of the Atomic Scientists, 165
Burger King, 114
Burke's Law, series, 117
Burns, George, 81
Butterfingers, 92*n.*
Byrne, Anna, photo, 18

cable television, 175-79
Cakes and Ale, series, 149, 151
Cambodia, 65, 127
Camel cigarettes, 191-92
Cameron, William J., 33
Campbell Soup, 91

Canada, 138, 146, 195
Candid Camera, series, 138
Cantor, Eddie, 33
Capital Cities, 158, 203
Carey, Norman D., 80
Carnegie Commission on Educational Television, 64, 179-80, 182
Carnivore, documentary, 147
Carter, Boake, 33, 35
Carter's Pills, 89
Castro, Fidel, 138
Catered Affair, A, drama, 106
Catholic War Veterans, 49
CATV, *see* cable television
Cavalcade of America, series, 34-36, 49, 66
CBS, *see* Columbia Broadcasting System
CBS Reports, series, 56, 132
CBW: The Secrets of Secrecy, documentary, 132-33
Center for Growth Alternatives, 144
Central Intelligence Agency: and global corporations, 84-85, 116-17, 127; as drama inspiration, 117-21; assassination policies, 117, 133*n.*; finances Advertising Council campaign, 143
Century, magazine, 17
Chain Store Management, magazine, 26
Chaos, Operation, 120*n.*
Charm Big Tops, 92*n.*
Charren, Peggy, 91
Chayefsky, Paddy, 105-7
Chevron, 135*n.*
Cheyenne, series, 46, 107
Chicago, University of, 31
children: as advertising target, 26, 63, 91-95, 115; and the NAB, 93-95; FCC, 91, 93-94; FTC, 91, 93-95; Action for Children's Television, 91-95; viewing patterns,

children (*Cont.*)
102-5; propaganda content of programming, 63, 120, 164
Chile, 85, 147
China: "China Lobby," 44, 201; dramatic treatment of, 120
Chips Ahoy, 92*n.*
Chlorodent, 48
CIA, *see* Central Intelligence Agency
cigarettes: as drama sponsors, 55; merchandising strategy, 95; newscast policy, 191-92
CIO, *see* Congress of Industrial Organizations
Cities Service Orchestra, series, 24
Civilization, series, 149
Clairol, 134
Clark bars, 92*n.*
Classic Theater, series, 66
Clio awards, 80, 194
Cliquot Club Eskimos, series, 17, 24
Close-Up, series, 56
Clyne, C. Terence, 54
Coca Cola, 135*n.*
codes, NAB, 24, 58*n.*, 89, 93, 128, 199
Colgate, 73, 91, 112
Collins, Judy, 147
Columbia Broadcasting System: formation, 25; in radio, 25-26, 31-32, 35-36, 39, 45, 188-90; in early television, 45-46, 48, 51-54; impact of quiz scandals, 56-57; stress on demographic ratings, 71-72; "cultural democracy," 123; news and public affairs programming, 129-38, 141, 145, 166, 192, 200
Columbia University, 87, 125, 133, 185
Columbia Workshop, series, 36, 45
Commerce, U.S. Department of, 13, 39, 144
commercials: early evolution, 14-18, 24-27; protest movement against, 27-32; institutional emphasis in World War II, 39-40; postwar escalation, 42-44; addressed to children, 63, 91-95, 115; analysis of television commercials, 79-99
Committee for Open Media, 145
Communication Satellite Corporation, 178
Communications Act of 1934, 61
Compañero, documentary, 147
Compton, advertising agency, 198
COMSAT, *see* Communication Satellite Corporation
conglomerates, influence over television, 95, 157-58, 203
Congress: actions affecting broadcasting, 10, 13, 22, 28-31, 37, 44, 64-65, 124, 133, 166-67; conflicts of interest in, 180-81
Congress of Industrial Organizations, 33
Connecticut State College, 28
Consumer Federation of America, 144*n.*
Cook, C. W., 140-41
Cooke, Alistair, 59*n.*
"cooperative broadcasting," 31-32
Corporation for Public Broadcasting, 64-65, 179
Corwin, Norman, 35-36, 189
Cosby, Bill, 119
Costigan, James, 110
Council on Books in Wartime, 41
Counterattack, newsletter, 44, 48
Cousin Bette, series, 149, 151
Cox Broadcasting, 158, 203
CPB, *see* Corporation for Public Broadcasting
Creative Person, The, series, 63
Cremo Military Band, series, 25
crime series, 104-5, 107-10, 117-20, 198

Cronkite, Walter, 125-26, 129, 166
Crosby, Bing, 38, 81
Cuba, 108, 120, 127, 147
Culp, Robert, 119
"cultural democracy," 123
culture, 67-68, 148-51

Damrosch, Walter, 22
Dance in America, series, 66
Danger, series, 48
Danger: Radioactive Waste, documentary, 168
Davies, Marion, 16
Davis, Elmer, 35, 39
Davis, Jerome, 28
Davis, Peter, 133
Day, Rob't, cartoon, 122
de Forest, Lee, 10
Dean Martin's California Christmas, special, 110
Defense, U.S. Department of, 63, 119, 127, 132-34, 162
demographics, 70-73, 114
Depression, impact of, 25-27, 29
Devil Dogs, 92*n.*
Dewey, Thomas E., 59
Dichter, Ernest, 196-97
Dies, Martin, 41
Dill, Clarence C., 30-31
DiMaggio, Joe, 80
documentaries: Murrow era, 51-52; rebirth after quiz scandals, 56-57; Vietnam War influences, 63-67; problems on commercial television, 130-39; documentaries on public television, 146-47; documentaries *re* atomic energy, 163-68
Documentary Showcase, series, 146
Dragnet, series, 107, 138
Drasnin, Irv, 136
drugs: role in early radio, 25-26; prominence in television, 48-49, 71-72, 142, 156; drug commercials, 89-90, 93-95, 98

du Pont, 34-35, 38
du Pont–Columbia University awards, 133
Dunedin, Florida, 71

Eames, Charles, quoted, 101
East Germany, 120
Eastman, 111
Edge of the City, film, 106
Egypt, 108
Eleanor and Franklin, specials, 110-11
Eli Lilly & Co., 61
Empire and Communications, 174
End of the Game, documentary, 147
Energy Research and Development Administration, 167, 203
entertainment: the term discussed, 101-2; "entertainment" surveyed, 102-21
environment: rising concern, 87-88, 132-33, 156-57, 160-62, 165-69, 204; treatment of theme in commercials, 88-89; cancellation of documentary series, 135; Advertising Council view of, 142, 172, 201
Environmental Action, 144*n.*
episodic series: defined, 103; crime series, 104-5, 107-10, 195-96; spy series, 104-5, 107-10, 117-20, 198; westerns, 107-10, 191, 196; children's series, 64, sitcom, 191
Essay on Hotels, An, documentary, 134
Essay on Women, An, documentary, 134
"Eve of Destruction," song, 63
Eveready Hour, series, 20, 24
Exploratory Project for Economic Alternatives, 144*n.*
Exxon, 61, 66, 68, 111

Facts of Medicine, The, series, 61

Fairness Doctrine, 87-88, 124, 130-32, 145
"fairness filler," 131-32, 157
Fall of the City, The, verse play, 35
FBI, *see* Federal Bureau of Investigation
FBI, The, series, 104, 117, 195-96
FCC, *see* Federal Communications Commission
Federal Bureau of Investigation, 50, 65, 104, 195-96
Federal Communications Commission: genesis of, 29-31; actions on non-commercial broadcasting, 45, 58-61, 67; network programming, 53-56; fairness disputes, 87-89, 124, 132; children, 91, 94
Federal Energy Administration, 139
Federal Radio Commission, 22, 25, 28
Federal Trade Commission, 21, 89-95
Felix, Edgar, 14, 16-17, 187
Feller, Bob, 81
Fessenden, Reginald A., 10
Field and Stream, magazine, 20-21
Field Enterprises, 61
Flamini, Roland, 113
Flanders, Ed, 147, 202
Fonda, Henry, 80
Fontaine, Joan, 81
Ford Foundation, 45, 58-60, 62, 68
Ford Motor Company, 33, 39-40, 51-52
Ford Sunday Evening Hour, series, 33
Foreign Intrigue, series, 117
Forhan's toothpaste, 26
Forsyte Saga, The, series, 149, 151
Fourth Network, The, 61
Franco, Francisco, 35-36, 44
Frank, Reuven, 131, 135
Friendly, Fred W., 51, 56, 130, 132
Friends of the Earth, 144n., 168

FTC, *see* Federal Trade Commission

Galbraith, John Kenneth, 83, 123, 156
Gallup Organization, 86
Garden, Mary, 22
Gardner, John W., quoted, 149
gas, natural, sponsorship by, 53-54
Gauguin's Tahiti, special, 134
Geneen, Harold S., 85
General Dynamics, 64
General Electric: in early radio, 10-12, 20-23; and Advertising Council, 140; as conglomerate, 158, 163, 167-69, 203
General Foods, 33, 141
General Mills, 35, 164
General Motors, 24, 39, 45, 135n., 169
General Motors Family Party, series, 24
General Public Loan, commercial, 43
General Tire and Rubber, 158, 203
Gerbner, George, 109
Geritol, 89-90
Germany, 108
Get Smart, series, 117, 120
Getty, J. Paul, 80
G.I. Joe army toys, 63
Gillette, 17
Gimbel's department store, 16
Girl from U.N.C.L.E., The, series, 117
global corporations, influence over television, 42, 83-89, 95, 116-21, 157-61, 178-79, 197-98
Global Reach, 159
Go Fission, documentary, 164
Godmilow, Jill, 147
Gold Dust Twins, series, 17
Goodman, Paul, quoted, 79
Goodrich, 16-17

Goodyear, 47, 105, 172
Goodyear Television Playhouse,
  series, 47, 105, 196
Goulet, Pierre-Marie, 147
Granada Television, 147
*Great American Dream Machine,
  The*, series, 65
Great Songs of Madison Avenue,
  80
Greene, Rosaline, 24
Guardian of the Atom, documen-
  tary, 164
Gulf Oil, 56, 66
Guns of Autumn, The, documen-
  tary, 136-37, 200
Gunsmoke, series, 73
Gussow, Joan, 92
Guthrie, Woody, 36

Halberstam, David, 128-29
"hams," 10
Handel Films, 163
Harding, Warren G., 12
Harney, John B., 29
Harper's, magazine, 128-29
Harper's Bazaar, magazine, 20
Harris, Julie, 113
Harris poll, 63
Harvard University, 28, 61, 93, 192
Harvest of Shame, documentary,
  132
Hatfield, Henry D., 29
Hazel Bishop lipsticks, 46, 56
Hearn's department store, 16
Hefties, 80
Helter Skelter, special, 110n.
Helvering, Guy, 38
Hennock, Frieda B., 45
Hershey bar, 92n.
Hertz rent-a-car, 80
Hewitt, Don, 137
Hill, George Washington, 25
Hill, John E., 145
Hitler, Adolph, 35-36, 39

Holloway Milk Duds, 92n.
Hollywood: production shift to,
  45-46, 107; program testing, 113-
  14; studios become conglom-
  erates, 158
Hong Kong, 108
Hooperatings, 33
Hoover, Herbert, 12-13, 17, 22, 24n.
Hoover, J. Edgar, 104
Hope, Bob, 33, 38, 46, 84-85
Hostess Cupcakes, 92n.
Hostess Twinkies, 92n.
Hubert, Richard, 134
Hudson Pharmaceutical Company,
  93
Hughes Aircraft, 134
Humble Oil, 61
Hunt, Stan, cartoon, 148
Huntley-Brinkley program, 126

I Dream of Jeannie, series, 117
I. F. Stone's Weekly, documentary,
  146
I Led Three Lives, series, 117-18
I Love Lucy, series, 107
I Spy, series, 117, 119-20
IBM, *see* International Business
  Machines
In Performance at Wolf Trap,
  series, 66
In Which We Live, series, 135
Incredible Machine, The, docu-
  mentary, 66
Incident at Brown's Ferry, docu-
  mentary, 168
Innis, Harold A., 174
Inside North Vietnam, documen-
  tary, 63-65, 192-93
Internal Revenue Service, 87
International Association of Ma-
  chinists, 144n.
International Business Machines,
  61, 68, 110-13, 134, 178
International Paper Company, 135n.

International Telephone and Tele-graph Company: strategies as global conglomerate, 84-85; commercials, 85-86; historical background, 177-78
Ipana Troubadours, series, 17, 24
Italy, 108
ITT, *see* International Telephone and Telegraph Company

J. Walter Thompson: introduction of commercial television in Britain, 107-8; overseas interests, 198
Jackson Heights, 16
Jakarta, 127
Japan, 108, 138, 180
Jara, Victor, 147
Jericho, series, 117
John Hancock Life Insurance, 61
Johnson, Laurence, 48-49, 136*n.*, 191
Johnson, Lyndon B., 62, 64-65, 119, 168, 181
Johnson, Nicholas, 142, 198
Johnson's Wax, 41
Joint Committee (Council) on Educational Television, 45
Jones, Jesse, 39
Jordan, Max, 35
Jude the Obscure, series, 149, 151
Junior Mints, 92*n.*
Justice, U.S. Department of, 111, 138-39

Kaiser Industries, 158, 169, 203
Kaltenborn, H. V., 35-36, 40-41
Kaye, Danny, 36
KDKA, Pittsburgh, 9-12, 22
Keesely, Nicholas Edward, 53-54
Kellogg, 26, 92*n.*
Kintner, Robert, 56
Kit-Kat, 92*n.*
Klauber, Edward, 36
KNXT, Los Angeles, 128
Kodak Chorus, series, 17

Kohlberg, Alfred, 44
Kolynos toothpaste, 26
Konner, Joan, 168
Korea, 42, 44, 116, 127
Korean War, impact on broadcasting, 42, 44
KQED-TV, San Francisco, 59, 66-67
Kraft Television Theater, series, 105, 196
KSTP-TV, St. Paul, 61
KTCA-TV, St. Paul, 60-61
KTRK-TV, Houston, 145

Labor, U.S. Department of, 13*n.*, 117
Laos, 65, 127
Lash, Joseph, 110
laxatives, as news sponsors, 72
Lebanon, 108
Leboyer, Frederick, 147
Ledbetter, Huddie ("Leadbelly"), 36
Lehman, Robin, 147
Lennen & Newell, advertising agency, 53
Lever Brothers, 48-49
Lewis, Fulton, Jr., 36
Life Savers, 92*n.*
Little Orphan Annie, series, 26
Lockheed, 84
Lone Ranger, The, series, 164
Lopez, Vincent, 22
Lorenz, cartoon, 78
Los Angeles, channel problems, 59, 192; *see also* Hollywood
Lot of the Policeman, The, documentary, 134
Lowe, David, 132
Luce, William, 113

McBride, Mary Margaret, 38
McCann-Erickson, advertising agency, 54, 198
McCarthy, Charlie, 33

McCarthy, Joseph, 44, 51, 132
McCarthy, Richard D., 133
McDonald's, 114
MacLeish, Archibald, 35
McLendon, Gordon, 124
MacNeil-Lehrer Report, series, 146

Macy's department store, 16
"magazine concept," 47
Magic of the Atom, The, documentary, 163
Magoo, 113
Man Called X, The, series, 117
Man From U.N.C.L.E., The, series, 104, 117-20
Man Who Never Was, The, series, 117
Mankiewicz, Frank, 138
Marshall Plan, 42, 173
Marty, drama, 106
Marvel Comics, 93
Masterpiece Theater, series, 66, 193
Mattel toys, 63
Mauldin, Bill, cartoon, 100
Maxwell House Coffee, 24
Menotti, Gian-Carlo, 45
Metro-Goldwyn-Mayer, 158
Metromedia, 158, 203
Mexico, 108
MGM, *see* Metro-Goldwyn-Mayer
Milky Way, 92*n.*
Millay, Edna St. Vincent, 35
Miller, Ann, 81
Miller, Arthur, 34
Miller, William, 80
Mineralava, 16
Minneapolis Farmers and Mechanics Bank, 60-61
Minor, Gregory, 167
Mirachi, Joe, cartoon, 154
Mission: Impossible, series, 117-18, 198
M & M's, 92*n.*
Mobil: as underwriter, 66, 148; on

"issue advertising," 88; as commercial sponsor, 111
Modern Talking Picture Service, 52-53, 139-40, 191, 201
Money Matters, series, 60-61
Montalban, Ricardo, 80
Morgenstern, Joseph, 62
Morley, Robert, 80
Morris, Philip, 51
Mr. Goodbar, 92*n.*
Mr. Rooney Goes to Dinner, special, 134
Mr. Terrific, series, 117
Müller, Ronald E., 159
Murrow, Edward R.: on radio, 35; on television, 51-52, 130-32
Mutual Broadcasting System, 32*n.*, 36

NAB, *see* National Association of Broadcasters
Nabisco, 89, 92*n.*
Nader, Ralph, 168
NASA, *see* National Aeronautics and Space Administration
National Aeronautics and Space Administration, 134
National Association of Broadcasters, 24, 47, 58*n.*, 74, 89, 93-94, 128, 155, 180-81, 199
National Association of Supermarkets, 48
National Broadcasting Company: formation, 21-24; in radio, 25, 31-32, 39, 41; early television, 45-48; impact of quiz scandals, 56-57; news and public affairs programming, 56-57, 125-26, 130-35, 168-69; role of ratings and "demographics," 69; view on "counter-advertising," 88-89; RCA ownership, 168, 203
National Education Association, 29, 144*n.*

National Educational Television: formed, 60; quest for corporate underwriting, 61-62; program disputes, 62-66, 146, 192; distributes AEC films promoting atomic energy, 164

National Endowment for the Arts, 67

National Endowment for the Humanities, 67

National Film Board of Canada, 146

National Geographic, 66

National Organization of Women, 144

National Rifle Association, 136-37, 200

Navy, U.S. Department of, 10-11, 163

NBC, *see* National Broadcasting Company

NBC Symphony Orchestra, 39, 45

NBC White Paper, series, 56

Nelson, Donald M., 37

Nestlé, 92*n*.

NET, *see* National Educational Television

NET Journal, series, 63

New York: in early radio, 14-27, 31-37; early television, 42-45; production shift from New York to Hollywood, 45-46; in noncommercial television, 59, 62, 67, 192

New York Philharmonic, 39

New York Times, The, 80, 91

New Yorker, cartoons, 78, 122, 148, 154

Newman, Edwin, 135

news: in radio, 33, 35-36, 40-41; in commercial television, 51-52, 70-73, 88, 104-5, 124-30, 166, 199; in public television, 146

Newsweek, 62

Nielsen ratings: influence, 69-70; use of audimeters, 70; demographic ratings, 70-73; share-of-audience figures, 110, 113

Nixon, Richard M., 65, 85, 133, 147, 166, 202

Noon on Doomsday, drama, 50-51

North American Rockwell, 134

Northshield, Robert J., 135

Nova, series, 167-68

NRC, *see* Nuclear Regulatory Commission

Nuclear Regulatory Commission, 167

Nuremberg Trials, 53-54

Office of War Information, 39

Ogilvy & Mather, advertising agency, 198

oil companies: as sponsors, 39-41, 111-12; as underwriters, 61, 66, 68, 148; political advertising, 84-85, 88, 135*n*.; stake in atomic energy, 164, 168-69

Old Crow Bourbon, 52

Olivier, Laurence, 80

Olympic Games, 115

Omnibus, series, 59*n*.

One World, 41

Operating Experience—Yankee, documentary, 163

Opportunity Unlimited, documentary, 164

Oreos, 92*n*.

Ortho, 67

Oscar Mayer & Co., 93*n*.

Our Master's Voice, 29

Ovaltine, 26

OWI, *see* Office of War Information

Pace, Frank, Jr., 64

Paley, William S., 25, 46-47

Pallisers, The, series, 149, 151

Palmolive Hour, series, 24

Paramount, 139, 158

Patterns, drama, 106
payola, 44
PBS, *see* Public Broadcasting Service
Peabody Awards, 133
Pensions: the Broken Promise, documentary, 132
Perdue, Frank, 80
Perry Como's Hawaiian Holiday, special, 110
Philco, 33, 47, 105-6, 196
Philco Television Playhouse, series, 47, 105-6, 196
Philip Morris, 51
Phillips Petroleum, 135*n*.
Pinkham, Richard A., 55, 178-79
Pittsburgh: role in radio boom, 9-12; in public television, 202
Plain Speaking, special, 147, 202
Playhouse 90, series, 53-54, 105
Plutonium Connection, The, documentary, 168
Poldark, series, 149
politics: in sales pitches, 84-89; campaign "commercials," 96
pollution, 142
Postal Telegraph, 177
Preview House, 113-14
Price-Anderson Act, 164-65
Printer's Ink, magazine, 15
Procter & Gamble, 112
Project Salt Vault, documentary, 166
PSA's, *see* public service announcements
Public Broadcasting Service: underwriting, 66-68, 147; public affairs programming, 146-47, 179-80; cultural programing, 149-51; policies, 193
"public interest, convenience, or necessity," 22, 187
Public Media Center, 144-45, 168
public service announcements, 40, 74, 136, 140-46, 162

public service programming, 32-33, 37, 123-47
public television, 64-68, 146-47, 149-51, 179-82
Public Television: A Viable Alternative, 67
Pursuit of Happiness, series, 36, 189

Queensboro Corporation, 15-16, 186-87
quiz programs: rise of, 33; escalation of prizes, 42; quiz scandals, 55-57, 111, 130

Radio Act of *1912*, 10; of *1927*, 22, 24, 28, 30-31, 61, 187
Radio Broadcast, magazine, 15
Radio Corporation of America: creation of, 11-12; early broadcasting activity, 20-21; role in formation of NBC, 21-23. For NBC history as RCA subsidiary, *see* National Broadcasting Company
Radio Dealer, magazine, 15
Radio Free Europe, promotion by Advertising Council, 143
Rankin, William H., 16
Rather, Dan, 137-38
Red Channels, 44
Remington Arms, 52
Requiem for a Heavyweight, drama, 106
Revlon, 56
Revson, Charles, 56
Richardson, Jack, 128-29
Richter, Robert, 168
Ring-Dings, 92*n*.
Robeson, Paul, 36, 189
Rogers, Will, 20, 22
Rolaids, 90
Roosevelt, Franklin D., 28, 33, 111
Roots, specials, 114*n*.
Roper polls, 74, 80, 94, 103-4
Rorty, James, 29-30

Rose, Pete, 90
Rose, Reginald, 105
Rosenthal, Benjamin, 144
Rosten, Norman, 34
Rubbo, Michael, 146
Ruffo, Titta, 22

Sad Song of Yellow Skin, documentary, 146
Salvation Army, 139
Sampson, Anthony, 85
San Francisco, 59, 66-67
Saudek, Robert, 59*n.*
Save the Children Federation, 139
"scatter" buying, 69, 178
Schaefer, Robert, 128
Schmertz, Herbert, 88, 193
Schrafft's Tearoom Orchestra, series, 20
Schramm, Wilbur, 103
Schulman, Harvey J., 87
Scientists' Institute for Public Information, 144*n.*
Screen Actors Guild, 81
Secret File U.S.A., series, 117
Secret Squirrel, series, 117
See It Now, series, 51-52, 56, 66, 130, 132
Selling of the Pentagon, The, documentary, 133-34, 200
Serling, Rod, 50
Sevareid, Eric, 35, 126
Shanks, Bob, 114, 198
Shirer, William, 35
Shoulder to Shoulder, series, 149
Simpson, O. J., 80
"singing commercial," 43
Singing Lady, The, series, 26
Six Wives of Henry VIII, The, series, 149
60 Minutes, series, 137-38, 200
$64 Question, series, 42
$64,000 Question, series, 42, 56
Smith, Adam, 155, 181-82
Smith, Howard K., 35

Socialist Party, 116
Sons of the American Revolution, 49
Sovereign State of ITT, The, book, 85
Soviet Union, 41, 44, 161, 176
specials: origin, 110; sponsorship, 111-13, 132-34, 136, 200, 202
Spiderman, 93
Sponsor, magazine, 46, 48*n.*, 52
spy drama, 104-5, 107-10, 117-20, 198
Stalin, Joseph, 49
Standard Oil of New Jersey, 135*n.*
Stanton, Frank, 56-59, 123
Studio One, series, 105
sub rosa sponsors, 42-44
Sumner, Charles A., 177
Super Bowl, 71, 110
Super Market Institute, 49
Super 6, series, 117
Superman, 164
supermarket, influence of, 48-49, 71, 112
Surviving the Future, 170
Susskind, David, 111, 147, 202
"sustaining" programs, 32
Swing, Raymond, 35, 36, 41
Sylvester, Arthur, 119

Taft Broadcasting, 158, 203
Talent Associates, 111
Tarzan, 117
tax, influence on programming, 37-40, 87
Ted Bates, advertising agency, 55, 178, 198
Tennessee Ernie Ford in Moscow, special, 110
Tennyson, quoted, 9
Texaco, 84-85, 178
Theater Guild, 49-51
Theater in America, series, 66
They Fly Through the Air, 36

This Is an Army Hitler Forgot! 39
Tidewater Oil, 16
Till, Emmett, 50
Today, series, 47
Tokyo, 127
"toll" broadcasting, 14-21
Tom Brown's School Days, series, 149
Tonight, series, 47
Tootsie Pops, 92*n*.
Toscanini, Arturo, 39
Toynbee, Arnold, 170-71
Transaction, magazine, 94
Tribal Eye, The, series, 149
Truman, Harry S., 37, 39, 147, 202
Turkish Taffy, 92*n*.
Twelve Angry Men, drama, 106
Twenty-one, series, 55

"underwriter," 20
United Artists, 117, 158
United Auto Workers, 144*n*., 201
United Brands, 84
United Fruit, 11, 21
United States Chamber of Commerce, 49, 163
United States Conference of Mayors, 144*n*.
United States Rubber, 39
United States Steel, 49-51, 169
United States Steel Hour, series, 49-51, 105
United States Supreme Court, 91, 124
Universal Pictures, 158
"Universal Soldier, The," song, 63
University of Chicago Round Table, series, 31
Upstairs, Downstairs, series, 149

Van Doren, Charles, 55-56
Vanity Fair, series, 149
Variety, weekly, 110*n*., 114*n*., 134

Veblen, Thorstein, 91
Vidal, Gore, 105, 107
videodisc, 175
Vietnam War, impact on broadcasting, 62, 117-21, 126-29, 135, 138, 164
View From Space, The, documentary, 134
violence, 108-9, 114, 117-20
Visit to a Small Planet, drama, 106
vitamins, market demographics on, 72
"Voice of Experience," 26

Wagner, Robert F., 29
Wagner-Hatfield bill, 29-32, 45, 55
"Waist Deep in the Big Muddy," song, 63
Waiting for Fidel, documentary, 147
Walker, Clint, 107
Wall Street Journal, 61, 128
Wall Street Week, series, 146
Wallace, Mike, 138
Wanamaker Organ Concerts, series, 20
War Advertising Council, 39-40
War and Peace, series, 149, 151
Warner Brothers: ABC-TV contract, 46, 107; conglomerate status, 158
Washington, Booker T., 34*n*.
Washington: radio conferences, 13, 15, 19; radio stations, 19, 21; public television problems, 59, 62
Washington Radio Conferences, 13, 15, 19
Washington Week in Review, series, 146
Wasilewski, Vincent T., 155
Watch the World Go By, series, 40
WCAC, Storrs, 28
WCAP, Washington, 19, 21
WDRC, Hartford, 28

WEAF, New York, 15-21, 186-87
Wealth of Nations, The, book, 181
Weaver, Sylvester L., Jr., 47-48, 110
Webb, Jack, 138
Weber and Fields, 22
Welles, Orson, 35
Western Electric, 10-11, 135*n.*
Western Union, 101, 176-78, 181
westerns, 107-10, 91, 196
Westinghouse: in radio beginnings, 9-12, 20-21, 23; interests as con-glomerate, 158, 163, 167-69, 203
WGBH-TV, Boston, 61, 167, 192
WGBS, New York, 28
Whalen, Grover, 14-15
What In the World? series, 45
Wheeler, Burton K., 27
Where the Girls Are, 70-71
White Owl Cigars, 41
Who Invited US?, documentary, 65
Why We Fight, films, 41
WICC, Bridgeport, 28
Willkie, Wendell, 41
Wilson, Charles E., 140
Wilson, Flip, 69
Wilson, Irving, 51
Winchell, Walter, 38
Winters, Jonathan, 80
WJZ, New York, 20
WNBC, New York, 15*n.*

WNET-TV, New York, 67, 193
Woman Alive, series, 67
women, as demographic targets, 67, 71-73, 89-90, 95-98, 115
Wometco, 158, 203
Wonderful World of Disney, series, 137
Words At War, series, 41
World in Action, The, series, 147
World Series, 110
World War I, effect on radio, 10-11
World War II, effect on radio and television, 35-42
WQED-TV, Pittsburgh, 202
WRC, Washington, 21
WRCA, New York, 15*n.*
Writers Guild of America, 130-31, 190-91
WTIC, Hartford, 28
Wynn, Tracy Keenan, 110

Xerox, 68, 110-12

Yankee Doodles, 92*n.*
Yankelovich, Daniel, 86
Yodels, 92*n.*

Zagnut bars, 92*n.*
Zenith, 24*n.*
Ziv, 117